GULLAH CULTURE —IN— AMERICA

WILBUR CROSS AND
ERIC CRAWFORD

—BLAIR—

Cover Art: *Two Baskets*, 2000
Oil on Linen, 16" × 20" © Jonathan Green
The Collection of Margaret and Jeffrey Lofgren

Library of Congress Cataloging-in-Publication Data
Names: Cross, Wilbur, author. | Crawford, Eric Sean, author, editor.
Title: Gullah culture in America / by Wilbur Cross and Eric Crawford.
Description: [Second edition]. | Durham : Blair, [2023] |
Includes bibliographical references.
Identifiers: LCCN 2022041318 (print) | LCCN 2022041319 (ebook) |
ISBN 9781949467963 (paperback) | ISBN 9781949467970 (ebook)
Subjects: LCSH: Gullahs—History. | Gullahs—Social life and customs. |
Sea Islands—Civilization.
Classification: LCC E185.93.S7 C76 2023 (print) | LCC E185.93.S7 (ebook) |
DDC 305.896/07375799—dc23/eng/20220912
LC record available at https://lccn.loc.gov/2022041318
LC ebook record available at https://lccn.loc.gov/2022041319

GULLAH CULTURE IN AMERICA

CONTENTS

GOING HOME

Rising from Oblivion

Emory Shaw Campbell

Since long before America's independence, the nation has had hidden pockets of a bygone African culture, rich in native history, with a language of its own, and long endowed with beguiling talents in its traditions, language, design, medicine, agriculture, fishing, hunting, weaving, and arts. Although thousands of articles and hundreds of books have been written on discoveries of Native American cultures and American Indian lore, the Gullah Geechee culture has been almost totally overlooked. It is known only to those living near these African American communities and select historians whose findings have been published in specialized journals and scholarly books. This new edition coauthored by Wilbur Cross and Eric Crawford explores what very few yet know as a direct link to the African continent, an almost lost culture that exists in the Sea Islands of the United States, along a corridor stretching from the northeast coast of Florida along the Georgia and South Carolina coastal shores to the Wilmington, North Carolina, area, and little more than fifty miles inland at any point.

The first published evidence of this culture went almost unnoticed until the 1860s, when northern missionaries made their way South, even as the Civil War was at its height, to the Sea Islands of South Carolina, where they established a small school to help formerly enslaved people learn how to read and write and make a living in a world of upheaval and distress. One of these schools evolved into the distinguished Penn School. There they noticed that most of the native island Black people spoke a language that was only part English, tempered with expressions and idioms, often spoken in a melodious, euphonic manner. Yet this was the barest beginning, for the language carried over into other forms of communication and expressiveness, ranging from body movements and the use of hand and head movements to the rituals of religion, work, dancing, greetings, and the arts.

The homogeneity, richness, and consistency of this culture were made possible by the fortunate fact that these peoples maintained a solidarity over the generations because they were isolated from other peoples and cultures. Thus, they were able to maintain their heritage, language, and traditions, unlike other peoples of African and foreign lineage who came to America's shores and over the years blended in with other cultures, as they did in the northern or southern cities and the more heavily populated upper regions of Georgia, South Carolina, and North Carolina. Even today there are more than three hundred thousand Gullah-speaking people living in the more remote areas of the Sea Islands, such as St. Helena, Edisto, Coosaw, Ossabaw, Sapelo, Daufuskie, and Cumberland.

Part of this book focuses on the engrossing story of Sea Islanders of Gullah descent who traveled in groups to Sierra Leone in 1989, 1998, 2005, and 2019 to trace their origins and ancestry. I was fortunate enough to have been involved with the research into these West African origins, along with one of the most noted authorities in this field, Joseph Opala, an anthropologist who had made some remarkable studies about Bunce Island, in the harbor of Freetown, Sierra Leone, where in the eighteenth century thousands of captured Africans were held temporarily to be boarded on ships bound for South Carolina and Georgia.

Many subjects of pertinent interest are included, beginning with a brief introduction to the Gullah culture in America, its roots, the location and extent of its peoples, its current history and beliefs, and, most importantly, its exuberance, imagery, color, and contributions to the world we live in. It should not be forgotten how a young African American linguist, Lorenzo Dow Turner, ventured into the remotest reaches of the Sea Islands of Georgia and the Carolinas in the early 1930s to begin the first scientific investigation of the Gullah peoples and culture. Astonishingly—unlike Native American cultures, which were studied many generations ago by sociologists—the Gullah history and heritage were virtually unknown, even in the Southeast, until the Turner studies were published.

Even so, his work eventually faded from public knowledge, and awareness of the Gullah culture lapsed again, almost into oblivion, until a slow revival began in the last quarter of the twentieth century. One book alone, covering an entire culture, cannot do more than give its readers a broad panorama of the subject. Yet, remarkably, the chapters in this history of Gullah culture present a wealth of detail that allows readers to experience the drama, the color, the romance, and the vitality of Gullah, and in effect "meet" many of the personalities who have played a part—past and present—in making it what it is today. The authors, using personal and historical research, recount interviews with Gullah people who have described what it was like to grow up in the old traditions. They take the reader on a tour of "praise houses," where enslaved Africans and their descendants practiced religion, not only with the familiar spirituals, but with expressions of faith, joy, hardship, hope, and repentance in "shouts," which begin slowly with the shuffling of feet and the clapping of hands, followed by louder and louder expressions of reverence. The authors introduce the reader to one of the most bewitching aspects of the Gullah culture—its practices of healing and folk medicine. Though originating hundreds of years ago, in many cases these practices have been proven to be scientifically effective, and some are the forerunners of medications developed in the present century.

As one who is recognized today for my fluency in the Gullah Geechee language and my many assignments to translate it, I was particularly pleased to see the chapter on our speech, which takes the reader on a rewarding and effective road to discovery of the origins and usages of words, phrases, and idioms. And I recommend to you the joys of reading about Gullah foods and recipes, festivals and celebrations, music, song, and dance, and the unbelievable origins of that side of the culture that brings joy to the heart. In retrospect, it is difficult to realize that so many of the uplifting aspects of this unique culture were born in the darkest days of slavery, inhumanity, torture, and discrimination. How Gullah people rose from the ashes to revive and live their culture in the most positive of ways is truly a fascinating and inspiring story.

This second edition expands very effectively the fundamental aspects of this culture and brings greater awareness of the Gullah Geechee traditions in North Carolina and Florida. Early studies by Michael Allen and Congressman James Clyburn confirmed the presence of vibrant Gullah communities existing in these states. Over the past few years, the culture has become like the coast. It is being paved over, and we are being influenced by the larger culture so much that we forget our own values. This book reeducates us about what is important. I can state without reservation that you will reach the end of the chapters with a sense of great human accomplishment, and you will want to pass the book along to others to let them know what the human body, spirit, and soul can accomplish under even the greatest duress.

Emory Shaw Campbell
Executive Director Emeritus, Penn Center,
Hilton Head Island, South Carolina

—CHAPTER ONE—

WELCOME HOME!

On a November day in 1989, unusually brisk for the Lowcountry and Sea Islands, fourteen Gullah Geechee leaders gathered in Savannah, Georgia, for a trip that would be more meaningful than any other in their lives. Although they appeared to have much in common with other groups of travelers, these passengers would experience a journey that would take them backward in time to their ancestral homeland in Sierra Leone. It had been said that the enslaved Africans carried nothing with them on their involuntary voyages from West Africa to the New World. However, members of the "Gullah Homecoming" delegation were living proof that the enslaved had indeed brought "indelible memories of their culture—music, folklore, language, art, and religion—to the Sea Islands."

The 1989 "Gullah Homecoming" was the culmination of pioneering work by Lorenzo Dow Turner, Peter Wood, and Charles Joyner, who established West and Central African cultural ties to the Gullah people. In his 1949 book

Africanisms in the Gullah Dialect, Turner, known as the father of Gullah studies, presented conclusive evidence of West and Central African linguistic origins of thousands of Gullah words. In 1974, Peter Wood published *Black Majority: Negroes in Colonial South Carolina from 1670 through the Stono Rebellion*, which showed the value white planters placed on the enslaved Africans, specifically from the Rice Coast of West Africa, because of their high degree of skill at rice cultivation. Lastly, Joyner's 1984 book *Down by the Riverside: A South Carolina Slave Community* expanded upon Turner's and Wood's research as he focused on the West African cultural and agricultural contributions made by enslaved workers along the Waccamaw River. Yet the visionary behind the Gullah Homecoming was Joseph Opala, an American historian living in Sierra Leone.

Opala was teaching African studies at Fourah Bay College in the early 1970s when he began research on the ruins at Bunce Island, a former British slave castle that operated between 1670 and 1807. Located on a tiny island about fifteen miles from the capital city of Freetown, Opala discovered Bunce Island's historical role in sending thousands of captives to South Carolina and Georgia in the eighteenth century. He obtained invaluable information through oral interviews in many of the rural villages near Bunce Island, where the elders pass historical accounts down orally to each new generation. But one elder had been taught an untruth about the slave trade. Alimamy Rakka, an old chief in Sangbulima village on neighboring Tasso Island, told him that the white people had taken his people away to Europe, where they had all "died of the cold." "No," Opala said in Krio, "they didn't take them to Europe. They took them to America, and many descendants are still alive there today." The elder spoke up, wide-eyed. "America. That is a rich country, yes?" and after Opala had nodded in the affirmative, he remarked with a broad smile, "That means I have family in a rich country. That is good news." Similar to Turner, Wood, and Joyner, Opala also found linguistic and cultural similarities between the people of Sierra Leone and the Gullah people. Sierra Leoneans were fascinated by Opala's findings, which he shared with the public via local radio and newspaper interviews and public lectures, and they were eager to meet their "Gullah cousins" in America.

OVERLEAF: Gullah father and son opening oysters on their wooden scows in 1904. *Negative/Transparency No. 478150. (Photo by Julian Dimock.) Courtesy of the American Museum of Natural History Library.*

In 1986, Opala contacted Gullah community leader Emory Campbell, then director of Penn Center, about his research and accepted Campbell's subsequent invitation to give a lecture to more than one hundred people on St. Helena Island, South Carolina. In 1862, Penn Center, formerly known as Penn Normal, Industrial, and Agricultural School, was established as one of the first schools in the South for formerly enslaved Africans. On this historic campus, Opala explained the value South Carolina plantation owners placed on enslaved Africans from the Rice Coast and Sierra Leone's particular cultural importance for the Gullah people. Those in attendance were surprised to learn about their ancestral ties to the slave castle on Bunce Island and the founding of Freetown, the capital city of Sierra Leone, as a British settlement in the eighteenth century by formerly enslaved Africans from South Carolina. All of this made sense to Campbell because Claude and Pat Sharpe, a missionary couple involved in the translation of the Bible into the Gullah language, had already told him how similar Sierra Leone's Krio language is to Gullah. The Sharpes used the Krio Bible as a guide while translating the Gullah Bible.

Opala also informed the islanders of an offshoot of the Gullah people living in such far-flung areas as the Bahamas, Oklahoma, Texas, and Mexico. These were the Black Seminoles whose ancestors escaped from South Carolina and Georgia rice plantations in the eighteenth and nineteenth centuries and fled to the Florida wilderness. After the Second Seminole War (1834–1842), they were forced to move west on the "Trail of Tears." Surprisingly, the Black Seminoles still speak Gullah and eat rice dishes similar to those prepared in the Lowcountry. The islanders were as amazed to learn about the long-lost family in the American West as they were about their links to Sierra Leone.

In October 1988, the president of Sierra Leone, the late Joseph Saidu Momoh, visited Penn Center. Having heard so much about the Gullah Geechee, the president wanted to see firsthand if their culture was as similar to Sierra Leone's as he had heard. Momoh was astonished at the common words shared between Gullah and Krio, the English-based Creole language spoken in his own country. To his amazement, he saw antique mortars, pestles, and fanner baskets in Penn Center's York W. Bailey Museum almost identical to farm tools still used in Sierra Leone today. Later, he was impressed with the meal served by the community and was heard saying that Gullah rice dishes were just like the food back home in Sierra Leone. President Momoh was so enthusiastic about the cultural similarities he witnessed that he invited Emory Campbell and other leaders to come to Sierra Leone—to return home!

Journey Home

Upon their arrival in 1989, the Gullah delegation was greeted at the airport with drumming and dancing and hundreds of Sierra Leonean citizens, many in traditional dress. When it was discovered that the airline had misplaced their bags, President Momoh presented every member of the homecoming group with a new set of traditional clothes. The president joked that "your ancestors left here without their clothes and now you've come back without them!" The Gullah visitors laughingly agreed, and one could see that in their new African clothing they felt at home instantly.

As they traveled around the country, they encountered cultural activities and idioms of speech that were so familiar to them back home. "It was as though the community in which I was brought up back on St. Helena Island, South Carolina, had been lifted up and transported to Africa," said a member of the group. "I listened to several youngsters chatting with each other; I heard songs and watched dancing; I looked at baskets and clothing in a marketplace; I ate gumbo and hoppin' john at a luncheon in our honor; and, do you know, they were all Gullah—the Gullah I had known since earliest childhood back home."

One of the ladies in the group sent a postcard to her pastor saying she had attended a church service in a village where she knew all the hymns and the words and could even understand the preacher when he spoke in Krio. "Everywhere we went, we were greeted with Gullah words, often accompanied by gestures that were as familiar to us as 'How are you?' or 'Have a good day' might be back in the States. They simply rolled off the tongues of our hosts and into our ears as though we were longtime neighbors: *'Wi gladi foh si una'* ['We're happy to see y'all']; *'Au una du?'* ['How y'all doing?']." She also witnessed examples of the Gullah use of body language as a substitution for speech: "There were those same subtle movements and gestures that we were brought up with as children—a twinkle in the eye, a thrust of the chin, a nod of the head, a lift of the eyebrows, and of course, movements of the hands and fingers."

Every one of the fourteen people on this homecoming journey had similar experiences and stories to tell about their encounters with the people of Sierra Leone as they moved about the streets of the capital, Freetown, or in the Mende village of Taiama in the interior, where they took part in the rice harvest and witnessed traditional dances and ceremonies. In every aspect of life in Sierra Leone, whether relating to religion, medicine and health, foods, cooking, traditions, beliefs, or family matters, they saw parallels to their own experiences back home. As one visitor commented, "Once a Gullah, always a Gullah."

"The people of Sierra Leone were magnificent," wrote Emory Campbell in an article about his own experience. "Like Gullah islanders in the Carolinas, they are proud, friendly, and industrious. We were warmed by their smiles, spoke to them in our common language, Gullah and Krio, which are similar, and were thrilled to see examples of their skills in the marketplace—so much like ours back home—where hundreds of entrepreneurs displayed and peddled baskets, carvings, musical instruments, paintings, weaving, produce, and cooked foods almost exactly like those in native markets in our own islands back home. And everywhere we went, we saw signs saying, or people greeting us with, '*We glad fo see oonah*,' or '*Tun roun ya le mi see who yo da*,' or other common expressions in the Gullah tongue. From village to village, children had been kept out of school to see us (*fa see we*'), and they kept us for hours, reluctant to have us move on, showing us their rice paddies, their dances, their weaving, and their neat, miniature homes, and gladdening our ears with their glorious singing."

Campbell's most poignant memories were of the group's visit to the slave castle on Bunce Island and their final day in Sierra Leone. "We saw the place from which our ancestors had been taken from their beloved homeland: Bunce Island, with its slave quarters, fortress, jetty, and cannons still standing that had been used to prevent theft of the captured Africans before they were boarded on the slave vessels. In a sacred libation ceremony, we experienced the most emotional moments of our visit, realizing that we were standing on the exact spot where our ancestors had begun their miserable trek into slavery far, far from their native land.

"On our final day, we visited the Regent Community, established by Africans who had escaped from slavery, where we went to church. The people joined heartily with the choir, singing songs familiar to our ears, such as 'Swing Low, Sweet Chariot,' 'Steal Away,' and 'Old Time Religion.' And we listened patiently to a lengthy sermon in which the pastor admonished Africans in the diaspora against complacency. In effect, he warned us that 'freedom is not free.' It was a fitting message to leave with us as we departed for home, where so often his warning was more true than false. You can now call me *Gullah*, for I have gone home." The film *Family Across the Sea*, produced by South Carolina Public Television, documents this groundbreaking homecoming.

Journey to the Past

In 1997, Joseph Opala organized his second Gullah–Sierra Leone trip, called the Moran Family Homecoming. This African American Georgian family, led by matriarch Mary Moran, knew an ancient song in the Mende language of Sierra Leone that had been passed down from mother to daughter for at least two hundred years. Lorenzo Turner, the pioneering linguist, recorded Mary's mother, Amelia Dawley, singing this five-line song when he visited her in Harris Neck, Georgia, in 1931. More than fifty years later, Opala became intrigued with finding a possible Sierra Leone connection to Turner's song, so he enlisted the aid of Cynthia Schmidt, an American ethnomusicologist, and Tazieff Koroma, an African linguist. Their task was formidable, however, because the Mende ethnic group numbers in the millions in Sierra Leone. Remarkably, Koroma recognized a dialect word in the song unique to a specific area. After going village by village, they eventually located a woman named Baindu Jabati in the remote village of Senehun Ngola who recognized the lyrics from a song "her grandmother taught her." It had been a Mende funeral dirge sung only by women because birth and death rites are women's responsibilities in Mende culture.

Later, Opala and Schmidt went to Georgia and met with Mary Moran to inform her of their wonderful discovery. When the Moran family finally came to Sierra Leone in 1997, the public there responded enthusiastically to their homecoming. Sierra Leoneans also loved the documentary film based on the Moran Family Homecoming, *The Language You Cry In*. Jabati recalled that her grandmother predicted such "a homecoming in their village one day, a return of lost family, and that the old funeral song would link them to their returned kinsmen." The Mende song remains the longest African text known to have been preserved by an African American family. Although Opala found a Gullah family with a traceable link to their country, Sierra Leoneans were still not satisfied. Many wanted a name of the Mende person who took the song to America. In their words, "We want the name of a Sierra Leonean taken away as a slave, and we want to meet his Gullah family in America today." Opala soon found such a person in a ten-year-old girl named Priscilla.

On a sultry June day in 1756, in Charleston, South Carolina, there were fewer planters than usual on the south quay, despite the fact that the sloop *Hare* had arrived with what a newspaper advertisement described as "Likely and Healthy Slaves, to be sold upon easy Terms" by merchants Austin & Laurens. The ship was arriving from Sierra Leone, where rice was the staple crop, and the captive Africans aboard were skilled at its cultivation. The few who were present were all rice growers, including one satisfied purchaser, Elias Ball II, a wealthy owner of a plantation on the Cooper River. Ball made an entry that day in the "blanket book" he used to record the expenses he incurred for his slaves. This book is still preserved at the South Carolina Historical Society, where Ball's original entry can be seen:

I bought 4 boys and 2 girls—their ages near as I can judge: Sancho, 9 years old, Peter, 7, Brutus, 7, Harry, 6, Belinda, 10, Priscilla, 10, for £600.

The last-mentioned person, ten-year-old Priscilla, was taken to Ball's Comingtee Plantation, located on the western part of the Cooper River. Within ten years, she had fallen in love with a slave named Jeffrey and shared his quarters. By 1770, she had three children, and upon her death around 1811, she had thirty grandchildren. Her descendants lived on Ball family plantations until early 1865, when Charleston was taken by Federal troops and an officer assembled the slaves and told them they were free. One of Priscilla's descendants, Henry, was among those freed. He took the surname Martin to signify the end of a life of servitude to the Ball family and the beginning of his life as a free Black man.

Edward Ball, author of *Slaves in the Family* and descendant of Elias Ball II, decided to write a book about the many Africans his family had enslaved and his interviews with their descendants. He states, "What I've tried to do is tell an honest story that included white people and black people in it and tries to create a context for a partial reconciliation between white folks and black folks." Ball describes how he traveled all over the United States to meet descendants of the enslaved, who were often reluctant at first to speak to him.[1]

Among the African American families I came to meet—and there were more than those who appear in the book—the most common chain of reactions went like this. When I first turned up in the life of a family, either by phone or personal introduction or by writing a letter, people were stunned. The shock fading, they agree to a visit. A day or a week later, some of the families were overcome with suspicion. What did the white man want, after all? In two weeks or a month, the mistrust was replaced by curiosity and a desire to take advantage of the strange event of our meting to make sense of the painful history we shared.[2]

While researching his prize-winning book, Ball came across the entry Elias Ball II made on his purchase of Priscilla and the other children in 1756 and details about their terrible ordeal aboard the *Hare*. Ball also discovered the graphic observations made by Austin & Laurens, the South Carolina slave dealers, when the *Hare* unloaded its human cargo in Charleston. As they described it, the unwilling passengers brought ashore in chains were "a most scabby flock," suffering from skin diseases, semiblindness, stomach "complaints," and various other infirmities. Three of the lot died within days of coming ashore, and the rest were so pitiful that barely half of them tempted any buyers. Priscilla had been lucky to survive the voyage from Sierra Leone.

Later, to his own amazement, Ball was able to trace Priscilla to one of her modern-day descendants, a Charleston man named Thomas Martin. "Mr. Martin was a very dignified, soft-spoken man...intensely curious about his history," says Ball. "He knew about his family's life after emancipation, but he knew nothing about his family in slavery. I knew about his family in slavery and nothing about his family after slavery, so we had something to share. That exchange characterized the encounters I had with all the black families."[3] But in the case of Thomas Martin, the exchange led to something extraordinary. One of the most moving parts of Ball's book is the moment he shows Martin the family tree he created linking him and his family back to a ten-year-old girl brought from Sierra Leone.

Priscilla and her surviving descendants in Charleston first came to the attention of Opala in 1997, when Ball visited Sierra Leone and asked him for a tour of Bunce Island. Opala immediately recognized the importance of Ball's discovery and the immense impact of bringing a person with provable family connections back to Sierra Leone. Unfortunately, the country's civil war delayed any immediate plans, but Opala continued to research Priscilla's story and found original records of the *Hare* slave ship in the archives of the New-York Historical Society. Among these records were the letters of Captain Godfrey, the ship's captain, sent from Sierra Leone on April 8, 1756, the day before he sailed for Charleston, and another he wrote on June 25, soon after arriving in America. To Opala's amazement, he also uncovered the actual records of the sale of the *Hare*'s slaves in Charleston with a specific mention of Elias Ball's purchase of three boys and two girls for £460. He said quietly to himself, "One of these girls must be Priscilla."

Opala had found something that had probably never been documented before: an unbroken trail for an African American family stretching from Africa all the way to the present day. But the question remains, how did Priscilla come to be captured? No account has ever been found. Judging from existing records of the slave trade in West Africa, she was possibly taken when her village in the interior was raided by African slave traders who profited by kidnapping people—especially those from rival kingdoms—and selling them to European slave traders. In Sierra Leone the African slave traders were often Fula, Mandingo, and Susu people, and the European traders were mostly British. The dragnet caught those who were kidnapped, prisoners of war, people who were convicted of crimes, and some whose families were forced to sell them to pay off debts. In each case, people were sold for guns, gunpowder, cloth, rum, metal goods, and various trinkets.

With the end of the Sierra Leone civil war in 2002, there was such interest in the story, that Jacque Metz, a Charleston filmmaker, offered to organize a "Priscilla's Homecoming" trip and document the return of Thomas Martin, Priscilla's modern descendant, to Sierra Leone. Although Opala and Metz learned that Martin had passed away, they proposed to the Sierra Leone government that Thomalind Martin Polite, Mr. Martin's daughter, lead the homecoming visit. They later returned to Charleston with an official invitation for Polite. A thirty-one-year-old primary school speech therapist with a soft voice and a contemplative manner, Polite immediately agreed. To Opala's and Metz's relief, she was excited to go to Sierra Leone. Also invited on this trip was noted actor, educator, and former executive director of the Gullah Geechee Cultural Heritage Corridor Commission Ronald Daise, who would serve as Gullah ambassador.

Before the homecoming could take place, there was a new wrinkle, though, that had to be considered. Edward Ball had concluded in his book that the *Hare*, the ship that took Priscilla to America, was a British vessel owned by London-based proprietors of Bunce Island. However, records Opala found indicated that the *Hare* was actually an American slave ship sailing out of Newport, Rhode Island. Newport was the largest slave-trading port in North America during the eighteenth century, and the ship was owned by Samuel and William Vernon, two of the richest merchants in colonial Rhode Island.

Publicity about Rhode Island's role in the Atlantic slave trade came as a shock to many northerners, and especially to New Englanders, who grew up equating slavery strictly with the South. However, Rhode Island was almost as active as Charleston in the slave trade, except that it sent slave ships to Africa rather than receive them. From 1725–1807, Newport vessels made more than one thousand voyages to Africa, carrying more than one hundred thousand slaves to the West Indies, Havana, and the American Colonies.[4] Rhode Island also had more slaves than any other northern colony. Before the Revolutionary War, almost 20 percent of Newport's population was Black, and it was said that one-third of the families in the region owned at least one slave—and many of them owned two or three slaves. It was common to see advertisements in the *Newport Gazette* with large black headlines:

NEW SHIPMENT: SLAVES FROM THE GOLD COAST—
MEN, WOMEN, AND YOUTHS. IN GOOD HEALTH AND
WELL TRAINED FOR WORK IN THE HOME OR FIELDS.
TRADING AT PIER TWO SATURDAY AT NOON.

Armed with these facts, Opala traveled to Rhode Island, where he was able to get historians and community activists to raise funds to bring Thomalind Martin Polite to Rhode Island after she returned from her trip to Sierra Leone. As he saw it, the documentary film recording her journey would have an interesting and unexpected twist—it would not just link Sierra Leoneans and Gullahs, but it would also link Gullahs to the Rhode Island community. Thomalind would later lay a wreath in the water in Newport at the very spot from which local historians believe the *Hare* sailed on its fateful voyage to Sierra Leone in 1756. Sierra Leoneans who came from their homes in various parts of the United States were on hand to stand beside her and say prayers to their shared ancestors.

Completing the Journey

According to an article in the *Charleston Post and Courier*, Thomalind Martin Polite is "a cheerful woman with hardly a trace of a Southern drawl, much less 'Charlestonese' or Gullah."[5] In fact she readily admits that she hasn't even heard much "true" Gullah, nor can she speak it. Her introduction to the language of her ancestors was through hearing storytellers at the library as a child. She has a master's degree in speech pathology and audiology and is currently a speech language pathologist practicing in North Charleston, South Carolina. She is following in the family footsteps.

Education runs in the Martin family blood, dating back to Thomalind's great-grandfather Henry, the first Martin. In 1866, Henry, now remembered as Peter Henry Robards Martin, received his first formal education in the one-room Nazareth Church School in Pinopolis, South Carolina. He himself would teach there before moving to Charleston, marrying, working as a carpenter, and finally answering the call to become a preacher. In the latter part of his life, he moved back to the country, where he built a church and taught his parishioners' children until his death in 1931.

With his wife, Anna Cruz, Henry had ten children. One of his offspring was Peter Henry Jr., born in 1886, who prospered as a roofer. Peter's son, Thomas P. Martin, born in 1933, was the dignified, soft-spoken man Edward Ball met. A career educator who taught English, Thomas Martin, Thomalind's father, eventually became assistant principal of Charleston High School before he retired.

In late winter of 2005, Thomalind, bright, talented, and energetic, was almost overcome by the expectations of what it would be like to return to the land of her ancestors. "I can hardly describe it," she exclaimed in an interview about her upcoming trip. "I'm ecstatic. I feel fortunate to be the one chosen to go. I wish my father was still alive because he should have been the one to go. But with Priscilla at the beginning of the family line and me at the end, I guess it's only fitting." She paused for a moment and added thoughtfully, "Still, it's not as though I'm just taking a vacation to see a foreign land. I'm actually going back to where Priscilla was born—something few African Americans today have ever experienced. How else can I say it? I'll be *going home*."

For most African Americans, there is a genealogical void in their family history, a line severed by slavery. The Martin family's ability to trace their ancestry to a particular African ancestor via an unbroken document trail that goes all the way back to Africa is a rarity and a truly historic event. To add to the excitement, it was reported that, for the people of Sierra Leone, Thomalind's arrival—"Priscilla's Homecoming"—was cause for national celebration. The invitation Opala and Metz brought from the Sierra Leone government read, "Your visit will promote a greater understanding of the family ties that link the Gullah people of South Carolina and all Sierra Leoneans and help further the bonds of friendship between Americans and Africans in general. I can assure you that your visit will be well-publicized here before you arrive and that thousands of our people will be anxious to greet you, their long-lost family come home from South Carolina."

This was by no means an exaggeration. A year before it happened, Opala gave a speech on Priscilla's Homecoming at the U.S. Embassy in Sierra Leone. "I spoke to a packed house, people from the arts, education, the government—

all areas of the community," he reported. "In my speech I said, 'We know that this little girl lost her family. She thought of her family every day, and she thought of her home every day until she died.' After I said that, the audience was completely silent. I looked up to see everybody nodding their heads in agreement, 'Of course, of course.' Because, you see, in Sierra Leone, family is everything. Home is everything. They lost people. Hundreds of thousands of their ancestors were taken away by slavery. To have Priscilla's descendant come back is almost like Priscilla herself returning. To the people of Sierra Leone, this is considered incredibly good fortune—a true blessing. A healing. When Thomalind arrives, she'll be greeted by complete strangers joyously calling to her, '*Pree-SEE-la! Pree-SEE-la!*' It will be a very emotional moment. This will be just a beginning, the first door of many to open as all of us, on both sides of the Atlantic, find ways to reconcile with this powerful past."

Creating a Home in America

The Gullah Geechee people are the descendants of West and Central Africans who were forced to work on the rice, Sea Island cotton, and indigo plantations along the eastern coastal areas of North Carolina, South Carolina, Georgia, and Florida. They were from many different tribes, including the Mandingo, Bamana, Wolof, Fula, Temne, Mende, Vai, Akan, Ewe, Bakongo, and Kimbundu, but over time these enslaved workers developed a unique Creole language and culture framed within their African ancestry. Historian John Tibbetts states, "The Gullah people managed to retain extensive African sources in their speech and folklore. The grammar of Gullah is African, and many aspects of Gullah culture—religious beliefs, arts and crafts, stories, songs, and proverbs—are also derived from African sources. The Gullah people have preserved more of their African cultural history than any other large group of blacks in the United States."[6]

Unlike other areas of the United States, there existed a Black majority in the Sea Islands region in the eighteenth and nineteenth centuries. In the first federal census of 1790, Blacks comprised 18 percent of the nation's total population but ranged from 47–93 percent in several coastal areas of South Carolina, including the port of Charleston, the center of the slave trade.[7] This overwhelming African American population with its African-infused culture was separated from the mainland by creeks, rivers, and marshes that formed a geographic barrier against outside influences. Furthermore, the summer season brought the threat of malaria spread through mosquitoes, leaving Gullah Geechee communities even more isolated when white owners and their families moved to the mainland.

The warm climate of coastal South Carolina and Georgia was excellent for the cultivation of rice, but it proved equally suitable for the spread of malaria and yellow fever brought over during the slave trade. Some enslaved Africans had an inherited resistance to malaria due to the sickle cell (red blood cell) trait; however, prolonged labor in high ambient temperatures "increased the probability of those with sickle-cell trait or disease experiencing symptoms of fatigue, joint pain, fevers and, in children, delayed growth."[8]

It is possible that many of the ill-defined malaise that enslaved people experienced and the slave owners labeled "malingering" were in fact episodes of "sickle-cell crisis." On the Ball plantations where Priscilla lived out her life, the enslaved born between 1800 and 1849 had a life expectancy of 19.8 years for males and 20.5 years for females. About half of the children did not live to adulthood.[9] From out of such tragedy came African Americans resolved to never forget where they came from and to impart survival skills to the next generations.

A powerful example is provided by an islander named George Hamilton, age seventy-three, who survived an experience that might have meant death for someone not brought up in the Gullah tradition. Born into the steady hands of a Gullah midwife in the Spanish Wells section of Hilton Head Island, South Carolina, he was indoctrinated early on into the native ways. By the age of six, he had learned how to row a handmade wooden boat, and within a few more years he was adept at pulling fat blue crabs from long drop lines baited with ham skin and earning his keep on a job with the local fishery.

"We had to learn what we had to do and make do with what we had," Hamilton said of his childhood, explaining how he and his siblings and neighborhood friends taught each other and learned through success and failure. They knew where to get berries and certain kinds of barks that would cure toothaches and stomach ailments; they knew the waters and the tides; they could foretell weather conditions by changing winds; they gained respect for the marshes and waters around them and knew what dangers to avoid and what animals and other wildlife to respect.[10]

So it was in the spring of 2006 that his sixteen-foot wooden-hulled boat broke loose while he was picking oysters and drifted away from him in a strong current. He suddenly found himself stranded on uninhabited and isolated Turtle Island, far from the cruising waters between Daufuskie Island and Savannah. Not too concerned at first, he expected that family members and friends would come looking for him or that he would spot one of the nature tour boats that occasionally ventured far from the usual courses. But one day faded into the next and the next, and it was nine days before he was found.

How did an elderly gentleman survive and remain in such good health? As one account detailed it, he survived on dew and plant juices. He ate cactus scraped open with oyster shells. He ate the soft, salty-sweet roots of marsh grasses. He sucked on tiny flowers and blooms and pine needles that were moist and dripping at sunrise. Water was made available when he found a cache of a dozen carelessly discarded water bottles. They were empty, but he turned them upside down in the grass at night with the caps slightly loose, and by early morning each one had half an inch of water that had condensed inside. During the day, he stuffed the bottles with shaved cactus plants and placed them in the sun, where the heat drained moisture from them. He was also able to open a few oysters and small mussels laboriously with the only metal implement he had in his pockets—a key ring.

Shelter was a problem because the nighttime temperature dropped into the fifties, and he was wearing only jeans and a T-shirt. But he found a small hillock that sheltered him from the wind, where he made a lean-to from a small pine tree and palmetto fronds, with a bed of pine straw. During the day, some of his most agonizing moments were when he saw U.S. Coast Guard helicopters off in the distance, rising and falling and lowering divers at a spot where he later learned his boat had been found capsized. No amount of waving with his T-shirt on a long stick got any attention, and his efforts served only to exhaust and dishearten him for several hours.

After his eventual rescue, he learned that the Coast Guard had given him up for dead, believing him drowned and swept away in the often strong currents between the islands. On the third or fourth day, he spotted a fishing boat offshore, but it vanished past the far end of the island, and in his haste to get attention by waving he slipped and bloodied himself from head to toe on the sharp oyster beds that rimmed the shorelines. When he was finally able to get back up, the boat had vanished. From his long experience as a striker on a shrimp boat, he knew of the potential for infection that can come from oyster cuts, so he splashed salt water over every affected part of his body, even though the pain of the salt on the sores was almost unbearable. Then he sat in the sun to bake away the saline.

"Mosquitoes were hard on me, nighttime was hard on me," he later recalled. "Family couldn't do me no good. Only thing that could do me good was a little prayer maybe."[11]

His savior, on the ninth day, was a charter boat captain who spotted him waving his shirt as the captain navigated his boat past the island while going after redfish. Because he could not land on the treacherous oyster banks, the captain radioed the Coast Guard for help. Hamilton spent three days in the hospital recuperating and getting treatments for his cuts, bruises, insect bites, and lack of food and water. During that time, he reiterated again and again to visitors that God and his Gullah upbringing had saved his life. He called upon those life skills learned from his parents and those ancestors who had survived similar hardships during slavery.

There are many views regarding the origins and meanings of Gullah and Geechee. In general, African Americans living in the coastal areas of the Carolinas are known as Gullah while those in Georgia and upper Florida are called Geechee. Georgian communities further distinguish themselves as either "Saltwater Geechee," those near the coast, or "Freshwater Geechee," those near inland rivers and lakes. But the historical roots of Gullah and Geechee are a bit more complex and difficult to substantiate. Historian Margaret Washington Creel offers two possible origins for Gullah:

> The name "Gullah" is generally believed to be a shortened form of Angola. Africans from the Kongo-Angola region, Bantu-speaking peoples, were imported in large numbers during Carolina's early colonial history. As early as 1742, the *South Carolina Gazette* advertised for a runaway slave called "Golla Harry." One of Denmark Vesey's coconspirators, "Gullah Jack" was reportedly born in Angola. An entry of the Charleston City Council for 1822 refers to "Gullah Jack" and his "Gullah or Angola Negroes." Another theory suggests that the name was group-initiated, yet from a different ethnic source. "Golla" was used in the eighteenth century while "Gullah" was a nineteenth-century term for slaves in the coastal region of South Carolina. A very large group of Africans from the Liberian hinterland was called Golas, sometimes spelled "Goulah." ... One early twentieth-century white South Carolinian, Reed Smith, wrote extensively about Gullah dialect, maintaining that the term refers to the Golas of Liberia.[12]

Lorenzo Turner points to the Kissi (pronounced GEE-zee) people, who live in the area between Sierra Leone, Guinea, and Liberia, as the origin of Geechee. More recent scholars, however, believe the term emerged from the formerly enslaved Africans living in the vicinity of the Ogeechee River in Georgia's Lowcountry.

The Gullah Geechee people in South Carolina and Georgia live in what is called the Lowcountry, the distinctive low-lying semitropical areas of the coastal plains. Tibbetts points out, although many people think of the Gullah culture in terms of major Sea Islands such as St. Helena, Johns, Edisto, and Wadmalaw, "the classic Gullah culture existed most notably on the mainland tidal areas along rivers for 30 miles inland known as the rice coast."[13] Actually, Gullahs live in rural areas from Pender County, North Carolina, down to St. Johns County, Florida, but "they maintained their separateness" according to Lawrence Roland, historian at the University of South Carolina. Their isolated existence, born out of slavery, enabled them to survive even today and continue cultural traditions dating back to Priscilla's young childhood in Sierra Leone.

—CHAPTER TWO—

CATCH THE LEARNING

The scene is Philadelphia in the year 1862. The spotlight is on a young woman of thirty-seven, Laura Matilda Towne, who was born on May 3, 1825, and raised in Salem, Massachusetts. She attended the Women's Medical College in Philadelphia, where she studied homeopathic medicine, a program based on the belief of "like cures like." Homeopathy is a treatment using "minute doses of substances to stimulate the individual's natural healing process in order to restore and maintain health."[1]

Laura also trained as a teacher, and she was well recognized for her devoted volunteer work with underprivileged children in "charity" schools. After moving to Philadelphia in 1840, she found herself in "socially progressive circles" interacting with families and individuals counted among the most elite in Philadelphian society. Eventually, she became an avid follower of William

Lloyd Garrison, editor of the antislavery newspaper *The Liberator* and one of the most outspoken and influential leaders in the battle for freedom. Unfortunately, Laura found little support in her own abolitionist efforts in Philadelphia because women were discouraged from such "unfeminine" crusades.

Described as "pragmatic, down-to-earth, and strong-minded—a born administrator," Laura soon added the role of missionary to her calling.[2] She closely followed news reports that Union naval forces had achieved a strategic victory in a battle in Port Royal Sound, South Carolina, freeing the town of Beaufort, South Carolina, and several of the adjoining Sea Islands, including St. Helena. St. Helena was home to numerous cotton plantations whose owners had fled inland and westward, away from advancing Union forces, abandoning an estimated ten thousand enslaved people. In response to this dramatic need, the federal government instituted the Port Royal Experiment to provide for these newly free Africans' basic needs and to help them become self-sufficient citizens.

Described as a "rehearsal for Reconstruction," this program eventually involved more than fifty abolitionists, many of them young and fascinated by the adventurous campaign "to tutor the freemen out of slavery and into freedom."[3] One of their recruits was Laura Towne, who wanted not only to teach but also to establish a school for the Black children. In early April 1862, she found herself, along with some twenty other abolitionists, mostly of her own age, on board the *Oriental*, a steam-and-sail vessel of such antiquity that it had been all but scrapped by the Union navy. Rough weather, the condition of the vessel, and the presence of young passengers who were not accustomed to life at sea all contributed to making the voyage a fearful one for most of those on board. To make matters even worse, several members of the crew took delight in faking terror as the old ship pitched and rolled, saying in loud voices they were not sure whether it could withstand the high seas without capsizing.

Despite the discomforts and gloomy anticipations, the *Oriental* arrived in the picturesque port of Beaufort, South Carolina, one of the largest natural harbors on the Atlantic coast, framed by waving palms and stately oaks, permitting its passengers to disembark in a setting far more civilized than they had imagined. Rich in history, Beaufort was one of the oldest settlements

OVERLEAF: Sweet potato planting on Hopkinson's Plantation, Edisto Island, South Carolina, circa 1862. *Library of Congress, LC-DIG-ppmsca-11398.*

in America, having been discovered by the Spanish in 1514 and chartered by the British in 1711 as a center of indigo and rice plantations. The town, long known for its charm as the "Queen of the South Carolina Islands," fascinated the newcomers. Mockingly called the "Gideonites" by Union soldiers, Laura and the other young northerners had high hopes of being able to ease the trials and tribulations of the formerly enslaved Africans and guide them on the road to true emancipation and independence through education. The Gideonites would soon discover that the way ahead was fraught with unseen difficulties and frustrations.

By April 16, Laura was temporarily situated at the Beaufort home of Caroline Forbes, a white woman who lived in a fine home with an expansive seawall on three sides, abutting the Beaufort River, Brickyard Creek, and the bay, with luxuriant shade trees and brilliant blankets of flowers. There she experienced not only the amenities of plantation southern living but also the precarious position she was in. During her first walk down the road into the town, she was pained by the desertion and desolation and somewhat unnerved by the presence of Union troops, some of whom galloped past on horseback in a reckless manner and others who lounged idly on street corners in dirty uniforms looking unfriendly.

Walking down the street with Caroline one day, she encountered her first Black children from the island, who had a "mode of speaking that was not very intelligible." (It was some time before she realized that when they referred to "befit" they meant Beaufort.) But she had kind words to say about these children, who "tumbled about at all hours" on the front porch and in the main hall of the house where she was staying—"all very civil, but full of mischief and fun."[4]

Laura also had a chance to visit two of the local Black schools, where she observed the children learning their letters, which were primarily the pronunciation and meaning of one-syllable words. When she asked why there were so few children in the schools, she was told that most Black women and children had been sent to the plantations to keep them away from the unpredictable soldiers, and that many of the men had been conscripted into the Union army or were given jobs at nearby encampments. Although the children seemed happy enough in school, there seemed to be no system in their education, and only a modicum of concentration. These early experiences informed Laura of the daunting educational challenges and laid the foundation for the northern-based curriculum she later implemented as principal of her own school.

Laura had expected to meet other young missionaries from Philadelphia and Washington, mainly affiliated with the Freedmen's Aid Society or Protestant churches, who were passengers on an earlier vessel from the North. But she learned they had already gone to plantations on St. Helena, Lady's Island, Dataw, and other nearby Sea Islands to begin their instruction of the freed people. Around this time, she learned of a disturbing reality that had never occurred to her or been discussed. The local families and even the Union officers not only tended to overlook the fact that the islanders were free, but they threatened to transport these poor Blacks back to their former owners if they did not continue in service to the white population. With little choice, many of them worked in private homes doing housework or washing, receiving miniscule wages. Other freedmen, like one referred to as "Uncle Robert," delivered milk, eggs, or butter to the homes of white families.

By the end of April, Laura was able to write home with the good news that she was fairly well acclimated to the southern climate and community and was happy to be tending to the maladies of Blacks on a nearby plantation who had contracted measles and mumps. She had even been invited to attend a "pray's house or "prayer house," a small cabin in the midst of splendid live oaks hanging with Spanish moss, where Laura heard the islanders singing, praying, and reading from a tattered old Bible. Later she attended a "ring shout" in the large cabin of a Black woman named Rina and wrote an invaluable early record of this West African tradition:

> Three men stood and sang, clapping, and gesticulating. The others shuffled along on their heels, following one another in a circle and occasionally bending the knees in a kind of curtsey. They began slowly, a few going around and more gradually joining in, the song getting faster and faster, till at last only the most marked part of the refrain is sung and the shuffling, stamping, and clapping get furious. The floor shook so that it seemed dangerous. . . . They kept up the shout till very late.[5]

Laura's later description of the shout as a "savage heathenish dance" and a "form of idol worship" reflected her unfamiliarity with this form of religion so unlike her own. By comparison, her own Unitarian religion stressed guidance through reason and rationality and internal spiritual devotion. Throughout her many decades on the island, Laura struggled to appreciate the West African–derived elements of the islanders' shout.[6]

By May, Laura ventured out of the town of Beaufort into the countryside, riding to farms and plantations to meet the Blacks—mainly women and children—who were trying to cope with the planting, care of livestock, gleaning, and other typical chores. She was surprised at the vigor with which they welcomed a "white lady," and she noted their emphasis on growing edible corn crops over money-making cotton. Corn would prevent them from starving. Laura Towne closely observed the islanders' needs to determine what methods and facilities would accomplish the immense undertaking for which she had volunteered. At first it seemed that no lone individual could ever hope to cope with the desperate needs of these people, who were adjusting to their new lives as freed people. Laura could see that just teaching them to read and write was not enough.

Laura's assessment of the job ahead was that religion would probably be her strongest ally down the road. Most of the freed slaves—at least the adults—relied on their faith, hymns, and prayer meetings to cope with their difficult lives. Moreover, the most influential individuals were the religious leaders who—though few had any formal training as ministers—attracted devoted followers to their worship services. To gain similar support from the community, Laura began Bible classes for her students, and there were daily scriptures in their reading curriculum, requiring students to recite from the book of Psalms and the Ten Commandments. Laura even distributed Bibles to every island family.

An unsettling truth about the Port Royal Experiment was the presence of only about four thousand Union troops in the Beaufort area while all around them were some twenty thousand Confederate soldiers, who might at any moment decide to rout their enemies. The Gideonites from Philadelphia, New York, and New England knew full well that they were sitting on a powder keg. In fact, Laura Towne herself was involved in several skirmishes that could have had fatal outcomes.

In late May, Laura made the decision to move from Beaufort to St. Helena Island some ten miles to the east. Her reasons were threefold: she was getting tired of the petty bureaucracy and the presence of so many military officers who had rules of their own; she found it difficult to try to establish a school with so few pupils and other programs already in operation; and she had just received some $2,000 worth of clothing, rations, equipment, and other supplies, making her less dependent on her Beaufort hosts. Another possible reason was the pending arrival of her good friend and associate Ellen Murray. She would be joining her as a teacher and partner. At last, it was time for Laura to venture into the unknown to help the freedmen become independent.

Off to St. Helena and a Site for the School

On Saturday, June 7, 1862, Laura Towne repacked her steamer trunk, ready for the hot and dusty cart ride over buggy roads and farm paths that lay ahead. She expressed great consternation and anxiety not only about leaving behind so many children and elderly people whom she had been treating, but also because recent skirmishes between Confederate and Union troops had forced the evacuation of many of the defending soldiers in Beaufort. Many of those in town were panicky because fleeing infantrymen had burned the bridge, but her own apprehension diminished considerably when she finally reached the deserted house on Oaks Plantation, which was the temporary headquarters of the Union Army. These accommodations were arranged by Edward L. Pierce, a young lawyer from Milton, Massachusetts, who had been assigned to aid the Blacks and oversee cotton production in the Sea Islands.

Even before trying to unpack and make living quarters out of semivacant rooms, Laura began planning where they could set up a classroom to entice students to begin lessons. She decided on the former parlor as the most likely classroom because of its reasonable space, light, and ventilation and then moved every bench, chair, and stool she could find into position. Her work was interrupted when one of the Black women living nearby rushed in to announce, "Miss Murray has come!" The news—though so long hoped-for—was so unexpected that Laura felt faint and had to sit down momentarily before going outside to greet Ellen and hear all the news about her trip down from the North.

Earlier, Ellen had twice traveled from Philadelphia to New York to board her expected ship and sail to Beaufort only to be turned away. The war made travel much more difficult now. When she finally embarked on her voyage, the passage was frightening, grim from beginning to end, leaving her in little condition to start teaching others the value and compassion of freedom. But the reunion with her lifelong friend and teaching associate Laura revived her, and their eagerness kept them awake for most of the night discussing plans for establishing their new school and for accomplishing their goals to teach their expected pupils. It should be pointed out here that Towne and Murray were only partially aware of the fact that, in South Carolina, just by teaching Black students how to read or write they were flouting a law whose breaking carried a fine of up to $100 and imprisonment. Yet their plans remained unchanged: they would teach basic literacy skills as the cornerstone of learning at their school, including not only reading and writing but multiplication, the alphabet, and the Bible. They were beginning an educational journey that would encompass the next four decades.

Several days went by, however, before they could spread the word about their new school and talk some likely pupils into attending. The potential students were shy and hesitant, if not confused by all the attention they were receiving. On opening day, June 18, they had nine pupils, all adults who were unsure about what would be expected of them. Towne and Murray named their fledgling school in honor of William Penn, who embodied the brotherhood of all humanity and their affiliation with Pennsylvania's Freedmen's Aid Society. Within a month, the enrollment multiplied tenfold when the two teachers gained the trust of the islanders, who initially believed there was imminent risk to their children by attending the school. Once the original parlor school was bursting at the seams, Laura and Ellen moved to larger accommodations at Brick Baptist Church in the center of the island.

From the standpoint of the two green teachers, however, instruction was going to be a challenge. As Laura Towne later recorded in her diaries, speaking of the female pupils' conduct, "They had no idea of sitting still, of giving attention, of ceasing to talk aloud. They lay down and went to sleep; they scuffled and struck each other; they got up by the dozen and walked off to the neighboring fields for blackberries, coming back to their seats with a curtsy when they were ready."[7] When an outbreak of smallpox occurred, Union officers encouraged Laura and Ellen to go North and leave the island like so many of the original Gideonites, but they refused to leave and give up their work. Penn School remained at Brick Baptist until a freedman named Hasting Gantt donated a fifty-acre tract of land across from the church. In 1864, the Pennsylvania Freedmen's Aid Society sent a three-room, ready-built schoolhouse by boat to St. Helena Island, and Towne personally donated a brass bell to the new school with the inscription "Proclaim Liberty." As it rang, the school's students, a heterogeneous group of men, women, and children, marched across the road and took their seats in one of the first schools for Blacks in the South.[8] The Freedman's Society was one of the few sources of income for the school over the ensuing years other than what the Towne family and close friends contributed whenever the financial situation became desperate.

Even though they had moved away from the military operations in the Beaufort and Port Royal Sound area, those at Penn School were constantly threatened by hostile skirmishes on St. Helena and even farther out toward

Fripp Island and the Coosaw River, where units of the Confederate Army were engaged in intermittent rearguard harassment. Again, Laura and Ellen were urged to return home at once, even if they had to leave their newfound friends and belongings, not to mention their aspirations, behind. James McKim, corresponding secretary of the Pennsylvania Freedman's Relief Association, expressed his concern for their safety in what he assessed as a "dangerous situation." Laura wrote in her diary, "Ellen and I are determined not to go, and I think our determination will prevail over his fears, so that he will not order us home, as he has the power, I suppose."[9]

The threat of an assault resulted in Laura's new role as a supervisor of a small detachment of freedmen ordered to train as recruits in the event Confederate soldiers invaded the area in search of supplies and equipment. For this purpose, she was given an assortment of muskets, pistols, and ammunition. Late afternoons she would run up a small flag, distribute the weapons from a locked cabinet, and drill the men for an hour, after which she would dismiss them and place the weapons back under lock and key. Although neither the leader nor the troops had much knowledge of either weapons or military strategy, these drills paid off one fateful night on October 24, 1862. "Three boats of rebels attempted to land on these islands last night, two at the village and one at Edding's Point," Laura wrote in her diary. "The Negroes with their guns were on picket; they gave the alarm, fired, and drove the rebels off."[10]

These new military responsibilities exacerbated Laura's already hectic daily schedule. She reported in one letter that she regularly got up at six, ate a hasty breakfast, and then saw three or four patients. Then, by nine o'clock, she was on her way to see patients living on one or two of the outlying plantations. She treated ulcers, injuries, respiratory ailments, measles, mumps, insect and snake bites, and an assortment of other ailments, as well as delivering babies and caring for colic and other infant-related maladies. "The roads are horrible," she wrote, "and the horses ditto, so I have a weary time getting around."[11] After returning home to grab lunch, Laura taught school until four o'clock, returned home at six o'clock for the military exercises, and ate dinner around seven o'clock. As it was, both Laura and Ellen now taught Sunday school lessons as well as their lay classes, and thus had not a single day of rest from one week to the next.

Once the military exercises concluded, the ladies would dress for dinner as was the custom, despite the environment, the sparsity of tableware, and the scarcity of customary food supplies. Fortunately, there was no real short-age of food. "We have nice melons and figs," Laura reported, "pretty good corn, tomatoes now and then, bread rarely, hominy, cornbread, and rice waf-fles.... We have fish nearly every day...and now and then turtle soup."[12] Meat of any kind was a scarcity because livestock was rarely raised for that purpose on the island, and the kinds of game—mainly squirrels and possums, caught by only a few hunters—were almost inedible.

Regardless of the demands and constraints of her self-imposed work sched-ule, Laura always found time to appreciate and comment about the beauties of the environment. "I wish you could see the wild flowers," she wrote to her friends up North, "the hedges of Adam's needle, with heads of white bells a foot or two through and four feet high; the purple pease [sic] with blossoms that look like dog-tooth violets—just the size—climbing up the cotton plant with its yellow flower, and making whole fields purple and gold; the passion flowers in the grass; the swinging palmetto sprays and the crape myrtle in full bloom."[13] Much as she enjoyed nature, there was always the constant torment from pests, especially the midges, punkies, fleas, and mosquitoes—the last-mentioned being so prevalent at certain times of the year that they had to sit in their room at night under netting. This restriction was a major aggravation for Laura because she could not write her daily diary or letters in the evening, having twice set the netting on fire from the candle she was using for light.

The tiny school staff was augmented in the early fall of 1862, when Char-lotte Forten joined Towne and Murray at Penn School. Charlotte, age twenty-five, was a Philadelphian born into an influential and affluent Black family who had started her teaching career in a school in Salem, Massachusetts—the first African American ever hired. Yearning to help her people and be part of what she hoped would be an upward movement out of slavery, she volunteered to be sent to the Sea Islands of South Carolina to join in the educational move-ment just underway. She immediately realized the challenges when she found that many of her pupils spoke only the Gullah Geechee language, and there was a lack of a formal school routine.

Charlotte's first day of teaching "was not a pleasant one," she wrote in her diary. "Part of my scholars are very tiny—babies, I call them—and it is hard to keep them quiet and interested while I am hearing the larger ones. They are too young even for the alphabet, it seems to me. I think I must write home and ask somebody to send me picture-books and toys to amuse them with."[14] Charlotte, however, had her triumphs with an adult student named Harry.

"He is most eager to learn...and is really a scholar to be proud of....I gave him his first lesson in writing tonight, and his progress was wonderful."[15]

Although enjoying many periods of accomplishment and satisfaction, Charlotte was often overcome with doubts that she could truly uplift her race. Also disturbing to her were the many instances in which the islanders had been mistreated, even by some of the northerners who were supposedly helping on the road to freedom. Suffering from recurring bouts of lung fever (pneumonia), she was finally forced to return home to Philadelphia after only two years on the island. On the eve of her first day of teaching she wrote this short prayer that sums up her noble intentions: "Dear children! born in slavery, but free at last? May God preserve to you all the blessings of freedom, and may you be in every possible way fitted to enjoy them. My heart goes out to you. I shall be glad to do all that I can to help you."[16]

Despite the failure and closure of most of the educational programs launched in the Port Royal Experiment, Penn School not only survived but continued to expand its enrollment and curriculum. The school's success was due not only to its demanding discipline but also to a rigorous, no-nonsense curriculum modeled after schools in New England and Philadelphia. Such an approach produced wonderful educational achievements from the students, but it came at the cost of the students' own culture, especially their language— Laura and Ellen discouraged its use. As one observer noted, "To Miss Towne and her faithful companion was turned over not only the task of teaching the Negro the three R's but also instilling in him the rudiments of civilization. The Negro had to be torn down and rebuilt according to the white man's conception of civilization."[17]

The teachers discovered that they could improve the quality of their classroom curricula by teaching songs to the students and observing various holidays to make the learning process fun as well as educational. The children sang favorites such as "My Country 'Tis of Thee" and "John Brown's Body," accompanied by homemade flutes and stringed instruments, and sometimes by drums and tambourines made by the students themselves. Murray, who played the organ, was responsible for much of the musical instruction and often challenged the students with northern hymns like "Pull for the Shore," "What Shall the Harvest Be," and "Sound the Loud Timbrel."

There was also the Fourth of July program, which they observed during the second year of Penn School. In addition to having discussions about the meaning of the Fourth of July and its place in America's history, the pupils made buttons, badges, and other typical tokens of the holiday and learned the verses of "The Star-Spangled Banner," which they sang "with great gusto." Charles F. Folsom of Massachusetts, who had arrived on the scene as temporary school superintendent, then read the Declaration of Independence, followed by a Black minister from the nearby Methodist church who gave an oration. Among the guests were a number of officers from the 54th Massachusetts Regiment (colored), including Colonel Robert Gould Shaw, who was soon to meet his death so heroically while leading his Black troops in battle at Fort Wagner on July 18, where nearly all of the officers of the 54th were killed or wounded.

The war was never far away. "We could hear the guns all day and night," Laura wrote later to her friends up North. Two weeks after the Fourth of July event, she was hastily summoned away from her classroom to Beaufort to help nurse the casualties who had been transported down by the hundreds from the fateful battle at Fort Wagner. Noticeably missing was Colonel Shaw, who was buried in a common pit on the battlefield as an insult to a leader of a Black regiment. The field hospital was inundated with food donations from the farmers, including melons, sweet potatoes, chickens, and other produce, but there was little that could be done for the gravely wounded. The citizens were further asked to send potatoes and other vegetables to the soldiers at Fort Wagner, who were suffering from dwindling food supplies as a result of the engagement.

The winter of 1865 was nasty and grim on St. Helena, with no stoves, plants frozen stiff, milk icing in the dairy, and the earth a hard ball. For the first time since arriving on the island, Laura was too ill to leave her room for the better part of a week. But many of the school families were even worse off. "The children are all emaciated to the last degree," she wrote, "and have such violent coughs and dysenteries that few survive. It is frightening to see such suffering among children." One of the problems was that the intense cold found very few families with blankets, and many children died of the cold before the government finally distributed blankets to the neediest homes.

Laura's medical training made her aware of what the problem was and how it could be alleviated, but she had insufficient resources to prevent the widespread tragedy. Even after the freezing winter waned and spring approached, the disaster had only partially abated. In the school area alone, there were nearly one hundred "almost naked and entirely filthy" people, most of whom were deathly ill, still awaiting boxes of supplies that had been promised but were endlessly delayed. "The people come to our yard and stand mute in their misery," she reported, unable to find even scraps of clothing, and there was no room to take many inside a building for relief. To compound the problem, the intense cold and freezing rains had destroyed the small winter crops, made fishing almost impossible, and sent what small game there might have been in the forests into hibernation, leaving the populace starving. The Penn School teachers did what they could to obtain grits and rice from Beaufort and the military bases, but these rations were far too little to meet the overwhelming need.[18]

The coming of spring also brought a great anguish for the freed slaves. On April 14, 1865, several from Penn School traveled to Charleston to see the United States flag raised on Fort Sumter by Union General Robert Anderson, who had been compelled to surrender the same fort four years earlier. On April 23, a town crier in the village of St. Helena announced that Abraham Lincoln had been assassinated—ironically, just at the time that the troops were celebrating the recapture of the fort. Many Black people had considered Lincoln to be a saint and their savior, and they went into a long period of mourning, conducting religious services and praying that the assassination had not taken place and that their president was only wounded and would recover. At Penn School, the children draped the classrooms in what pieces of black cloth they could find, and some pinned scraps of the cloth to their shirts or hats to show their sorrow.

Oddly there is no record that the schoolchildren, teachers, or residents of St. Helena actively celebrated the end of the Civil War. There was simply very little to celebrate in the Sea Islands, and soon the twelve-year Reconstruction period in the South would bring broken promises and even more heartaches to Blacks. The remoteness of Penn School and St. Helena protected the teachers and the islanders from most of the southern backlash following the Civil War. However, Laura Towne and Ellen Murray found it increasingly difficult to cut through the shattered communications network to order badly needed supplies and equipment. To make matters worse, most of the Union officers they knew who had been stationed in the Beaufort area and who had helped them greatly in times of need had been transferred or relieved of duty.

Crop problems would be one of the biggest concerns for Towne, Murray, and others associated with Penn School during the next thirty years. Yet it is remarkable that in every case of agricultural disaster, they managed to take courses of action to keep the school functioning and in some cases even to use these situations to train their young pupils who would have to face such set-backs all of their lives. Penn School had been founded, after all, not simply to acquaint students with the arts and letters but to alert them to, and train them in, the ways of living against all odds. On May 7, 1871, Laura Towne wrote a note in her diary: "Just think, forty-six years of age! Almost half a century and with so much history in it too!"[19]

Little did she realize that her work was not only helping these Black people on a remote island but also laying the groundwork for the upward mobility of an entire race. These people, though unknown in her time by any specific name, would later be called Gullah Geechee.

CHAPTER THREE

A QUANTUM LEAP

We jump from the nineteenth century to St. Helena Island in 1989, when the Gullah contingent left their Sea Island shores to explore their ancestry in West Africa and see an unfortunate reality. Over the past several decades, the predominantly African American community of St. Helena Island, like many island communities on the southern part of the U.S. Atlantic coast, experienced the rapid encroachment of aggressive and often carelessly planned development. The result is a profound sense of displacement among the African American population, a separation from a way of life that evolved out of slavery, through emancipation and then Reconstruction, and into the twentieth century. The rapid expansion of luxury residential complexes, commercial businesses, resort and tourist attractions, and the infrastructure to support them has drastically changed the once idyllic rural farming communities of the islands. Although St. Helena is not as totally transformed as some of the neighboring islands, the people are fully aware of the fact that vigilance is now a way of life they must maintain to guard against further displacement.

The disappearing presence of Gullahs on the islands raises questions about real estate development in the southern coastal states and the importance of honoring communities' farming and cultural legacies. All too often, decisions in these areas are driven by profit without the inclusion of the voices of those most impacted. It should not be forgotten how thousands of enslaved Africans used their agricultural skills to build highly successful rice, cotton, and indigo plantations. Equally so, their relative social and geographical isolation allowed these people to create unique artwork, music, food, and language— Gullah Geechee culture. After emancipation, freed Blacks purchased valuable land for the first time upon which to make their new lives and fashioned compounds reminiscent of the family complexes of West African villages.

Until well into the mid-1900s, small farms, saltwater creeks, and streams that flowed nearby gave the people of St. Helena Island most of what they needed to be self-sufficient. The rest was up to their own hard work and ingenuity and the strong sense of interdependence that was fostered among them since Reconstruction and even before. Families and extended families worked the fields, fished the waters, and shared goods and labor. Everything that went on their tables and most of what their families used came from the island's natural environment. What cash was needed was earned by taking produce by boat to mainland markets or by working at Penn School, for many years the island's most prominent establishment.

With the coming of development in the latter half of the twentieth century, the self-sufficient way of life changed for the islanders. Emory Campbell explains:

> The biggest impact has been the need for cash. The old culture known as the Gullah, and just now being recognized as a major heritage, had existed without the need for cash. Everything the Gullah people needed was done by them, among them, and, you might say, in coordination with the entire community. If you needed a net knitted, you knew where the net knitter was. You shared information. All of a sudden, develop-

OVERLEAF: Slave quarters on a plantation at Port Royal Island, South Carolina, circa 1862. *Library of Congress, LC-USZ62-67818.*

ment and the need for cash comes. Now on the island people have to buy food, look for better ways to fix the roof or equip their homes, but since they don't grow crops or maintain a tool shop, and since they have a job that takes all their time, and hardly ever get to go fishing, they realize they have changed day-to-day occupations and a way of life.[1]

In a story circle, arranged to present an insider view of life in the Sea Islands, three African American islanders, Ursell Holmes, Ethel Green, and Martha Chisholm, recall how different life was when they were growing up.

Holmes: My grandparents worked mostly in the fields. They tried to support themselves with the fieldwork to grow tomatoes and cucumbers, corn, and vegetables, and sometimes okra, beans, and peas. They would take them to Beaufort and sell them. They did not do too much outside work, although sometimes my grandfather worked on the Penn School farm. Everybody had cows and horses that they used to help farm because they had no farming equipment like you have today. At certain times of the year, they did hog killing, and in our community, everyone shared the meat from the hogs. So that's how we lived.

Chisholm: And you had the sweet potatoes, and corn. Folks grew their own corn and ground it, so you got the cornmeal, you got your husk, you got your grits. We grew sugarcane and ground it and then made syrup. They also grew rice, and the little children had to shoo the blackbirds out of the field so they would not eat the rice. I cried many a day when the birds would fly over my head, and I could not make them go away because the rice was taller than I was. Turkeys, they raised and sold them at Thanksgiving. The marine base at Parris Island was always a good market. Folks would come by and find out what you had and buy it—the city folks who lived in town who weren't able to farm. Or the insurance man and the mailman would say, "Miss So-and-so, I need two quarts of lima beans" or "I need some eggs" or "I need me a chicken for Sunday." You'd supply what was needed and then get paid—usually less than what was charged at local stores.

Green: I lived with my grandmother. I didn't do a lot of fieldwork, I was just there tending my grandmother's garden, but it was a big garden. She had field peas, butter beans, okra, peanuts, greens, corn. During the summer, we had fig trees, peach trees, pear trees, plums, and so forth. So we picked all those fruits, and Granny preserved them in jars and put them aside for the winter. My uncles were the farmers, so when it was time to learn about the crops, I worked on my uncles' farms. My mother was gone a lot of the time because she was a domestic with a U.S. Marine major on nearby Parris Island, and then went with his family when he was transferred to another base at Quantico, Virginia. She sent money back home for my upkeep, to send me to school, and for my clothing. I went out on nearby farms to work. I didn't have to go, but it was a chance to get away from home. That was where the other children of the neighborhood were, so I could have some playmates and enjoy some fun. Those were the farms of the white folks who were able to have costly equipment like tractors and trucks, and that was where you made your money in the summertime.

Chisholm: The river was our "supermarket." The river was always there. Before my grandfather went to work at four o'clock in the morning, he would go in the river, throw his net, and pull up a bucket of fish to bring home. Then we had to get up and clean those fish before we went to school and lay them out for Grandmother to cook. Whenever there was nothing to eat, they would say, "Go get something." There were always plenty of crabs, oysters, clams, or different kinds of fish. We had a wood-burning stove and often my grandmother would fry up a batch, so we could always have some that were ready to eat.

Due to outside intervention, the ability to "go get something" out of the river has changed. Whereas people once fished for food and income, now it is mainly just a recreational sport with rules and regulations controlling when and where you can fish. The South Carolina State Wildlife Commission established a sixty-day annual season for baiting shrimp and limited the amount of shrimp that could be caught, frustrating island fishermen who preferred the old, traditional method of baiting. Equally impacting the amount and quality of seafood is the growing problem of pollution in waterways caused by waste runoff from cars, boats, golf courses, homes, and hotels. Developers did not anticipate the effects of the large volume of sewage from septic tanks—more than the land would hold. As a result, yards are often flooded and sewage lines

overtaxed, causing seepage into the creeks and streams, and shellfish beds often had to be closed at times because of the heavy pollution. Albert George,
the first director of conservation at the South Carolina Aquarium who was
raised Gullah Geechee, worries that these environmental changes will affect
the Gullahs' unique cuisine:

> Shrimp, for example, is an integral ingredient in several Gullah Geechee
> dishes eaten throughout the South, such as the popular Lowcountry
> boil, which to the Gullah Geechee was considered a "slop pot," a way
> to use all the leftovers from the fridge before they went bad. But "shell-
> fish need a certain level of water quality and salinity. Oysters, clams—
> you see serious shifts in their ability to propagate in [the] environment,"
> George said. "These people are experiencing changes to their land, a shift
> in habitat and shift of what's in the water itself . . . taking away hundreds
> of years of cuisine and culture.[2]

Many islanders further lament the lack of wild animals they used to see
when they were growing up, including rabbits and deer that would run across
the fields or slip into the backyards to nibble cabbage and collard greens in the
garden. There was enough food for everybody, but now the wildlife no longer
have any place to go. Even the turtles that would come out of the water to sun
on the banks seem to be fewer and fewer.

Some of the older Black people on the Sea Islands still maintain small gardens, and a few farmers like Walter Mack do small-scale farming:

> I'm doing something different, though. I am trying fruit trees, and I
> want to get into herbs and flowers. People think some fruits don't grow
> around here, but I don't believe that. I have been very successful in grow-
> ing apples. Blueberries thrive down here, as well as figs and pears. The
> muscadine grape is another one that is easily grown because muscadines
> are indigenous to this area. Growing up I remember my grandmother
> had citrus fruit trees—oranges, tangerines, and lemons. I want to try to
> get back to doing some citrus because I think they can make it here, you
> just have to get the right variety.[3]

Mack, former executive director of the Penn Center, is one of the local
farmers who believes that the family farm and the traditions of self-sufficiency
so important to island families of the past can be adapted to have a place in
the twenty-first century. Some years ago, Tuskegee University introduced lo-

cal farmers to "u-pick" fruits and vegetables farms and other strategies of the modern farm entrepreneur, with the idea that tourists would be attracted to farms not only for the fresh produce but also for the visual appeal of fruits and vegetables in their native surroundings. "People love to see things growing in the natural setting," said one of Tuskegee's researchers. "If you ask kids where a tomato comes from, most of them would answer, 'out of the store.' The idea that you can take children to see tomatoes growing is a selling point—almost like going on an outing to a petting zoo."[4]

Of the small Black farmers in his area, Mack could think of only one person, Jackie Frazier, who is currently able to make a living from farming as a full-time job.

> He has a large u-pick operation. One thing that he started was a greenhouse to grow strawberries year-round. If nothing else, it's a big attraction. He decided that a tour of his farm operation would be successful. Everything is based on the tourist industry, and he is in a good location. He still does some truck farming along with his u-pick. He has truckers coming in from New England buying up loads of produce from him, especially his main crop, which is watermelon.[5]

Frazier is well known locally for his produce and for the fact that he never wears shoes; thus, his business is called Barefoot Farms.

Small farmers argue that governmental regulations have favored the corporate farms and big businesses. The large farm owners, many of whom live outside the area and even outside the state, have been able to influence legislation and regulatory agencies unfavorable to small farmers. For example, they have changed the way tomatoes are cultivated. As one local grower complained,

> All of a sudden, the big farmers were not going to plant the sweet soft tomatoes any longer. The breed they selected was one that was local to Florida—beautiful to look at but with a skin so tough that, if they dropped to the ground, they would practically bounce back at you. The homegrown variety was more easily bruised and thus less marketable in bulk, but it is a sweeter and more tender tomato. Then the requirements specified that growers had to cover the fields with plastic, maintain a certain amount of irrigation under the plastic, and intake gas to kill the weeds. . . . All of these procedures, equipment, and labor priced the small farmer right out of the market, as well as ending up with a product that has led to many complaints from consumers.[6]

Mack remembers the farming practices of old: "When I was growing up, all the local farmers grew what were called 'hotbeds,' which were small nurseries where they used their own seeds and planted their own seedlings. Lately, it has been required that you have to buy your seedlings.... Right now, if you plant tomatoes, they can't touch the ground and you have to spray almost every other day to keep the diseases away, since the hybrids are developed in greenhouses and are not resistant to local diseases." Mack's complaint is that such rules focus on the large farmers, while the small farmers have to adapt the technology the best way they can. He says, "Maybe these techniques or practices just were not right for small farmers, but they were good for larger farmers who had the equipment to produce those types of crops using that technology."[7]

Two of the most sizeable tomato farm operations on St. Helena Island are among the largest in the nation. Following the seasons, these corporations transfer their migrant workers to farms in other states ranging from Florida to New England. The Gullah community views these temporary and absentee neighbors the same way as many of the plantation owners of old: people who did not live there and, other than owning the property and reaping its benefits, had no connection to the land or the community.

St. Helena Island has been designated by the county as a Rural Agriculture District, a not-so-small feat accomplished through the active participation of local community leaders who successfully negotiated a plan that excludes the development of golf courses, condominium complexes, waste treatment facilities, and other environmental intrusions on St. Helena. It calls for the island to remain a place where homes, family gardens, small farms, and limited large truck farms can coexist. Penn School graduate Lula Holmes says, "We feel that we want this to remain rural. Let it be rural. Its beauty and the people are rural. For one thing, you get to know your neighbor. You are on speaking terms with people. You look out for one another. You share food, share crops from the field. They send you potatoes, they send greens, and especially to indigent persons."[8]

The challenge of preserving the spirit of interdependency and self-sufficiency that defined life on St. Helena in the past will depend on the ability of small farmers to run profitable operations, whether that be u-pick farms, farm tours, trucking to markets, roadside farmers' markets, or other innovative ventures suitable to the twenty-first century. It will also depend on demonstrating the desirability and profitability of farming to younger generations, to explain just how such an age-old livelihood as farming can fit into the computer age. Equally important, however, it will depend upon public policies that make it possible for small farmers to compete in the marketplace, fair lending practices and access to relevant information and assistance from government-supported agencies engaged in agricultural research and demonstration projects. The rest, as before, will be up to the hard work of the island people who have relied upon the land for subsistence and income since the days of emancipation.

The Hardships of Nature

Despite the abundance of fertile soil, valuable timberlands, glorious foliage, and plentiful foods from the rivers, inlets, and shores, there were several natural disasters that permanently altered the way of life in many Gullah Geechee communities. Most notable was the Sea Islands storm of 1893 and the arrival of the boll weevil in 1918. Following these destructive events, many Gullahs moved away from the islands, and those who stayed had to find new food sources and jobs in order to survive.

On the night of August 27, 1893, a storm made its way from the Gulf of Mexico, and instead of following the Gulf Stream, it veered inland in a curve like an archer's bow, not only with hurricane-force winds but also with a tidal wave that averaged almost ten feet high and in many places much higher, ravaging the land and drowning many of the occupants. The "tide of death," as it was referred to, made landfall just south of Beaufort, South Carolina, and claimed more than two thousand lives (only two of them white) in a single night. Margaret Weary, of the Beaufort Industrial School for Girls, gave this account the day after the storm:

> Next morning we went home, but there was no house there, nor anything left. All had been washed away into the marsh, and the sedge and seaweed were piled up all around higher than my head. We saw dead cats and dogs, dead horses and hogs all along the shore, and some dead men and women and children. We saw one dead woman holding on to a timber of her house by her teeth.[9]

The gaunt figure of famine silently stole across the land because all vegetable growth was destroyed, livestock was swept away, and fresh water was turned to saltwater. The noted founder of the American Red Cross, Clara Barton, directed a ten-month relief effort in the area, conscripting what few boats were still intact or could be brought to transport survivors to the mainland. However, it took almost a month from the time the governor finally sent his urgent message to Washington, D.C., until help actually arrived, resulting in hundreds more deaths from injuries, storm-related disease, or starvation. As was later determined, this outrageous delay was to a great extent caused by the fact that African American segments of the population were deemed to be more accustomed to suffering and less in need of help than their white brothers and sisters.

Despite horrid conditions, Black and white residents labored together to bring back their ravaged land, digging drainage ditches to carry away stagnant, mosquito-breeding waters, planting seeds supplied by state and federal governments and the Red Cross, and building emergency shelters from lumber supplied by relief agencies, private citizens, and church congregations. Looking back on the Great Hurricane of 1893, Emory Campbell attributes the remarkable resilience of the population to the fact that such a large percentage of those affected were the descendants of the enslaved families and later freedmen whose very lives had been day-to-day struggles to survive. So even though thirty days elapsed before any assistance came from beyond the island's shores, the people were taking positive steps, often strengthened by their religious faith. At the core of this kind of inner strength were Laura Towne and Ellen Murray at Penn School, which, being far from the shore and whose buildings remained more or less intact, served as a center of hope.

Not so lucky, however, was the phosphate mining industry, which would never recover from the storm. Phosphate companies employed nearly three thousand workers, many of whom were Black males in their twenties and thirties, bringing an economic boom to the poor region. From 1870–1893, 60 percent of the phosphate produced in the United States came from South Carolina, and half of that was mined in Beaufort County.[10] With such success, mining companies could afford to pay their Black workers well (about $1.75 per day), and these men supplemented this income with a "two-day system that included sharecropping, farming their own land, hunting, fishing, and odd jobs."[11] The end of phosphate mining placed an even greater reliance on profits from long-staple cotton, which was still being grown on the islands. Since emancipation, Gullah farmers had grown sweet potatoes and vegetables for subsistence and cotton as their cash crop; however, the arrival of the boll weevil ended the era of cotton forever.

Native to New Mexico, the boll weevil is a small beetle about a quarter inch long with a pronounced snout sometimes described as a cross between a "termite and a tank." From the late nineteenth century until 1920, it infested all of the U.S. cotton-growing states and completely decimated Sea Island cotton. The long-staple cotton was highly susceptible because it "demanded a long growing season, which meant that its bolls ripened in late summer when the boll weevils were at full strength."[12] At the height of the production of Sea Island cotton in 1911, there were 119,293 bales produced, but with the arrival of the boll weevil in 1919, this figure dropped to only 6,916 bales; in 1924 only 11 bales of the once-great Sea Island cotton were grown.[13] To many, the devastation from the boll weevil was a contributing factor in the Great Migration as African Americans left the South for better jobs in the North. The boll weevil's massive destruction inspired a popular blues song with humorous lyrics conveying the less than happy end to so many farmers' dreams:

> Oh, the boll weevil's got half the cotton and
> The merchant's got the rest
> Didn't leave the farmer's wife
> But one old cotton dress
> And it's full of holes
> And it's full of holes
> It's full of holes
> It's full of holes
>
> Now if anyone should ask you
> Who was it made this song
> Tell 'em a poor old farmer
> He done been here and gone
> He ain't got no home
> He ain't got no home
> He ain't got no home
> He ain't got no home[14]

One of the Gullah Geechee communities most affected by the boll weevil's arrival is the beautiful and isolated Daufuskie Island, South Carolina. Daufuskie, also called Yamacraw, once had a thriving cotton industry supporting two thousand residents on the island. "Before the Boll Weevil destroyed all the cotton fields in the early 1900s, the waterways around Daufuskie were busy as boats transported cotton, oysters, timber, pears, pecans, produce and freight between island and mainland—either to Savannah, Bluffton, or Beaufort and even as far away as Charleston. Sometimes there could be as many as five steamships docked at the public landing or anchored offshore. Daufuskie was bustling."[15]

After the boll weevil's destruction of Daufuskie's cotton crops, many residents left the island or turned to shucking oysters, a delicacy rumored to be favored by the czar of Russia. Later, water pollution destroyed the island's oyster industry in the 1950s, and most of the remaining people moved away. Where once there were two thousand residents, now only sixty remained. Noted author Pat Conroy, who wrote *The Water Is Wide* about his life as a teacher in the one-room schoolhouse on Daufuskie, describes the great migration on the island: "A steady flow of people faced with starvation moved toward the cities. They left in search of jobs.... The population of the island diminished considerably. Houses surrendered their tenants to the city, and signs of departure were rife in the interiors of the deserted homes." There were also dramatic changes to Laura and Ellen's Penn School, threatening the very survival of this renowned institution.[16]

Penn Center

By the time Emory Campbell became the executive director of Penn School in 1980, it was now called Penn Center and had not offered classroom instruction to students in thirty-two years. Gone were the eighty years of educational programs established by Laura Towne (1825–1901) and Ellen Murray (1834–1908) and their successors Rossa Cooley (1872–1949) and Grace House (1877–1961). Cooley and House had implemented an industrial educational model favored by Booker T. Washington, featuring classes in wheelwrighting, harness making, masonry, mechanics, and midwifery. The midwifery program was so effective that the infant mortality rate on St. Helena Island dropped to 48 per 1,000 or 4.8 percent in the years 1920–1928. This accomplishment is even more impressive when compared to the national average for African Americans at this time, which was 100 deaths per 1,000 or 10 percent and the national average for whites of 60 per 1,000 births or 6 percent.[17]

Cooley and House retired in 1944 after forty years of service and were replaced by Howard Kester, who inherited a school deeply in debt and struggling to stay open. Although Kester proposed new adult education courses, an expanded boarding school, and a seminary school, none of these programs ever materialized, and Penn School was dealt one final blow. The school's trustees hired Ira Reid, an African American sociologist from Atlanta University, to evaluate Penn and design a more cost-effective curriculum, but to their surprise he recommended "the transfer of the formal educational program of Penn School to public authorities." His report included this passage:

> There are at least two St. Helena Islands. One is part memory and part myth; the other is stern reality. There are at least two Penn Schools. One is a romanticized Institution located and working in a land-holding Negro community with its "praise houses," "just laws," and simple, unaffected folk. The other is a real social institution working through Northern benevolences in a rapidly changing rural South Carolina community with people caught in the eddy of that change.[18]

Reid viewed Penn School as outdated and unable to meet the needs of a 1950s African American community. Penn School soon was closed and turned into the Penn Community Center. In his overview of the school, historian Michael Wolfe writes:

> Penn evolved into much more than a local private school. Its leaders embraced that most ancient of American Puritan dreams, "the shining city on the hill," and these missionaries came to believe that from their lonely island outpost, led and empowered by God, they could change the world.... Furthermore, the Penn School's history sheds enormous light on American ideals of social progressivism and the religious motivations of those ideals. Like so many other social progressives in American history, Penn's leaders were not merely building a better society, they were dreaming of the Kingdom of God on earth.[19]

The Penn School educators succeeded in producing highly skilled teachers, tradesmen, and midwives, and future college graduates whom they believed reflected the best of the Black race in such a kingdom. Unfortunately, there was little room for the Gullahs' language and form of religious expression in this utopia. Penn School graduate Ralph Robert Middleton recalls that "Penn teachers did not recognize Gullah. They tried to get us out of Gullah. Our training was not to speak the Gullah language, but we were taught English."[20]

Remarkably, Penn School, now the Penn Community Center, found new purpose in the 1950s and 1960s under the leadership of devout Quakers Courtney and Elizabeth Siceloff. Courtney took advantage of the relative seclusion of St. Helena Island to bring together Blacks and whites in meetings centered around political consciousness and social equality. Penn routinely hosted national and international conferences held by the Student Non-Violent Coordinating Committee (SNCC), Congress of Racial Equality (CORE), National Association for the Advancement of Colored People (NAACP), World Peace Foundation, American Friends Service Committee, and the Southern Christian Leadership Conference (SCLC), led by Martin Luther King Jr.

Beginning in March 1964, King visited Penn on five occasions during which the SCLC had week-long planning meetings designed to "promote understanding within SCLC and to forge a renewed dedication to the struggle for civil rights."[21] Also present was the biased white media who described the SCLC members gathered at the 1964 workshops as a group of "radicals under orders from the communist leaders."[22] David Garrow, author of the Pulitzer Prize–winning book *Bearing the Cross: Martin Luther King, Jr., and the Southern Christian Leadership Conference*, views these sessions at Penn as among the most important of all of the national SCLC staff gatherings because King articulated to his staff the evolution of his thought.[23] A few months before his death, King spoke of a new approach he termed *aggressive nonviolence* during his last SCLC retreat from November 27–December 2, 1967:

> We black and poor people who have dreamed for so long of freedom are still confined in a prison of segregation and discrimination. Must we respond with bitterness and cynicism? I insist that we shall not—for this can lead to black anger so desperate that it ends in black suicide. Must we turn inward in self-pity? Of course not, for this can lead to a self-defeating black paranoia. Must we conclude that we cannot win? Certainly not, for this will lead to a desperate black nihilism that seeks disruption for disruption's sake. Must we, by fatalistically concluding that segregation is a foreordained pattern of the universe, resign ourselves to oppression? Of course not, for passively to cooperate with an unjust system makes the oppressed as evil as the oppressor. Our most fruitful course is to stand firm, move forward with aggressive nonviolence.[24]

King saw a need to adapt his nonviolence strategy to urban conditions and urban moods to address what he termed "heightened black impatience and stiffened white resistance."[25]

In 1959, Courtney Siceloff invited Myles Horton, leader of the Highlander

Folk School, to conduct citizenship workshops at Penn. Horton had worked with Esau Jenkins and Septima Clark at their pioneering citizenship school on Johns Island, which dramatically increased the number of registered African American voters, and Siceloff hoped to begin similar adult education training on St. Helena Island. In the minds of many, citizenship schools made the single most profound contribution to the civil rights movement, and in the words of former Congressman Andrew Young, the citizenship schools "really became a foundation of Martin Luther King's non-violent movement."[26] Soon, local churches on the island became involved in citizenship training and helped many residents to pass the literacy test required for voter registration. Church leaders also organized boycotts against the local Piggly Wiggly store because the southern supermarket chain would not employ Black residents.

Courtney Siceloff served for nearly twenty years as executive director of the Penn Community Center, bringing to his position a humility and a creed he would follow during his time at Penn: "God is known in love. Loving your neighbor and acting on that love."[27] A central aspect of Courtney's faith was to listen attentively to the needs of the islanders. "Projects initiated should arise out of the community," he believed, then "the community should feel that it is its own . . . then assume as much responsibility as practical in implementing the decision."[28] When compared to Penn's previous leaders, Wolfe offers this critical assessment of Siceloff's importance:

> This attitude of appreciating the African American voice and culture proved a decisive step. Back in 1862, the first missionaries arrived believing that the islanders were merely "ignorant savages" who needed to be Americanized. . . . Far from being in need of Americanization . . . [Siceloff] believed that Black men and women had a life of faith needed in America. Never desiring to alter island Gullah culture, Siceloff took practical steps to preserve it.[29]

Beginning in the middle 1950s, Siceloff began a field recording project aimed at capturing the memories of the elderly residents on St. Helena Island. He made audio recordings, now housed at the Library of Congress, of various church services, Penn Center community sings programs, and special holiday programs. The Siceloff collection represents an invaluable preservation of a disappearing Gullah Geechee culture on St. Helena Island.

Siceloff's work with the Gullah community and his views on civil rights, however, made him very unpopular among many whites in Beaufort County. He states,

> I acted personally in ways not normal for Whites. It was confrontational in terms of speaking and acting. But I did not seek to confront people. I lived my example.... In Quaker thought, there is part of God in everyone. You must respect your opponents whatever crimes committed.... Courtney believed it important to live in a "subversive manner, working quietly and unnoticed, modeling his ideas until others accepted a new way of living."[30]

As mentioned, Towne and Cooley wanted to purge aspects of the Gullah Geechee culture in order to create an educational and religious community on par or better than any northern example, and their success can be measure by the many students and world leaders who revered these educators. Yet their legacy can also be seen as an example of the larger, dominant society trying to interact with a smaller, local culture. Although the "outside world" was focused on St. Helena and the Sea Islands, the African American islanders went about their own lives, practicing their religion, and seeking God through visions and ecstatic rituals. The arrival of the Siceloffs gave new voice to the Gullah community and a say-so in their own destiny. Eventually, Courtney resigned to allow for an African American to assume leadership for the first time at Penn. Thus, the story of St. Helena is really about how two vastly different traditions, white and islander, "emerged from their own environments, how each sought particular goals for the island, and how they eventually merged into a living faith community."[31]

Despite the fact that the Port Royal Experiment fell short of its ambitious mission to educate enslaved peoples and help them learn skills and trades to support themselves, Penn School must be given credit for its many successes, despite often being on the verge of closure. In 1900 when the school faced financial and leadership problems, Rossa Cooley and the Booker T. Washington model saved the day, bringing in educators from the North to conduct what was initially called an "experiment" in educational salvation. Focusing on "character development" among the African American islanders, Penn School "linked hands with a worldwide network of Christian organizations, progressive educators, and government agencies."[32] Rebranded as Penn Center in the 1950s, it regained center stage during the civil rights movement. Remarkably this school continued to remain at the forefront of the uplifting of Gullah Geechee culture and the Black race.

CHAPTER FOUR

GROWING UP GULLAH

On Hilton Head Island, South Carolina, there is a common phrase used by the older generation of African Americans—"before the bridge," referring to the days when the only access to the island was by small boat and a sometimes unpredictable little ferry. Such an isolated existence enabled many Gullah Geechee communities to develop strong social, religious, and familial bonds even against the backdrop of "Jim Crowism." The subsequent "after the bridge" period threatened to loosen many of these cultural bonds, but notable Gullah leaders, artists, and educators have been at the forefront of efforts to highlight the culture and ensure its continued survival. These remarkable people come from communities all along the federally recognized Gullah Geechee Cultural Heritage Corridor, encompassing the states of North Carolina, South Carolina, Georgia, and Florida.

Emory Campbell, "Humble Greatness"

Emory Shaw Campbell, executive director emeritus of Penn Center and leader of the first Gullah Homecoming delegation, is a native son who left his early environment temporarily and returned not only as a leader but also as a visionary and proponent of constructive policies and programs. He was born on Hilton Head Island, South Carolina, in October 1941, the sixth of twelve children. His parents were both teachers—as were his paternal grandparents. He attended classes in a tiny one-room schoolhouse, and when it came time for further schooling, he took a bus across a narrow swing bridge to the all-Black Michael C. Riley High School in Bluffton. "I remember my teacher would hike us down to the old fort in Port Royal [Fort Walker] every spring, to that old steam gun mounted down there. He tried to teach us about Civil War history, about the sound," Campbell recalled—the teacher did not succeed.[1]

In 1960, he graduated as class valedictorian and faced the decision of migrating to the urban northeast for work, like so many of his peers, or choosing to be the first among his siblings to attend college. Campbell decided to pursue a degree in biology at Savannah State College, and he later earned his master's and doctorate degrees from Tufts and Bank Street College, respectively.

"'Family values' perfectly explains the remarkable success attained by the Campbell family," says Don McKinney, an editor, author, and book reviewer who himself is a former resident of Hilton Head. Everyone is a success story in the Campbell family and can "trace their roots to the Civil War and beyond.... All but two of the living family members live on a thirty-five-acre tract of land in Spanish Wells, part of an African American community that has flourished for centuries. The Campbells meet once a month to talk about what they are doing, discuss family business, and reinforce the ties that have held them together for so long."[2]

The Campbells are noted for their record of service to the community. One brother, Melvin, for example, is a former Hilton Head representative for the

OVERLEAF: Enslaved people sitting in front of a building on Elliott's Plantation, Hilton Head Island, South Carolina. In a written inscription on the back of the original photograph, this structure was described as the "nursery" where enslaved children were cared for. *Library of Congress, LC-DIG-ppmsca-11384.*

Beaufort County School Board; another brother, Morris, is the former deputy director for community services for Beaufort County; and several other siblings are former teachers or administrators in local social services programs.

One of the reasons that there is so much family participation in community and educational services is that in the strict Gullah tradition, they were all brought up to understand personal values, discipline, learning, family loyalty, traditions, and the importance of church attendance and worship. "My grandmother, Mama Julia, used to teach in our little schoolhouse," explained Herb Campbell, "and I'd meet her up at the fork of the road to walk to school in the morning. If I wasn't there, she'd go on without me and boy did she walk fast! I'd have to run like crazy to catch up with her, because if she got there first and rang that school bell, I was late. And everybody that was late got whipped on the hand with a switch. I learned my lesson." Mama Julia also had a remedy for pupils who complained that another pupil was calling them names and should be punished. "No way," came the reply. "Don't care what somebody else calls you. You know who you are."[3]

Herb's younger brother Emory Campbell is credited with instituting the much-heralded Heritage Days program during his tenure at Penn Center. This three-day event has done much to present and enhance the Gullah culture, not only to the public but to many African Americans themselves who were not fully aware of their distinctive heritage. Emory has won many honors, including the Governor's Award for Historical Preservation (1999), induction into the Penn Center 1862 Circle (2003), and the Carter G. Woodson Award for Civil Rights (2006) from the National Education Association, presented to him in recognition of "his work at Penn Center to preserve Gullah, the language, lifestyle, and culture of a people with roots in Africa and the Southern Sea Island plantations."[4]

Thin, lithe, and about six-foot-three-inches tall, with tousled gray hair and a ready smile, Emory is one of the most familiar faces on Hilton Head Island, St. Helena Island, and locations all up and down the South Carolina coast. He is constantly on the go, heading up his Gullah Heritage Consulting Services, escorting groups on his Gullah Heritage Trail Tours bus, giving more than fifty speeches and presentations each year, guiding local farm and historical programs, and contributing extensively to newspaper editorials, scholarly publications, documentaries, and television news shows. Yet if a stranger approaches him in a museum, school, or even on the street and requests information, he thinks nothing of spending fifteen or twenty minutes of his time to be of help.

Ayoka Campbell, Emory's daughter, recalls her early indoctrination into the Gullah culture: "My father would always talk to me in two languages—one African and one American. 'Ye yent!' is what he would exclaim whenever I made what seemed to him to be an unbelievable statement. After my astonished reaction to this and other Gullah terms, he would translate them to English for me. 'Ye yent' meant 'Is that true?' in English. . . .

"While listening to a man from Liberia, Africa, speaking on the Howard University radio station, I was surprised by how much he sounded like my father. All of my life, I heard him, his brothers and sisters, his mother [intensive mainland schooling had virtually erased his father's Gullah speech pattern] and other native islanders of Hilton Head and surrounding islands speak Gullah language—a mix of African and American words using an African grammar pattern."[5] Emory views this language as his culture's greatest asset because "it allowed Gullah people to remain one big family. It has kept us intellectual, esoteric, and protected."[6]

Many people who meet him for the first time would agree with Gary Lee, a *Washington Post* staff writer, who spoke of him as a "fountainhead of inspiration, whose graying hair and thoughtful speech [give] him an elegant Old World demeanor."[7]

Vertamae Grosvenor, "Travel Notes of a Geechee Girl"

Vertamae Smart-Grosvenor (1937–2016) was a prominent Gullah Geechee woman who hosted National Public Radio's award-winning documentary series *Horizons*. Although she grew up in Fairfax, South Carolina, which is a small town about forty-five miles outside of the designated Gullah Geechee Corridor, she considered herself Geechee. In the view of food author Mayukh Sen, she "inhabited the skin of [a] Gullah Geechee woman publicly, long before the world around her was willing to swallow what that even meant."[8] In the 1980s, Vertamae was a frequent contributor to NPR with a series of documentaries, including "Slave Voices: Things Past Telling" and a special about Daufuskie Island, South Carolina, once populated almost entirely by Gullah residents, which won her a Robert F. Kennedy Award. She was also honored by the National Association of Black Journalists for a segment on "South Africa and the African American Experience," which aired on *All Things Considered*.

Vertamae, a premature twin, was born and raised in Hampton County in the South Carolina Lowcountry, where her first language was Gullah. Affectionately known as "Kuta," which means turtle in the Gullah language, she weighed only three pounds and barely survived. "My brother weighed, like, a five-pound bag of sugar," she explained on one of her broadcasts, but "he died and I was very, very weak. My maternal grandmamma, Sula, put me in a shoebox and placed the box on the oven door of the wood-burning stove. When folks came to look at the 'shoebox baby,' they exclaimed, 'It looks like a *kuta.*' So the name stuck." Her mother was too weak to nurse her, so she was fed on goat's milk.

When Vertamae was ten, her parents moved to Philadelphia, but life was difficult because the kids at school teased and taunted her about her Gullah accent and manners. Feeling different forced her into a kind of isolation, where she began reading many books, especially those that guided her to different places and peoples around the globe and sharpened her imagination. Later, during a trip to Europe at the age of eighteen, she met some of the kinds of people she had read about and began to appreciate the richness of other heritages, including African and the Gullah Geechee heritage.

Vertamae learned the fundamentals of cooking under the tutorage of her maternal grandmother, Sula Ritter, and her paternal grandmother, Estella Smart, and her father, Frank Smart, was a gifted cook. From this background, which was influenced by the culinary traditions of the Gullah people and her continuing association with people from many lands, she became fascinated with cooking and publishing cookbooks. Her first book and masterpiece, published in 1970, was *Vibration Cooking: or, The Travel Notes of a Geechee Girl.* This book not only provides recipes but also delves in depth into the cultures and the peoples who created them, hence she describes herself as a "culinary anthropologist." She ingeniously coined the term *vibration* as a method of cooking, spontaneously adding ingredients here and there without measuring them, and she also referred to "making do" with leftovers. She further explained *vibration* as "different strokes for different folks. Do your thing your way."

Vibration Cooking contains recipes written in a conversational manner with wit and storytelling as important as the ingredients. Take the Harriet Tubman ragout, a brown beef stew simmered in peanut oil with potatoes, carrots, onions, turnips, and okra, just as her Uncle Costen told her it was served in the Underground Railroad. Or the simple pound cake she made with sugar, butter, flour, eggs, salt, vanilla extract, lemon extract, and mace. (It got her a marriage proposal from a "fine fly young man"—she did not accept.) Consider the eight-line recipe for terrapins, which "ain't nothing but swamp turtles" in her view. "Now they are the rare discovery of so-called gore-mays," she would write. "White folks always discovering something... after we give it up."[9] In addition to recipes for food, Vertamae includes recipes for cocktails, herbal teas, herbs and spices, and home remedies from her Gullah Geechee roots. She wanted to create an understanding of "soul food" as a tradition passed on from Africa, not one based on the myth of coming from master's leftovers. "The definition of "soul food" has to be broader. What I call it is Afro-Atlantic cookery, meaning a touch of Africa that is all throughout the Americas."[10]

She considered cooking the highest of the art forms and, like any art form, believed it could be taught to anyone regardless of their nationality or background. She notes that "soul food" resists any racial designation—"It's how you put your soul in the pot." Vertamae is the subject of the documentary *Travel Notes of a Geechee Girl* by well-known filmmaker Julie Dash (*Daughters of the Dust*). Dash says, "Vertamae's story is important to our history and culture as well as the international artistic, intellectual, and social movements of which she was an active participant."[11]

Cornelia Walker Bailey, "I Am Sapelo"

Cornelia Walker Bailey, author of *God, Dr. Buzzard, and the Bolito Man*, referred to herself as "a saltwater Geechee" born and raised on Sapelo Island, Georgia. She was the kind of Geechee storyteller who enjoyed life in the present but also relished the experiences of the past. She captured in her writing the spirit of the community, the people she had known there throughout a lifetime of rich experiences, and her love for departed family members and friends. Cornelia was of the last generation to be born, raised, and schooled on Sapelo Island.

"I am Sapelo," she proudly stated. "Life goes on much as it does anywhere else, but if you get to really see and feel what's here, you will see the difference. The proud faces as well as the angry walk, the easy smile as well as the hard frown, the easy life as well as the hardship—it's all here, reflected in the faces and stature of each individual. The old who don't want to change and the young who does. But get to know the young ones and you will see tradition and hear pride. We are all proud of our heritage."[12]

Cornelia looked back on her life as a young girl and recalled seeing women at such places as Raccoon Bluff fishing with a drop line and cane pole from a bateau boat, "trusting in the Lord because they couldn't swim." She had not forgotten the drama of watching men fishing at night with flambeaus, looking for alligators with a long pole and giant hook. Nor could she forget "the smell and sweat of the men as they walked behind oxen and mules, plowing task after task of fields."[13] Her memories took her back to other elements of her Gullah life, such as the taste of fresh-dug sweet potatoes cooked in hot ashes, watching older brothers and sisters dancing the "Buzzard Lope," and observing a group of young men on a Saturday night with their moonshine, playing the guitar, blowing the comb, and trying to do the tap dance or the soft shoe with somewhat hesitant girls.

One of her favorite characters when growing up Gullah was Grandpa Bryan, a "mysterious fellow" who was one-half Creek and one-half African, who was said to have come from the Okefenokee Swamp in southern Georgia. He was a self-made barber who would use a bowl when cutting men's hair, clipping all around it and then lifting it for a bit of trim so that the neck ended up in a perfectly straight line—which would cause the kids to snicker when they went to church and sat behind one of Grandpa Bryan's customers.

Church held many memories for Cornelia Walker Bailey, especially the music. "The songs we used to sing in church," she said, "we've been singing for years and years. Nobody really goes to the hymn books—they sing from memory. When Grandma used to sing, she had a captivated audience. She'd sing 'When I Get to Heaven' and 'Things I Used to Do.'"[14] Grandma was unusually expressive when she had a little bit from the bottle before setting off for church!

Cornelia recalled many little things about her father when she was growing up on Sapelo Island—how he used to sing around the house, though without such an appealing voice as Grandma's, how he could hold the children spellbound with his stories, and how he showed them how to make fishnets or fox traps. But his prime skill, much appreciated, was his ability to cook hominy grits, which they all considered a real treat. She says, "Papa provided for us the best he could. We had alligator dishes, along with pork greens. We had game birds and shore birds—wild turkey and gannet. We had fish of all kinds. We had turtle of all kinds. We had deer, squirrel, rabbit, raccoon, and possum. Some only in season, some by means of poaching. Sometimes nothing at all."[15]

One of Papa's most unique skills, appreciated by all of his own and the neighborhood's children, was his ability to take the bladder from a fresh-killed hog and make a balloon out of it by rolling it in warm ashes until it was thin and then blowing it up—"our first balloon!" He could also make whistles from spent shotgun shells, or whittle toys to play with, or show everyone where to find the tastiest kumquats and other fruits in the forests, fields, and neighboring orchards.

Much of what Cornelia Walker Bailey remembered as vital parts of her life and family activities growing up Gullah are now mostly gone. "Our old schools are closed down," she said. "Our churches have only a handful of worshipers left; our neighborhood organizations, such as the Farmer's Alliance, the Eastern Stars, and the Masons, are no longer; and there are no more pray's [praise] houses. It is even hard to find the kinds of boys and girls who used to giggle in the dark under the stars, with a chorus of frogs and crickets for company. Even our ghosts don't walk anymore. There is no one for them to scare now. No one walks the road at night. No jack o' lantern leads the weak-minded or drunk-minded away to some dark woods for a night of fright."[16] She was sometimes sad, sometimes even angry, at what has been lost since the time when she was growing up. Still, she was happy for her childhood memories and an understanding of who she was. "For in many ways we are still living in the days of the *Buckra* [name for a white person] and the *Buckra* fields. I am still in *Massa* fields. I can see and hear traces of the old days, and there in those fields I can also retain my dignity and be myself without undo influences. It's not easy, but I watch the birds and my mind is free."[17]

Anita Singleton Prather, "The Gullah's Aunt"

Anita Singleton Prather was born and raised in the picturesque and historic city of Beaufort, South Carolina, the sixth of eight children of Julius Caesar and Inez Singleton. "Education was a driving force in the Singleton family," says Cathy Harley of the *Beaufort Gazette*, "with her mom as a teacher at Broad River Elementary School who helped prepare children for desegregation and her dad as a second-generation graduate of Tuskegee Institute." She attended first and second grade at the all-Black Robert Smalls School but elected to transfer to Beaufort Elementary in the third grade under the new "freedom of choice" plan offered to Black students. Forced now to sit at the back of the classroom, she had to deal with the "N-word" and white students claiming she had "cooties" or body lice that supposedly all Black people had. But she was outspoken and not to be ridiculed, and she frequently answered lesson questions when the teacher was about to pass her over. "I was very competitive, even with boys," she recalled. "If you were going to play football with me, you were going to get tackled no matter what!"[18]

After receiving her bachelor's degree in psychology from Howard University and her master's in education from the University of South Carolina, she continued the family tradition in education by teaching math and social studies at various elementary, junior high, and high schools in Beaufort County. But she showed such talent as a storyteller—in the classroom and out—that she was soon filling requests to appear on stage and radio. And thus began a whole new career, all based on her own upbringing in a Gullah household and her ability to convey the ups and downs, the humor and despair, and the very essence of the individuals and families she had known all her life. Her one-woman show, *Tales from the Land of Gullah*, became a hit nationally on PBS, prompting her to create the Gullah Kinfolk, with twenty-five members from age two to seventy-five, who have recorded compact discs and feature films with such titles as *A Gullah Kinfolk Christmas* (2002), *Songs uv dee Gullah Pee'puls* (2007), *Circle Unbroken: A Gullah Journey from Africa to America* (2014), and *The Gullah Kinfolk Live* (2015). Anita and Marlena Smalls cofounded the Hallelujah Singers, who performed in the blockbuster film *Forrest Gump*, filmed in Beaufort.

Anita Singleton Prather's most popular effort may be her creation of Aunt Pearlie Sue, a character she is referred to as much as her own birth name. Aunt Pearlie Sue is based on her grandmother Rosa Singleton, also known as "Ronnie," whom she describes as her mentor and role model. She was "always pleasingly plump, stylish, and her hair always done. Growing up in a large family, everybody had their special person, and my grandmother was my special person when I needed attention." As Aunt Pearlie Sue, she has appeared widely and continuously in broadcasting, on the stage, and at major events, such as Beaufort's Original Gullah Festival, San Francisco's Festival of the Sea, Charleston's Spoleto Festival, and the Arts Midwest World Fest. Recently, the Children's Museum of Houston created an exhibit based on Aunt Pearlie Sue called *Cum See Gullah*, introducing more than a million young people to the Gullah Geechee culture.

Anita is featured in South Carolina ETV's 2019 documentary film *Gullah Roots*, which follows Gullah Geechee leaders as they travel from South Carolina and Georgia to Sierra Leone. Aunt Pearlie Sue and the Kinfolk can be heard performing many of their trademark songs to enthusiastic crowds around this West African country, even before Freetown Mayor Madame

Yvonne Aki-Sawyer at her annual mayor's ball. A highlight is certainly the crowning of Anita as a paramount chief, Mahei Jiagie, in the village of Taiama in southeastern Sierra Leone. Of her homecoming journey, she says, "When you get there, you finally realize that you're where your family started from. It empowers you in such a way, I can't even begin to express it."[19] Anita Singleton Prather is currently a minister at New Covenant Fellowship Ministries of Beaufort.

Althea Sumpter, "Documenting the Ghosts"

Althea Sumpter, Anita's classmate at Beaufort Elementary and a native of St. Helena Island, has also gained recognition for a remarkable career dedicated to capturing "the memories of those who survived enslavement and hard times in the South."[20] She recalls "running around the grounds of Penn Center so often that I could find my way around blindfold, since my mother and many other family members and friends were graduates of the school." As a Quaker she also finds Penn Center dear to her heart because it was founded by Quakers, and for many years it was closely associated with this denomination. Her Penn roots and early cultural experiences influenced her decision to dedicate her life to researching, writing about, teaching, and promoting Gullah Geechee culture and heritage. She received a master's degree in media arts from the University of South Carolina, writing a thesis titled "Civil Rights in South Carolina: Desegregation in Clarendon County," and received her doctorate in African American studies from Clark Atlanta University with the dissertation titled "Navigating the Gullah Culture Using Multimedia Technology."

From 2005 to 2007, Althea conducted extensive oral interviews of eighty- and ninety-year-old Black elders at the Coosawhatchie Senior Center in Jasper County, South Carolina. The center "served the elders from hamlets and crossroads of Coosawhatchie, Gillisonville, Pineland, Grays, Ridgeland, Point South, Early Branch and Pocotaligo for many decades," recalls Althea. "Through regular activities, meals, and creating crafts passed down from one generation to the next, the elders gathered to share their lives shaped by the experiences of rural South Carolina and the Gullah Geechee culture."[21] The seniors shared stories about growing up in a rice culture, forgotten cultural practices, and the uniqueness of their Gullah language. Althea views these interviews as even more important because most of these individuals have since passed. She explains the need for this kind of work:

The ghosts are dying—the way my grandmother would describe the link with those who have come before. Linking with the past is what I felt I was doing when an elder cousin asked for me to sit with her to hear more stories, and then she told me about her grandfather who "came over in the boat." I was holding the hands of a cousin who learned about life from an enslaved African. She died a few weeks later—the link to that ghost, broken.[22]

Althea's mentor was the pioneering linguist Dr. Keith E. Baird, whose examinations of the African diaspora "focused on language as a tool for liberation and self-definition, not as a political tool against marginalized groups."[23] In the 1960s, Baird argued persuasively for the use of "Afro-American" in lieu of "Negro," a term applied to the "enslaved and the enslavable," and he is considered a true visionary in the field of African American studies. Althea is currently compiling Baird's extensive library and papers, and she will be adding these materials to the more than ten thousand volumes of Baird's research now housed at the Auburn Avenue Research Library on African American Culture and History in Atlanta, Georgia.

On October 12, 2006, Congress authorized the creation of the Gullah Geechee Cultural Heritage Corridor—the first of its kind in the United States. Althea Sumpter is a founding member and past chair of the federal commission responsible for facilitating an understanding and awareness of the significance of Gullah Geechee history and culture within the coastal communities north of Wilmington, North Carolina, south along the South Carolina and Georgia coasts, and into northern Florida. She was asked about the early beginnings of the Corridor by WABE radio host Steve Goss:

> There had been a constant growing interest from a group of people in the '90s trying to figure out how to form a recognition of who we are. Through this collective you had people who were saying we need to push forward for preservation because we are losing our culture, we are losing our land. The culture is linked to the land. It started with a committee formed of people from South Carolina and Georgia who really pushed in 2000 for a resource study, which is the first stage in the National Park Service looking at a specific location in preparation for becoming a national heritage location.[24]

During her impressive career, she has directed media and productions with the Martin Luther King Jr. Center, served on the faculties of several universities, lectured in many capacities, produced films both independently and for television, written and edited extensively, and organized numerous workshops. In almost every instance, the characters, plots, and topics she presented were grounded in the Gullah Geechee culture she knows so well. One of her most important moments occurred while she was in graduate school, when she proposed the inclusion of a short story about her Gullah childhood as part of her dissertation: "I was able to include that short story in my dissertation as an example of a participant-observer. It was difficult to defend my role in a traditional academic arena. But I was successful."[25]

All along her road to success, she developed new ways of approaching an ancient culture with roots back to West and Central Africa. As an ethnographer and producer with training and experience in both cultural preservation and digital technology, Althea Sumpter is able to document her own culture through her access as a trusted insider. By using digital video, still photography, and audio documentation to create interactive design tools on Gullah culture, she offers a model for other researchers and communities wishing to employ digital technology to document persons and cultures.

Jonathan Green, "Capturing the Humanity in Gullah"

With its broad sweep of triumph and tragedy, history and personalities, and elation and despair, the Gullah Geechee culture has spawned fine artists of many schools with works in many galleries in the South, both large and small. Undeniably, Jonathan Green is one of the most important painters of the southern experience who is preeminent in capturing the traditions, people, and scenes of African American culture. Described as "one of South Carolina's treasures," his work spanning more than two decades has been exhibited at major national and international venues and published in many periodicals and books.

Green was born in the small Gullah community of Gardens Corner in the Sea Islands of South Carolina, where he was raised by his grandmother in a matriarchal society that relied heavily on oral traditions. Looking back on his early life, he explains that he was always interested in how crafts of all kinds were studied and created and was curious about the nature and hopes of the people in his family and community. "I had all this stuff in my head," he once explained, "but I didn't have a place for it until I started painting. I know I can't save a whole culture, but as an artist I can help create better awareness perhaps." And he has done just that by helping people all over America and abroad to understand his heritage.

"Through the years many African American artists, such as painters Eldzier Cortor and Ellis Wilson, photographer Jeanne Moutoussamy-Ashe, and the late folk artist Sam Doyle, a native to the area, have featured the colorful Low-country and its people in their work," wrote Carroll Greene Jr. in a profile of the artist, "but Green's body of work, about 150 Gullah works, is perhaps the most ambitious artistic expression of Sea Islands culture ever successfully undertaken." Jonathan Green's most vivid memories of Gullah life are culled from the 1960s. "I can remember things as a child, such as hair wrapping, men weaving fishing nets, farming, and hunting. There is very little of these ac-tivities going on now. What fishing and hunting that goes on is mainly sport and not out of necessity as before. Food used to be preserved in various ways, drying, canning, and smoking. Now, only gardening seems to continue. Mat-tresses were made of Spanish moss, and men made furniture for use in the community."[26]

"Within the community, each family was known for providing some spe-cific goods or services. For example, one family would sell seafood, another family would sell produce, and another family moonshine, and so it went. My grandmother was a quilter," Jonathan Green recalls.[27] One must bear in mind that the first bridge connecting the Sea Islands to the U.S. mainland was con-structed only after World War II. Indeed, many of the island residents had never been on the mainland before that time. He readily admits that he did not always have much appreciation for his Gullah heritage. Like many others, he had to leave home and journey to faraway places to comprehend the value of his Gullah roots.

Jonathan served in the U.S. Air Force, which took him to North Dakota, Colorado, and Texas. He also traveled through Europe and Mexico. After all of this, he reminisces, "I wanted to go back to my roots. The older people were dying, and I began to see people [the Gullahs] differently. I saw them as a people with a strong link, probably the strongest link with Africa of any of the black American people. I had studied African art, and I began to appreciate a certain uniqueness."[28] Jonathan completed his formal training at the Art Insti-tute of Chicago, earning a bachelor's degree in fine arts in 1982.

Jonathan Green's background provides him with an insider's understanding of the Gullah people and their traditions. For instance, in his painting *Tales*, there is a group of men at the end of the day gathered under a huge live oak listening in varying degrees to the yarns of a storyteller. The scene is a continuation of the strong African oral tradition transplanted to America. Another painting, *Banking Yams*, illustrates an unusual method of storing yams by putting them in little huts made of dried corn stalks and straw. His painting, *Two Baskets*, is featured on the cover of this book.

Jonathan Green's Gullah art is a testimonial to harmony of style and content:

> Human figures, which have always been the artist's favorite subject, are rendered featureless in the Gullah paintings. The viewer is not permitted past the dark oval faces. At first the figures seem to bar introspection, but these featureless persons are not anonymous beings. In their communities they are recognized by size, shape, stance, and gesture, the way one recognizes a familiar person whose back is turned toward you. The lack of features seems to suggest an archetypical human being and, in this instance, serves to universalize a people in their daily routines and special occasions. Jonathan Green's earlier works showed considerable cubist influence, perhaps Picasso, Cezanne, or others, though his strong interest in the human figure is evident.[29]

William Starrett and the Columbia City Ballet premiered the production *Off the Wall and Onto the Stage: Dancing the Art of Jonathan Green* in 2005 as a tribute to the world-renowned artist, and critics acclaimed this work as one of the most original in the ballet company's repertoire. In describing the southern influences in his art, Jonathan states, "While the southern soul is often portrayed as angst and peace, the southern spirit is filled with creative healing energy, always evolving and growing in its creativity and adaptability. While there are pains in life and survival, I view the South today as appropriating the best of cross-culture heritage constructing a new sense of place and an enhanced sense of purpose."[30]

Philip Simmons, "The Keeper of the Gate"

The most celebrated ironworker of recent times in Charleston, South Carolina, and most probably in all of the Lowcountry and Sea Islands, was Philip Simmons (1912–2009). When visitors take tours near the southern areas of Church Street and Bay Street, they are more than likely to marvel at the magnificent iron designs on gates and other functional metal work in the shape of hearts, diamonds, egrets, cranes, turtles, snakes, and many other objects found in nature. Much of this unique artwork was done by Philip Simmons, who was born on nearby Daniel Island in the summer of 1912, but like thousands of African Americans who lived in Charleston, was a freed man even before the advent of the Civil War. According to a Gullah tour guide in Charleston, most tourists are surprised to learn that "nearly everything you see around here, in this historic district, was built by blacks—the houses, the walls, the streets, and sidewalks—and not just by slaves either."[31] In his Gullah language he said, "*Dem cyapentas, boat mekkah, iyon wukkah, net mekkah, en pleny mo' is wuk dat de Black people bin doin' ya fuh shree hunnad odd yea.*"

Simmons, who has been described as a national treasure, got started in his profession when he was only thirteen years old and long finished with any kind of regular schooling. He was brought up in a family that insisted on continuing work and education. "I used to stand in the door of the blacksmith shop," he said, "and see the sparks flying, and I liked that. The blacksmith let me help out, hold the horse while he was putting the shoe on, turn the hand forge, clean up the shop. And after a while he taught me names of everything. He'd say, 'Boy, hand me the three-inch swage,' and I had to know just what he wanted. I learned that way." This blacksmith was Peter Simmons, a formerly enslaved man, who offered Philip an apprenticeship that lasted for five years.

Later, after learning at work and studying everything he could about ironwork in his free time, he took the plunge and started his own business. But it was rocky. "I had to make those changes, 'cause the horses was going out; the cars was taking place of the horse and wagon. And all I knew about cars is ride in 'em. And the cars was coming. We would say, when I first went in the shop in 1920, we would see a car in the streets once or twice a year. Everything—when being poor, all the delivery in Charleston—vegetable, fruits, and other things was being delivered, the merchant had horse and wagon. And after things have changed, cars, machines, and I have to make changes. People will come by the shop just before I start doing wrought iron and say, 'Hey, Philip, how you doing?' 'I say I'm doing [fine].' 'Did you heard the blacksmith is becoming now a lost art?'"[32]

In the 1920s and early 1930s, customers primarily called upon a blacksmith's practical skills, says John Michael Vlach, author of *Charleston Blacksmith: The Work of Philip Simmons*. "They wanted their tools repaired or sharpened, or perhaps a wagon wheel needed a new metal rim. Fishermen ordered various forms of 'boat iron' or farmers required new points for their plows. Philip Simmons was trained to complete all of these utilitarian tasks but, importantly, he was also trained to do more. Peter had, on occasion, shown his young charge how to make pieces of decorative wrought iron. It was this branch of smithery that appealed to Philip in the 1930s."[33]

In 1931, Charleston adopted a historic preservation ordinance that required demolitions and alterations to the existing historic structures. As work began on these buildings, there were urgent requests for decorative ironwork on gates, balconies, window grills, fences, and stair railings, and Philip had the opportunity to finally utilize his artistry through ironwork. "By the late 1930s, Simmons was able to replicate the older designs with replacements that appeared to have been original to the ironwork. The quality of his work soon spread around Charleston by word of mouth."[34] Although he tended to call himself a "general blacksmith," meaning that he did accept the special tasks of the angle smith, farrier, wheelwright, toolmaker, and ornamental ironworker, he said, "I could mash out a leaf the same as a horseshoe. They both got the same principle. An angle is an angle."[35]

The 1950s and 1960s found Philip in even more demand with commissions from prominent Charleston locations such as First Baptist Church, the Christopher Gadsden house on East Bay Street, and the Rhett House on St. Michael's Alley. Featured on these gates are images of animals such as a rattlesnake at the Gadsden house and a delicately profiled egret for the Rhetts, the first examples of animal sculpture in Charleston wrought iron.[36] In 1976, Simmons returned to this snake motif for a Smithsonian Institution commission, but he added several pieces of curved iron to convey the allusion of the snake swimming.

Honors and expressions of appreciation for Philip included lunch at the White House with President Ronald Reagan, the presentation of a lifetime achievement award from the South Carolina State Legislature, a major commission from the South Carolina State Museum, a mayoral declaration that his eightieth birthday be known throughout the city of Charleston as "Philip Simmons Day," and an honorary Doctor of Fine Arts degree from South Carolina University in 2006. In response to these many accolades, Philip Simmons was notoriously modest, and he repeatedly stated, "I owe all that I have to the people of Charleston."

His work and decisions paid off well. He said, "I put my children through school. I have given money to my church. I have everything I want. And I am rich in friends." He was also rich in prestige as a result, not only because of his talents but also because of his dedication to the arts and the help he gave to talented young people all throughout his career. In 1982 the National Endowment for the Arts awarded him its National Heritage Fellowship, the highest honor that the United States can bestow upon a traditional artist.

Minnie Evans, "The Visionary Artist"

Born in a log cabin in Long Creek in Pender County, North Carolina—the northernmost part of the Gullah Geechee Cultural Heritage Corridor—Minnie Evans (1892–1987) became one of the most important visionary folk artists of the twentieth century with works at the Museum of Modern Art, the Smithsonian Institution, and the American Folk Art Museum. Minnie's originality stemmed from "her devoted faith, brief formal education, low income, advanced age, and isolation from an arts community."[37]

Her mother, Ella Jones, was only fourteen and working as a domestic worker when she was born, so Minnie was taken to live with her grandmother, a seamstress, who essentially raised her as her own daughter. As a child, Minnie often heard voices and had waking dreams and visions. In fact, she could not recall a night without having dreams, causing her to have a confused sense of reality. According to author Gylbert Coker, "there were times when Evans could barely distinguish between dreams and visions, as well as between dreams and wakeful experiences."[38]

When Minnie worked as a "sounder," going door-to-door selling shellfish, she met Julius Caesar Evans, whom she married at age sixteen. Although Minnie was too young to legally marry at the time, she wrote her age as eighteen on the marriage license, which became something the couple often joked about in a long marriage that produced three sons. The young couple got jobs working for Wilmington, North Carolina, industrialist Pembroke Jones—Julius was a valet while Minnie worked as a domestic worker. "After the death of Jones, his widow remarried and moved with her new husband to the estate called Airlie where the Evanses worked for them. The 150 acres were developed into an expanse of gardens and opened to the public in 1949. Minnie Evans became the gatekeeper, collecting admission from visitors, and eventually retired from her post in 1974 after 25 years of service."[39]

The inspiration for Minnie's works often came from the spirit-filled religious services held at Saint Matthew AME Church in Wrightsville Beach, where she occasionally spoke, and Pilgrim's Rest Baptist Church. When asked about her training, she would reply, "I am without a teacher, a worldly teacher. God has sent me teachers, the angel that stands by me and directs me what to do." She was particularly moved by Ezekiel's vision of the Chariots of God. Art historian Theresa Leininger-Miller believes that Minnie was the embodiment of a "tradition of God-directed literacy or 'spirit writing' evident among the Yoruba people in West Africa."[40] Minnie's husband, however, was concerned about her visions and drawings until their pastor explained that they were part of God's plan.

On Good Friday, 1935, Minnie had her strongest spiritual encounter. "Something told me to draw or die," she stated. "It was shown to me what I should do.... When I get through with [the paintings], I have to look at them like everybody else. They are just as strange to me as they are to anybody else."[41] Beginning in 1948, she started selling her paintings to visitors at Airlie Gardens for fifty cents each, a sum equaling half her daily wages, and these works eventually came to the attention of New York photographer and art critic Nina Howell Starr. Over time, Starr gained Minnie's trust and arranged for a 1966 exhibition of her works called "The Lost World of Minnie Evans" at the Church of the Epiphany and St. Clement's Episcopal Church in New York. While in New York, Minnie visited the Metropolitan Museum, where she was amazed at the large canvases and pieces of art, influencing her to expand her own existing artwork. Following a successful New York premiere, she was the subject of several articles in 1969 and had larger gallery showings and a solo exhibition at the Whitney Museum of American Art in 1975. To date, Minnie's work has been shown nationally and internationally in nineteen solo exhibitions and is held in numerous museums and private collections.

A vital part of Minnie's art is the presence of African-derived elements. For example, there is a striking similarity between her use of color and the textile and the beadwork commonly found in Western Africa, and Minnie's stylization of her central heads evokes the shapes of African masks.[42] These cultural retentions connect to Minnie's family history of strong women, who passed down to each generation the experiences of their ancestor, Moni, who was an enslaved worker in Trinidad before being brought to North Carolina.[43] Minnie continued to draw all of her life, eventually moving into a nursing home in 1982, where she died on December 16, 1987, at the age of ninety-five. A few months earlier, she had a solo show at the North Carolina Museum of Art.

Bessie Jones, "Called to Teach"

Mary Elizabeth "Bessie" Jones (1902–1984) was born in Smithville, Georgia; however, her family moved to her uncle's farm in nearby Dawson when she was only an infant, and it was there that she called home. Her education was limited due to responsibilities at home and in the community that often kept her out of school. She says, "I never went to school a whole term, and I didn't get past the fifth grade; every school day I had to keep other people's babies and sometimes I had to work in the fields."[44] Her formal education ended at age ten when she was offered a job as a nursemaid for a white family. These early experiences shaped Bessie's love of children, their songs, and their games. At the early age of eleven, she met and married Cassius Davis, who had come from St. Simons Island looking for work inland. During her visits to her husband's home, she found a world very different from her own.

Bessie's first trip to St. Simons Island occurred in 1919, when she attended a funeral for Cassius's baby sister who died from influenza. She recalled, "I had never heard Geechee people talk before—I call them Geechees, but ain't no such thing as Geechees—no more than Cassius and some of the boys he was with up there.... Well, I love the children.... They had the funniest sound I had ever heard in my life when they talked, and I'd give them pennies—I'd go and get a dollar's worth of pennies just to give them—to hear them talk."[45] After the death of her husband, Cassius, she married George Jones, who was also from St. Simons Island, and the couple decided to settle on the island. At this time, she was introduced to the Spiritual Singers of Coastal Georgia, who were formed by folklorist Lydia Parrish for the purpose of preserving the old Gullah Geechee songs. They were so impressed with Bessie's vibrant personality, extensive repertoire, and experienced singing style that they invited her to join their group; she became one of the first mainlanders so honored.[46]

Although Bessie was considered an outsider or mainlander, she had already amassed an impressive repertoire of old spirituals from elders such as her husband's grandfather Jet Sampson, a formerly enslaved person in the community of Dawson; thus, she was familiar with the form, texts, and performance style of the music sung by the Spiritual Singers of Coastal Georgia. She said, "With the old group we used to get together, and it was 'You know this song here?' 'You know this song?' We'd sit right there singing the old-time songs. We taught one another."[47] In 1955, she met famed folklorist Alan Lomax, who was so impressed with her that he returned to make a recording of the Spiritual

Singers in 1959. Lomax also collaborated with Bessie on a children's book titled *Step Down: Games, Plays, Songs, and Stories from the Afro-American Heritage*, a favorite among elementary music teachers everywhere.

At the urging of Lomax, Bessie renamed the group the Georgie Sea Island Singers, and they appeared in a Lomax-sponsored film set in Williamsburg, Virginia. It was in Virginia, the birthplace of her husband's grandfather Jet Sampson, that she found her "calling to teach." Lomax asked her to sing for a young white girl's birthday party, but before she performed the lullaby, Bessie held the audience spellbound as she spoke about a nearby trough in Williamsburg that had deep meaning to her family: "'When I see that trough out there,' I told them, 'I think about what my grandfather said. He said that if I ever came here, I would see the trough that he used to eat out of.' And my grandfather said that they had to eat from that trough on a Sunday, and they be playing games that they had learned in Africa."[48] One of the games they often played was called "Juba" with the following texts and Bessie's interpretations:

Juba thus and Juba that	That means a little of this and a little of that
Juba killed a yellow cat	That means mixed-up food might kill the white folks
And get over double trouble, Juba	Someday they would get over double trouble
You sift-a the meal, you give me the husk	You see, so that's what they mean— the mother
You cook-a the bread, you give me the crust	wished she could get that good *hot cornbread*
You fry the meat, you give me the skin	or hot pies or hot what not. But she couldn't
And that's where my mama's trouble begin	She had to wait and give that old stuff
And then you Juba	That was leftover.
You just Juba	Then they begin to sing and play.[49]

This pivotal moment in Williamsburg showed Bessie how to communicate to a wider world the little-known history of African Americans and slavery through the stories, songs, and dances that she had learned as a child. Beginning in 1963, the Georgia Sea Island Singers, featuring singers John Davis, Peter Davis, Emma Ramsey, and Bessie Jones, performed around the country at venues such as Carnegie Hall, the Newport Folk Festival, the Montréal World's Fair, the Ash Grove in Northridge, California, and the Smithsonian Folk Festivals in Washington, D.C.

At the Sing for Freedom Workshop May 7–10, 1964, in Atlanta, Georgia, Bessie Jones's "calling to teach" would have another dramatic influence on an audience. Organized by Guy Carawan, Andrew Young, Dorothy Cotton, and Bernice and Cordell Reagon and sponsored by the Highlander Folk School, SCLC, and SNCC, this workshop brought together civil rights leaders in heated discussions centered around race and the role of music in the fight for freedom. Many in attendance felt the old songs or Negro spirituals were outdated, and some whispered "Uncle Tom" when the Georgia Sea Island Singers sang during the Saturday morning workshop. Charles Sherrod, organizer for SNCC, asked, "Why? Why these songs here?" An older woman stated, "We can hear those songs any time back home. I came here to sing freedom." Bessie replied, "Slave songs were the only place where we could say we did not like slavery, say it for ourselves to hear!"[50] The impact of these words was so great that the Georgia Sea Island Singers were the only group to receive a standing ovation at the evening concert from both young and old. There was a consensus that the Negro spirituals or the sea island songs would continue their important role in the movement. Bessie was also part of a traveling prayer band that marched with Martin Luther King Jr.

A highlight for the Georgia Sea Island Singers was their performance at the 1976 inauguration for President Jimmy Carter, and in 1982, Bessie received the National Heritage Fellowship from the National Endowment for the Arts, the highest honor for folk and traditional arts. Despite such honors, Bessie knew her place as an outsider within the Black community on St. Simons Island. "Here on the island, I'm a visitor. I'm a stranger. And it wouldn't make any difference whether I had been here twenty or forty years, I'm still a stranger.... Let me die and you'll see where I go. I ain't going to King's Cemetery, no sir. I'm going to Stranger's Cemetery. On July 17, 1984, the legendary Bessie Jones died and was buried in the Stranger's Cemetery on St. Simon's Island.[51] When Alan Lomax learned of Bessie's passing, he said, "She was on fire to teach America. In my heart, I call her the Mother Courage of American Black traditions."[52]

McVynee Betsch, "The Beach Lady"

McVynee Betsch (1935–2005) was born in Jacksonville, Florida, the southernmost part of the Gullah Geechee Cultural Heritage Corridor, where she worked tirelessly to ensure the survival of a stretch of beachfront property on Amelia Island called American Beach. She was known as the "beach lady," and her great-grandfather Abraham Lincoln Lewis, Florida's first Black millionaire and president of the Afro-American Life Insurance Company, had purchased the land in the 1930s so Blacks could have a beach of their own.[53] According to author Russ Rymer, "For decades it flourished as an ocean-side paradise for blacks from around the country, who admittedly had little choice."[54] During the Jim Crow period, Florida's beautiful public beaches were for the most part off limits to African Americans, who were only allowed in the most remote, polluted, and hazardous areas.

McVynee grew up at the height of American Beach's popularity when "commercial establishments—motels, guest houses, restaurants, nightclubs—sprang up along with new summer homes. . . . Visitors could find rooms at the A. L. Lewis Motel, Williams's Guest Lodge, and Cowart's Motel and Restaurant. . . . Out on the beach, there were surf fishing and shell gathering, beauty contests and automobile races, and the warmth of friendly faces."[55] Her family's connection to this iconic beach and her memories of its importance to the Black community would stay with McVynee even when she left home to attend Oberlin Conservatory of Music, in Oberlin, Ohio; studied voice in Paris and London; and enjoyed a stellar operatic career in Germany during the mid-1950s and early 1960s. She eventually returned to Florida but faced a diagnosis of ovarian cancer in 1975 that caused her to reevaluate her life and find new purpose in the preservation of American Beach.

During McVynee's absence, American Beach had fallen on hard times partially due to the passage of the Civil Rights Act of 1964. One of the unfortunate consequences of the ending of segregation in public spaces was the loss of Black support for the Black businesses on American Beach. They could now go to former all-white beaches in Miami, Daytona, and even on St. Simon's Island that were closer to home. The final nail in the coffin was the closure of McVynee's great-grandfather's Afro-American Insurance Company in 1991. Now only twenty-five families remain on American Beach. Rymer states, "Most of its homes are aging and modest; a few of the grandest have been torn down. And its businesses—the nightclubs, hotels and restaurants that used to throb with activity all summer night—are boarded up."[56]

The greatest threat to American Beach in more recent years has been resort companies looking to buy up the American Beach property. In 1995, Amelia Island Plantation bought a huge section of the property, including a large sacred dune, for golf and vacation resorts, but McVynee protested the sale and loss of the dune that dominates the town. The resort company agreed to leave the sand dune intact and build behind it, and they supported the transfer of the 8.5-acre sand dune, the largest dune in Florida, to the National Park Service, now part of the Timucuan Ecological and Historic Preserve. In her efforts to protect the land, McVynee established a local historical society, named in honor of her great-grandfather A. L. Lewis, and the original thirty-three acres of American Beach are listed on the National Register of Historic Places in 2002.

In the last years of her life, there was one project most dear to McVynee—the creation of a museum dedicated to her great-grandfather. For years she had kept her great-grandfather's papers, artifacts, and books in her mobile home, but she envisioned a proper memorial to his memory. She became aware that Nassau County was looking for a voting site for Amelia Island residents and asked if a museum and elections site could be under the same roof. To the surprise of many, the county agreed, and the American Beach Museum had a home in 2014. Although McVynee had died nine years earlier, her lifelong dream had come true. Carol Alexander, founding director of the American Beach Museum states, "McVynee was the museum itself!"[57]

McVynee was a figure considered by some to be a shaman or witch because of her almost supernatural ability to persevere against all odds and her unusual appearance. According to her friend Rymer, "Her fingernails [were] very long—until they got clipped in the hospital, those on her left hand spiraled to more than a foot and a half. Her hair, coiffed into a wheel over her head, [cascaded] in graying dreadlocks down her back and past her ankles. Her hair and clothes [were] festooned with political buttons, unfailingly radical."[58] After her death in 2005, a memorial service was held at American Beach, where McVynee's ashes were spread upon her beloved sand dune named "NaNa" and upon the waters of American Beach.[59]

The Opposite Side of the Coin

Could a white person "grow up as a Gullah"?

It's an interesting question. Take the case of Robert Lee, executive director of Seabrook, a retirement community near the southern part of Hilton Head Island, South Carolina. Many employees who work with him are African Americans, and a large percentage are of Gullah extraction. Although he is white, he says that he feels right at home because, as he puts it, "I really grew up Gullah." Much of his childhood was spent in Bluffton, South Carolina, which was then a small village on the May River. His grandmother was born in the Huger-Gordon Home, a large wooden house on the river that was built around 1800.

My grandmother's only brother, Percy Huger, with the help of a mule and one worker, built the causeway to Myrtle Island, and my grandparents built their house on the island in 1931, where my uncle still lives. The house is long and thin, so that all the rooms caught a breeze from the river. Each room had a fireplace, and on the second floor there was a screened area called the sleeping porch, to stay cool in the summer.[60]

Lee has great affection for the house and what it meant to his family and to him during the long summer visits.

Other than a brother and sister and some relatives, there were very few other white families. Many of my father's playmates and fishing buddies were from the local black families. It was not long before everyone picked up a thick Gullah accent. When I was young, they would read me Br'er Rabbit stories in Gullah, and I learned native songs, such as "The Beaufort Boat Does Not Come." I was very grateful for my heritage. I love the song-like quality of the language, and moreover, I found that many of the phrases had a great deal of personal meaning in the messages they conveyed so persuasively.[61]

Rob even enjoys talking in Gullah, and at a moment's notice will pop up with one phrase or another. Some of his favorites are:

"Dog got four feet but can't walk but one road."
"No matter how many things you'd like to do, you can do only one at a time."

"Fox da watch de henhouse."
"A fox [crook] is watching the henhouse [money]."

"Milk ain't dry off e mout yet."
"The person is too young for the assignment."

"Evry frog praise e ownt pond."
"Everyone praises his own family."

"New breom sweeps clean but old breom gets corners."
"To get the job done use someone familiar with it."

"Li 'i pitcher got big ears."
"Be careful what you say around children."

Rob's Gullah phrases and memories reflect the willingness of Gullahs to share many aspects of their culture, but these Blacks often had little choice in their service as playmates or nursemaids to white babies. Historically, the Lowcountry was filled with whites who could speak the Gullah language fluently, but the language is not the entire culture. Just as his whiteness gave Rob free entry into the Black world it served a barrier for Blacks who could not freely express themselves, complain, or even think of themselves as equal to, let alone better than whites. The imposed dogma of slavery was equally unfair to the white child who rarely got to know the dreams, anger, joys, and passions of the Black child.

A GULLAH SONG IN MENDE

The following song text, recorded in Harris Neck, Georgia, in the early 1930s by Dr. Lorenzo Turner, the foremost African American linguist of his time, shows the strong connections between the language spoken by Gullah Geechee and those in West and Central Africa.

> *A wohkoh, mu mohne; kambei ya le; li leei ka.*
> *Ha sa wuli nggo, sihan; kpangga li lee.*
> *Ha sa wuli nggo; ndeli, ndi, ka.*
> *Ha sa wuli nggo, sihan; huhan ndayia.*

Modern Mende

*A wa kaka, mu mohne; kambei ya le'i; lii i lei tambee. A wa kaka,
  mu mohne; kambei ya le'i; lii i lei ka.*
*So ha a guli wohloh, i sihan; yey kpanggaa a lolohhu lee. So ha
  a guli wohloh; ndi lei; ndi let, kaka.*
So ha a guli wohloh, i sihan; kuhan ma wo ndayia ley.

English

Come quickly, let us work hard; the grave is not yet finished;
  his heart [the deceased's] is not yet perfectly cool [at peace].
Come quickly, let us work hard; the grave is not yet finished;
  let his heart be cool at once.
Sudden death cuts down the tress, borrows them; the remains
  disappear slowly.
Sudden death cuts down the trees; let it [death] be satisfied,
  let it be satisfied, at once.
Sudden death cuts down the tress, borrows them; a voice
  speaks from afar.

HOPES AND FEARS AND ASPIRATIONS

"As the ox carts creak and the buggy wheels swish through the sand, a voice may be heard rolling over the marshes," wrote T. J. Woofter Jr., a renowned sociologist who was one of the few scholars studying the lives of the formerly enslaved Africans in the 1920s. On St. Helena, Woofter captured the singing of this island favorite:

> *Lawd, I wish I had an eagle's wings.*
> *Lawd, I wish I had an eagle's wings. o*
> *Lawd, wish I—O Lawd, wish I, o*
> *Lawd, wish I had an eagle's wings*
> *I would fly all de way to Paradise.*
> *I would fly all de way to Paradise. o*
> *Lawd, fly all—O Lawd, fly all o Lawd,*
> *Fly all de way to Paradise.*

IN THE LAND OF THE GULLAHS

What is it like for a person who is not of Gullah descent and generally unfamiliar with the Sea Islands to visit a Gullah community, attend a local church, and meet native residents who have lived there all their lives? The following is an excerpt from an account by just such a person, Gary Lee, a *Washington Post* staff writer who found his experience to be "refreshing and heartwarming indeed."

When I entered the village church the congregation was in full swing, belting out the day's scripture in what sounded like an African dialect. I did not understand a word, but that didn't matter. As I looked with uncertainty into the faces of the crowd—from a matronly villager with skin the color of cocoa to a burly brother with a '60s Afro—all returned heartfelt smiles. Uplifted by a Sunday morning of African-style worship, I followed the scent of catfish and collard greens to a favored local hangout. Along the wooden porch a couple of women in braids were setting out sweetgrass baskets, a handicraft common in West African markets. Under a sagging willow, a few village elders chewed the fat of the week. Inside, families were digging into bowls of gumbo and platters of rice and okra. In nearly every town along Africa's Gold Coast from Sierra Leone to Senegal, I imagined, similar scenes were taking place.

The catch was, I was not in Africa. I was on St. Helena, an island off the marshy shores of South Carolina and home to the Gullahs. Descended from slaves brought from Africa to the Georgia and South Carolina coast in the 18th and 19th centuries, the Gullahs have clung passionately to the languages, foods and traditions of their origin. While the rest of America, including much of the African American population, is swept up in a tide of cultural homogeneity marked by Nike shoes, baseball hats and Top 10 hits, the Gullahs have held resolutely to the rice dishes, prayer rituals, rites and chants that their grandfathers' grandfathers brought from the Motherland. Although they probably descend from different African countries and disparate tribes, Gullahs today are identified by their common language. Gullah Geechee is a Creolized language composed of words from English and several African tongues.

An intriguing destination for any traveler, the stretch of the South that many Gullahs call home seems to offer something particularly attractive to Americans descended from slaves. It is a dramatic reminder that, in the vast multicultural forest of the contemporary United States, African Americans have roots as deep as any other ethnic group. My introduction to the world of Gullah came through cinema and literature. The 1991 movie *Daughters of the Dust* depicted a community of Gullahs battling to keep the mores of the New World from subsuming their tight-knit social circles. *Down by the Riverside*, a historical account of life on South Carolina Lowcountry plantations, gives rich details of how slaves brought from Africa to South Carolina worked to retain aspects of their

African heritage, from songs to burial traditions. But neither the book nor film renderings of the Gullah story fully prepared me for my wanderings through the settlements where Gullahs live and gather. To observe the Gullahs is to see a people who have been resolute about preserving their culture on American soil.

—Gary Lee, "In the Land of the Gullahs," *Washington Post,*
September 20, 1998

A GULLAH PASSING

"February is alive with the vivid sounds and tastes of the Hilton Head Island Gullah Celebration," wrote David Lauderdale, one of the South's most noted and expressive columnists, on February 11, 2007, "but amid the pageantry, the home-going of Brother William Brown, Jr., during the celebration is a reminder of the foundations of the Gullah culture. Mr. Brown's long life shows both the past and potential future of an abundant culture being squeezed out by modern America.... Mr. Brown came into this world almost ninety-two years ago on Pinckney Island. Today, Pinckney Island is a blur at sixty miles per hour between the two bridges to Hilton Head."

As Lauderdale explains in his obituary to this Gullah gentleman of the old school, Brown took over his father's store, known as the Mr. Boney Brown Store, on the tiny island, and it became something of a center of learning and manners for the children of the neighborhood. Mr. Brown brooked no deviation from honesty, and if he detected any youngsters with their fingers in the candy jar, or climbing the pear trees outside to steal a little fruit, he gave them an instant—and meaningful—lesson in doing unto others as you would have them do unto yourself.

But those days, says Lauderdale, have vanished forever, to the bad luck of present generations. "Today's Gullah descendants face a harsh business world. Instead of a Mr. Boney Brown Store, we have giants like Publix. The odds of success seem insurmountable. But what do you think the odds looked like the day Mr. Brown was born? What did he lean on? How did he make it? Those odds are worth celebrating this and every year."

A GULLAH MEMORIAM

A legend of leadership is eulogized in the passing of Leroy Edgar Browne Sr., a proud but humble man who graduated in 1934 from Penn School, the first school for freed slaves, a few hundred yards down the road from the site of his funeral. He also graduated from Hampton Institute in 1940. He was proud of the education, and he turned it into wisdom and a place in history. Browne became the first Black elected official in America after Reconstruction, which according to long-time friend Thomas Barnwell Jr. "set the pattern for all of the United States," and was elected to the Beaufort County Board of Directors in 1960, five years before the passage of the historic Voting Rights Act of 1965. Browne rubbed shoulders with luminaries of the civil rights movement, including Dr. Martin Luther King Jr. and members of the Southern Christian Leadership Conference. While he moved among the great men of that era, he never forgot his roots. And he left a legacy of service that has paid dividends to the community. He was a champion of the poor and worked to improve the standard of living for people on the Sea Islands. He pushed for clean water and indoor plumbing, which helped prevent disease among island children. In 1980, the community named the Beaufort-Jasper Comprehensive Health building in his honor.

Browne also was a servant to the community. He was a member of the NAACP, the Low Country Regional Council, the board of directors of the Sea Island Federal Credit Union, the Sea Island Farmers Co-op, and the Democratic Party Executive Committee. Many people looked to him for wisdom and leadership. Indeed, all of Beaufort County will miss the ninety-one-year-old leader.

—*Penn Center Newsletter*, St. Helena Island, South Carolina

—CHAPTER FIVE—

HALLELUJAH!

"**N**o practice is more meaningful in the life of the Sea Island people, better illustrates how the different streams of influence flow together, and better reflects the synthesis of an ancient heritage with the culture imposed . . . than religion."[1] This statement, from a study of Gullah religions and spiritual matters in the *Low Country Gullah Culture Special Resource Study*, reflects the importance of religious faith and the celebration of God to the Gullah Geechee people. The slow move to freedom, though beset with every imaginable obstacle, did not dim their belief in a "better day a-comin."

Gullah Afro-Christianity

The religious practices enslaved Africans brought to America were similar in many ways to the Christian doctrines they encountered in southern plantations and in camp meetings. Religious scholar Albert Raboteau says, "Common to many African societies was belief in a High God, or Supreme Creator of the world and everything in it."[2] The Mende people living in parts of Liberia and Sierra Leone referred to their Supreme Being as *Ngewo* while the Akan-Ashanti called their God *Onyame*. "The Supreme Deity was generally considered omniscient, omnipotent, and creator of all life. God represented the highest values—kindness, justice, sincerity, and mercy.... Evil came from other sources, not the Creator."[3]

West and Central African religions believe in the survival of the soul after death, and Gullahs found great comfort when Christian ministers preached about the existence of a soul apart from their human form. This allowed them to continue in their great reverence, respect, and even fellowship with the spirits of departed loved ones. "An important departure from mainstream Christian belief," says a historical report, *Gullah Language and Sea Island Culture*, published by the Beaufort (South Carolina) Public Library, "is the Sea Islanders' belief in multiple souls. The soul leaves the body and returns to God at death, but the 'spirit' stays on earth, still involved in the daily affairs of its living descendants."

A unique tradition among the Gullahs was passing a baby back and forth over a coffin to prevent the spirit of the deceased from entering into a small child. If a parent or loving grandparent suffers a painful, accidental, or untimely death, the spirit of the deceased will return to visit the children the departed person loved during his or her lifetime. Evidence of this "return" might be seen in the unusual bedtime restlessness of a child who suffered the loss of a close relative or in some physical ailment or unusual fretfulness that had no apparent cause. But in the Gullah tradition, all of these undesirable problems could be solved by "placating" the spirit with the simple maneuver of holding up and passing all of the youthful relatives back and forth over the coffin at the burial site.

"Grave decorations were another way to quiet restless spirits," says Pinckney. "In a tradition still practiced in central Africa, the last articles used by the deceased were placed upon the grave in the belief they bore a strong spiritual imprint. Bottles, pots, and pans were common, [but] in later years, they were

OVERLEAF: The Brick Church in the Penn School Historic District near Frogmore on St. Helena Island, South Carolina. Construction on this oldest building in the complex started in 1855; enslaved workers built the church and the pews. *Library of Congress, Prints & Photographs Division, HABS SC,7-FROG.V,4.*

augmented by unused medicines, eye glasses, telephones, toasters, electric mix-
ers, even sewing machines and televisions." Pinckney even encountered one
grave "marked with a telephone, perhaps indicating a link between worlds."[4]
All of these objects were broken before being placed on the grave, not so much
to prevent them from being stolen as to accentuate the belief that the act of
breaking and rendering useless was part of the ritual itself, symbolizing the
ending of things of this world. Historical research shows that the origins of
this practice in Africa often involved more than just a few personal and household items but valuable pieces of furniture, jewelry, painted portraits, clothing, and antique chinaware.

Gullahs were familiar with the Christian funeral practice of throwing hand-
fuls of earth on a casket as it is being lowered into the grave. However, traditions from West Africa called for dirt to be placed in small containers called
juju bags, which could then be worn around the neck by surviving family
members to bring them good luck. To make certain that the spirit of the departed was well protected, it was advised that the grave should be ringed with
conch shells. Why? Because as one descendant of a slave from Africa explained
it, the shells represent the ocean water that had to be crossed from their homeland, and now the water was the medium for taking dead persons back to the
land of their ancestors. "The sea brought us, and the sea shall take us back."

It's Prayin' Time

Despite finding common ground with many Christian teachings, enslaved
Africans had little patience and tolerance with the preaching of obedience
imposed on them by white ministers. Brought to the plantations by white
owners, these preachers favored the letters of St. Paul, who was by far the apos-
tle most quoted by proslavery advocates. Many white people felt it far too
dangerous to let their enslaved workers understand that the life and teachings
of Jesus meant freedom. Theologian Howard Thurman tells the story of his
grandmother, a formerly enslaved African, who was forced to hear these obedience sermons. He questioned her one day about why she forbade him to
read from the Pauline letters. He never forgot her response:

> During the days of slavery, she said, "the white minister used as his text
> something from Paul. At least three or four times a year he used as a
> text: 'Slaves be obedient to them that are your masters . . . as unto Christ.'
> Then he would go on to show how it was God's will that we were slaves

and how, if we were good and happy slaves, God would bless us. I promised my Maker that if I ever learned to read and if freedom ever came, I
would not read that part of the Bible."[5]

Instead of Bible texts focused on obedience, the enslaved preferred stories
about liberation, such as Moses leading his people out of bondage or Daniel surviving the lion's den, from which they crafted the spirituals "Go Down
Moses" and "Daniel in the Lion Den." But secret prayer services and revival
meetings helped the enslaved find their greatest connection to Christianity
in the figure of Jesus Christ, whose suffering, crucifixion, and resurrection in
the New Testament offered them hope through their own ordeals. Jesus' life
seemed to parallel their own, and Christianity was for Gullahs somewhat of
an apocalyptic fulfillment.[6] Through prayers they could speak to him alone
or before a congregation on Sunday morning and know that he understood
their pain. This outlook has changed very little through Gullah generations.
Linguist Patricia Jones-Jackson describes a typical prayer in the 1970s on Wadmalaw Island after the minister selects a member of the congregation to pray:

> They usually begin with a quotation from the Bible, a poem, or, more
> traditionally, some lines from the Lord's Prayer. The speaker usually
> has no prior knowledge that he will be asked to pray. Thus, the quo-
> tation gives him time to organize his thoughts and prepare himself to
> deliver an effective prayer.... After the quotation, the speaker begins
> his personal prayer.[7]

Although any member of the congregation could be chosen to pray, the
minister (pastor) knew which persons had the special ability to pray. Such
ability was "considered a 'gift' like the ability to sing or play the piano," says
Jones-Jackson. "Those gifted with the technique are often singled out when
they are very young and encouraged to practice speaking in the church at special feasts, weddings, or holidays, especially Easter and Christmas." The prayer
was never written down or even rehearsed, but the most effective ones contained wonderful imagery, maxims, puns, understatements, and cultural references designed to elicit enthusiastic responses from the congregation.[8]

Traditionally, Gullah Geechee prayers had a half-spoken, half-sung quality and were performed in an open dialogue between the supplicant and the
congregation. Historian Michael Wolfe provides these words from a Gullah
prayer he observed: "Master, could I come this evening excepting my knees
are down at the floor? . . . Father, we down here this evening. Heavenly Father,

asking for your mercy.... Hallowed be thy name, They kingdom come, Oh Lord. Let thy holy and righteous will be done on this earth."[9] The petitioner (usually a deacon or trustee) often performed these repetitive phrases and allusions in what Wolfe calls a "rhythmic incantation," which is maintained by the congregation through responses such as "Yes, Lord," "Amen," foot tapping, swaying, and groans.[10]

In many ways, the islanders approached their prayers in the same manner in which they performed their songs. Just as spirituals relied upon accentuations and body movements in their performance, so did this prayer style, and congregants often swayed back and forth and inserted their own responses in regular intervals to the established musical beat. On occasion, members almost took over the prayer with their own personal pleas for mercy or salvation or acclaimed their full acceptance of what was being said. It was not uncommon to have a buildup of emotions during a prayer and a climactic moment before a gradual decrease in emotion and even volume as the petitioner brings his prayer to an end with the expected words, "In Jesus' name we pray, Amen."

"Call and response" characterized much of Gullah worship services but was best observed during the minister's sermon. When the minister or a speaker chanted, for example, "God is the bread of life; God will feed you when you are hungry," responses from individuals in the congregation might have been, "O, yes, I know he will," or simply, "All right. Yeah. Amen." Similar to the prayer's dialogue, but on a grander scale, the Black preacher and the congregation exchange their deepest emotions in a tradition born of the African past. Religious scholar Henry Mitchell states, "Authentic dialogue in Black preaching, therefore, is profoundly healing. There is a freedom granted in Black worship and specifically during the preaching moment, which allows the full range of human emotions to be expressed in God's presence, from the greatest joy to a healthy purging of guilt, sorrow, pain, and frustration."[11]

The Black preacher's chanted dialogue and audience response produced fragments of texts and melodies that gave birth to many Negro spirituals. Georgian Ella Clark witnessed this phenomenon during "religious services where emotions were stirred, and excitement was at a high pitch. The words and music were spontaneous and extemporaneous, and were in a large measure their own, suggested by some strong sentences in the sermon, or some scripture emphasized and repeated. More often than not the preacher was interrupted in his sermon by a song leader who was moved to answer him in song."[12]

The National Park Service study reported that "religion and religious cere-mony have been among the primary research interests within Gullah Geechee studies, and with good reason":

> Religion has played a central role in community life, organization, lead-ership, and survival within the various Sea Islands of South Carolina and Georgia and continues to be the most powerful force in Gullah com-munities. Gullah religious belief and practice can be compared to the broader belief systems of African Americans as they pertain to the doc-trine of Christianity and worship of God; however, a fair portion of Gul-lah religiosity remains grounded in African cosmology and worldview. There are many components to this body of research: spiritual beliefs and practices, music and song associated with religion, African cultural retention within Sea Island religiosity, and the role of the church within the community.[13]

The Pray's House

Described by one observer as a "paintless, cheerless-appearing building of boards that "looked as if a heavy gale might lay it low," the pray's house was a safe haven where the enslaved could freely express themselves and encourage each other out of view of the overseer or white planter.[14] Dating back to the 1840s, enslaved Africans called this structure a prayer or pray's house, but in more recent times, the standard English spelling "praise" is commonly used.

In her fascinating book, *Yankee Missionaries in the South*, Elizabeth Jacoway covers the subject in depth: "At the center of island religious life was the *praise house*, an inheritance from the days of slavery. The old plantations . . . still gave geographic definition to the island, and on each of these was located a little tumble-down building with rude benches, where the islanders gathered three nights a week for simple, informal, spontaneous worship." As one observer described a praise house service, "In the prayers and songs the emotional ex-perience of the islanders takes on a vividness and depth which is hardly to be entered into by a member of another race."

Jacoway gives historical accounts of prayers and songs by pray's house mem-bers that contain simple yet effective poetic imagery.

> *"Pray on de knees ob yo' heart,"* the leader directed, and an old woman would pray, *"May de bird ob love be in moo heart an' de Lam ob Christ*

*in moo bosom, an' oh, God, who tuk up de sun in de palm ob yo' han' an'
t'rowed her out into de sky to be Queen ob de day, listen to we.*" All through
her prayer the murmurs of response could be heard, slowly building into
a rhythm and finally breaking forth in the gentle singing of a spiritual.
Soon the song would blend with the prayer; and as the singing grew in
power, the prayer would fade out and the spiritual go on. Soon another
prayer would rise, and the congregation would join in again: "*Now as we
bend our hearts equal to our knees, Lord Jesus, wilt Thou climb up on dat
milk-white steed called Victory, an' ride ober de mountains an' t'rough de
valleys of our sins an' backslidin's.*" The images were vivid, and there can be
little doubt that they were real to these simple folk for whom the Bible
gave the only suggestions of life beyond their island.

> *I look all aroun' me*
> *It looks so shine,*
> *I ask muh Lord*
> *Ef all were mine.*
> *Oh, ebery time I feels de spirit*
> *Movin' in-a muh heart*
> *I will pray.*
> *Hallelujah!*[15]

In his book *The Gullah People and Their African Heritage*, William Pollitzer
writes, "Slaves could 'hold prays' on weekday evenings as well as on Sundays."[16]
Commonly, Gullah communities on many of the Sea Islands held their pray's
house services on Tuesday, Thursday, and Sunday evenings, but today only a few
islands continue this tradition, and its continued survival is in jeopardy.

During the antebellum period, the initial purpose of pray's houses was to
prevent enslaved workers from "stealing away" in the night to meet in "brush
arbor" services. These evening services, often termed "the invisible church,"
drew Blacks from various plantations, and white planters worried about runaways or a repeat of the Denmark Vesey Rebellion. Due to South Carolina's
law prohibiting the assembly of Black people, white planters made sure that
these structures were small in size; however, large numbers of Black people
still managed to fit within these structures. William Allen, a missionary on St.
Helena Island, witnessed "more than half of the population" of one plantation
gathered within a pray's house, resulting in a "monotonous thud of the feet"
that prevented sleep within half a mile of the structure.[17]

On St. Helena Island, there were pray's houses on more than forty plantations, and each structure was affiliated with and maintained by a specific Baptist church where members attended. Despite this relationship, all matters concerning the pray's house fell under the jurisdiction of its Black elders, who were chosen by white owners to preside over membership examinations, religious court proceedings, and worship services. These elders were experienced, highly respected church members, "deacons" or "watchmen," who took seriously their role in ensuring the spiritual welfare of their plantation community. "They visit, pray with and exhort the sick, rebuke the impenitent, counsel the weak, conduct social meetings for prayer, whenever such meetings are permitted by the proprietor of a plantation, and especially have vigilant watch over the young, striving to keep them in the path of rectitude."[18]

Pray's house elders were also called upon to settle disputes between members, and their religious court was referred to as "just law" as opposed to the white man's "unjust law." After a pray's house leader received word of a dispute, he assembled a committee to hear the case. When the proceedings began, each party "thrashed out" or gave their side of the story while committee members asked questions and interjected possible solutions. "The aggrieved party always speaks first," observed anthropologist Patricia Guthrie, and "after a peaceful settlement is reached, the quarreling parties confess to any wrongdoing and 'take hands' (shake hands); and are ideally friends again. Finally, the committee reports back to the leader that the case has been resolved."[19]

This religious court was highly effective, and rarely were cases not resolved because both parties feared the power of pray's house elders to "turn dem outen de pray's house if dey ain't fur walk right." Losing membership within the pray's house removed a person from the plantation community and jeopardized their spiritual welfare. They were now out "de Ark ob Safety." As a result, many Gullah Geechee communities were nearly crime free. A news reporter visiting Sandy Island, South Carolina, in 1972 found that no one had remembered a police officer setting foot on the island.[20] In the 1920s, Beaufort's sheriff, Ed McTeer, rarely had reason to come on St. Helena Island. He stated, "The Praise House kept Gullahs law-abiding even as freedpeople, because they 'fears the Lord more than [they] fears the law.'"[21]

Seekin'

When a young person decided to become a member of a pray's house, they had completed a period known as "catching sense." According to Guthrie who did field work on St. Helena, this period "begins at approximately two years of age and continues for the next ten years, and involves . . . learning right and wrong, good and evil . . . when they come to understand and remember the meaning of social relationships."[22] In West and Central Africa, many believed that the child's mother carried the sins of her son or daughter until that age. It was at this point that a young person went through a conversion experience known as "seekin'," which required them to remove themselves from the community until completing a test of Christian faith within the pray's house. Seekers usually wore white bandanas and untidy or ragged clothes, and females sometimes covered themselves with ash, thus informing any who crossed their path not to distract them. A lengthy entry in the *Southern Christian Advocate* by a Methodist clergyman gives a thorough account of the seekin' process:

> When one of these people becomes serious, or "begins to pray" as he would say—and this is seldom the result of preaching, but most commonly a "warning in a dream"—it is customary for him to select, by the direction of "the spirit" of course, with some church member of influence, as his spiritual guide. Females are often chosen. Soon after the "vision" in which his teacher is pointed out, he makes known to him his revelation and puts himself under his instruction.
>
> The role of the teacher is two-fold in nature: He is now a prophet to teach him how to conduct himself, and particularly how to pray. He is also "an interpreter of visions" to whom the seeker relates all his "travel." This word *travel* . . . is one of the most significant in their language, and comprehends all those exercises, spiritual, visionary, and imaginative, which make up an experience. . . . These travels may differ in some things, and in others they all agree. Each seeker meets with warnings—awful sights or sounds, and always has a vision of a white man who talks with him, warns him, and sometimes makes him carry a burden, and in the end leads him to the river. When the teacher is satisfied with the travel of the seeker, he pronounces "he git thru"; and he is ready.[23]

The seekin' experience was, in essence, a religious rite of passage for teenage boys and girls as a prerequisite for membership in a pray's house. Enslaved

Africans combined ancestral initiation rites from their West and Central African secret societies, which mirrored Jesus Christ's wilderness experience, and newly adopted Christian teachings during a process lasting from three days to three weeks. At camp meetings, Methodist missionaries first introduced the term *seekin'* to the Gullahs when they asked them if they would like to come forward and "seek Jesus." All who were repentant would come to the altar or pen area and sit on the mourner's bench or seeker's bench, "waiting for the signal that they had been saved."[24] Within the Gullah community, seekin' candidates received instruction from their spiritual guides on how to pray, the Holy Trinity, and the attributes of a good Christian in anticipation of the ending examination by pray's house elders. Afterward, a successful candidate was baptized, given communion (Lord's supper), and received a right hand of fellowship, a formal recognition of their membership.

Baptism

Following the seekin' experience was the dramatic baptism service as successful candidates were led into the river or creek. Similarly, African initiates returning from their trials in the bush were said to have "crossed the water," signifying the end of childhood and the beginning of their life as adults. Once back at the village, "they underwent a washing ceremony in the creek or river. After 'washing', new members were dressed up for their final return ... where in a public ceremony they were handed over to their parents with great acclamation."[25] The Gullahs' ancestral ties to this water ritual influenced their preference for the Baptist Church's total immersion in water over the Methodists' sprinkling of water on the head.

The Gullahs questioned the effectiveness of baptism without total immersion, so many Methodist churches had no choice but to consent to river baptisms. David Thorpe, superintendent of the Fripp Plantation on St. Helena Island, confirmed this fact in a letter in 1863: "They all insist upon immersion.... Sprinkling wouldn't do, none at all." As he described it, the candidates, 140 in all, came dressed ready for the waters, in "miserable clothing," with their heads tied up in kerchiefs, and they marched from the church to the nearest local creek, where they entered the water and were pushed down until totally immersed and baptized before being herded back to dry land and off "into the bushes" where they dried themselves and donned "shiny robes," to the accompaniment of song from the surrounding crowd of relatives and friends. There was then "a great difference in their looks when they came into the church a second time" for a long service, after which the sacrament of communion was administered to them, and they were considered "full members of society."[26]

As was the custon, deacons had to work on Saturday or early Sunday morning to prepare the creek or river for the Sunday baptism. "Dey dammed up de crick on Sadday so as it would be deep enough on Sunday" for baptism, remembered a Georgian sea islander.[27] In the case of a river baptism, the deacons had to wade in the water early Sunday, tapping the ground with tall sticks "to ward off the snakes" and check the depth of the water.[28] Although there was a real threat of water moccasins or even drowning, the singing, shouting, and rejoicing overcame any fears a young person had. The baptisms took place after high tide, allowing for the outgoing tide to wash away all sins.

These baptismal ceremonies were often all-day affairs, with various related activities pertaining to old and young alike. Unfortunately, as several resource studies along the Gullah Geechee Cultural Heritage Corridor have revealed, many of the historic ocean sites for Gullah baptisms have disappeared because the valuable ocean properties have been lost to beach resorts, boat landings, marinas, and other commercial developments. On St. Simons Island, Georgia, for example, one of the beaches was traditionally the site of Emmanuel Baptist Church's baptisms of its members for generations, but in the mid-1960s, it had to throw in the towel and, like many other rural churches, build an indoor baptismal pool.

Shoutin'

Pray's houses served as the primary space for the shared religious occurrence known as the *shout*. This West and Central African ritual, a combination of music, song, and movement, offered enslaved Africans a rare opportunity to openly express themselves. William Allen gives one of the earliest accounts of a ring shout:

> The benches are pushed back to the wall when the formal meeting is over, and old and young, men and women, sprucely-dressed young men, grotesquely half-clad field-hands—the women generally with gay handkerchiefs twisted about their heads and with short skirts—boys with tattered shirts and men's trousers, young girls barefooted, all stand up in

the middle of the floor, and when the "sperichil" is struck up, begin first walking and by-and-by shuffling round, one after the other, in a ring. The foot is hardly taken from the floor, and the progression is mainly due to a jerking, hitching motion, which agitates the entire shouter, and soon brings out streams of perspiration.[29]

Before the shout began, pray's house elders presided over a devotional service containing scripture readings, prayers, personal testimonies, and hymn lining, which is a responsorial singing method led by a worship leader, who read or chanted lines of a hymn in couplets, and then congregants responded by singing these words to a tune known to all.[30]

As Allen's account shows, once this service ended, the people moved the benches aside to give room for the performance of the shout. Generally, there were two main performance spaces within the tiny pray's house: the shouting area, where the movement took place; and the baser area, where the clapping and singing occurred. Those who were shuffling were careful not to cross their legs or lift their feet off the ground, and any offender was quickly taken out of the ring by the elders. Pray's house leaders were aware that white missionaries viewed the shout as a "heathenish dance," so they made sure that participants followed these strict performance rules. The basers used their hands, feet, and voices to serve as the musical accompaniment for the shout, but Geechees from Georgia often featured the stick.

Georgia has the most celebrated ring shout tradition, beginning with the George Sea Island Singers in the 1930s and continuing with the McIntosh County Shouters and the Geechee Gullah Ring Shouters today. The close-knit Black families in McIntosh County and Bolden County are committed to the continued survival of an art form lost and, in some instances, forgotten in other areas of the Gullah Geechee Cultural Heritage Corridor. Shouter Freddy Palmer of the McIntosh County Shouters says, "I knew from early childhood that it was important for me and my brothers, sisters, and cousins to keep this tradition alive."[31] Through the leadership of Bessie Jones and Frankie and Doug Quimby, Lawrence McKiver, and Griffin Lotson, to name a few, Georgia has truly become the home of the ring shout, and each of these groups has gained national and international recognition for their contributions to this art form.

"There is a specific repertoire of songs for the ring shout that range in expressive mood from playful to fervently apocalyptic," says folklorist Art Rosenbaum. "The shout songs would never be sung in church in place of spirituals, hymns, or gospel songs ... nor would these serve the needs of the shout."[32] The most popular songs, such as "Move, Daniel" and "Eve and Adam," feature vivid pantomimes that add great drama to the performance. For example, the McIntosh County Shouters are known to extend their arms in a birdlike fashion as they shuffle and sing "Move, Daniel."

Leader: Move, Daniel, move. Daniel
   Move, Daniel, move
Basers: Daniel.
Leader: Move, Daniel, move
Basers: Daniel.

During their performances, the Geechee Gullah Ring Shouters bend over to pick up leaves as they perform "Eve and Adam." This shout song is also popular in South Carolina, where it is known under the slightly different title "Adam in de Gaardin."

Leader: Oh Eve, where is Adam?
   Oh Eve, Adam in the garden
   Pickin' up leaves.
   God called Adam

Basers: Pickin' up leaves
Leader: God called Adam
Basers: Pickin' up leaves.

The counterclockwise circular direction of the shout relates to ancestral West and Central African burial practices. In his book *Four Moments of the Sun*, Robert Thompson discusses a West African funeral in which the body of the deceased is laid out in state in an open yard "on a textile-decorated bier" as bare-chested mourners dance to the rhythms of drums "in a broken counterclockwise circle, their feet imprinting a circle on the earth, as cloth attached to and trailing on the ground from their waists deepen[s] the circle.... If the deceased lived a good life, death, a mere crossing of a threshold into another world, was a precondition for being 'carried back into the mainstream of the living, in the name and body of grandchildren of succeeding generations.'"[33]

Sierra Leonian Earl Conteh-Morgan confirms a similar counterclockwise movement around the deceased during Bandu burial services in his country. This circular tradition represents an unbroken circle of life processes such as marriage, the birth of children, and death and permeates much of Sierra Leone society, predating the transatlantic slave trade. In Kongo, there is a similar belief in an unbroken circle, which applies to the four moments of the sun: dawn (birth), noon (life at its fullest), sunset (the end of life's journey), and, finally, a second dawn (rebirth), represented by a cosmogram. This symbol, often in the shape of a cross, has been found on the base of colonoware bowls in living quarters of formerly enslaved workers. English scholar Corey Stayton concludes that the cosmogram "provides a unique model of religious and social values which have paved the way for the very foundation of many African-American traditions."[34]

According to historian Sterling Stuckey, "wherever in Africa the counter-clockwise dance ceremony was performed...the dancing and singing were directed to the ancestors and gods, the tempo and revolution of the circle quickening during the course of movement. The ring in which Africans danced and sang is the key to understanding the means by which they achieved oneness in America. Knowledge of the ancestral dance in Dahomey contributes to that understanding and helps explain aspects of the shout in North America."[35]

There is no doubt that the pray's house and the shout were vital parts of the religion of the enslaved Africans and the Gullah peoples of that day. But not all historians have treated the subject with the respect it deserves. In his book, *The Abundant Life Prevails: Religious Traditions of Saint Helena Island*, Michael C. Wolfe quotes one writer's description of a typical shout ritual: "Then began one of those scenes, which, when read, seem the exaggerations of a disordered imagination; and when witnessed, leave an impression like the memory of some horrid nightmare—so wild in the torrent of excitement...sweeping away reason and sense."[36] This writer failed to understand the African cultural practices on display and the need for these enslaved persons to release the painful emotions they were unable to express outside of the pray's house. Indeed, "de Ark ob Safety" within this structure was the only true place where they could be themselves.

Gullah Religion in Print

Although many elements of the Gullah culture and tradition have faded and even been threatened with extinction, the religious heritage has become stronger and stronger in many ways. Often, for example, in attempts by translators and scholars to re-create the Gullah language and determine its origins, samples of translations relating to the Bible or sacred teachings are used. One of the most common is saying grace, as in the following manner:

*Gee we da food wa we need dus day yah an eby day. Fagibe we da bad ting
we da do. Cause we da fagibe dem people wa do bad ta we. Leh we don habe
haad tes wen Satan try we. Keep we from ebil.*

For many Gullah people, saying grace was akin to the pouring of libations,
a tradition that goes back thousands of years, it is said, to the time when Jacob
erected a pillar of stone in the place where he had spoken to God. He poured
oil on it, made an offering of wine, and made an expression of commitment.
Expressions of grace in Gullah were followed by more elaborate translations,
both from ecclesiastical history and from the Bible. Quite common were versions of the Lord's Prayer:

> *We Fada wa dey een heaben*
> *Leh ebrybody hona ya nyame*
> *We pray dat soon ya gwine rule oba de wol.*
> *Wasoneba ting ya wahn,*
> *Leh um be so een dis wol*
> *Same like dey een heaben.*
> *Gii we de food wa we need*
> *Dis day yah an ebry day.*
> *Fagibe we fa we sin*
> *Same lik we da fagibe dem people*
> *Wa do bad ta we.*
> *Leh we dohn hab haad test*
> *Wen Satan try we*
> *Keep we fom ebil.*

For many years, there was resistance to translating almost any kind of pas-
sages into the Gullah Geechee language, let alone the Bible and other religious scripture. "It was like breaking the King's English," said Mary Ravenell, a
middle school teacher and minister from South Carolina. "But Gullah is not
'broken English.' It has a distinct grammar and vocabulary, and it originated
with the slave trade that brought West Africans to the Sea Islands beginning
in the 1700s. Traders wanted to thwart uprisings and escapes, so they mixed
slaves who spoke different languages. Slaves developd Gullah to communicate
with one another." Amazingly, the enslaved passed down their language from
generation to generation without need of any written form.[37]

Beginning in 1979, there came a heroic challenge: to translate portions of
the Bible and eventually the entire New Testament into Gullah. This proj-

ect endeavored to help Gullah speakers, who were accustmoed to words and phrases in their native tongue, understand much more of the Bible than they could from the standard English translation. Emory Campbell explained, "Even I, who have a graduate degree and have read the Bible in English all my life, can better understand the New Testament in Gullah. It makes a whole lot more sense to me."[38] He should know, for he was at the forefront of the translation that was completed in 2005. But he almost missed his chance.

In the early 1980s, a visiting linguist from the University of Southern California convinced Campbell that Gullah was more than broken English and its survival was vital to the preservation of the culture of the Sea Islands and the Lowcountry of Georgia and the Carolinas. "Along with my friends and people my age, I had actually rejected Gullah in my student years," he admitted, "as a kind of stigma that set us apart as outsiders. So everybody I knew in my age bracket wanted to speak standard English."[39]

Shortly thereafter Campbell met the late Pat Sharpe and her husband, Claude, who lived on nearby Daufuskie Island, one of the Sea Islands whose inhabitants were, for many years, largely of Gullah origin. As professional translators, they had begun a Gullah translation of the New Testament, and they convinced Campbell that he should join in this unique venture. Another key person was David Frank, a linguist and translation consultant, whose most challenging assignment was to recruit competent volunteers who would commit to a process that could take fifteen to twenty years to complete. It was decided, however, that their task would not seem as daunting if they released advance Gullah Geechee translations of the Gospel of Luke, which was published in 1994, and the Gospel of John, which was published in 2002. As it turned out, the New Testament (*De Nyew Testament*) was thirty years in the making, actually appearing in November 2005 under the bylines of the Wycliffe Bible Translators and the American Bible Society.

The most remarkable achievement of this project—though secondary to the accomplishment itself—was the fact that within a matter of only a few weeks from the date the nine-hundred-page edition was released to the public, the entire initial printing—ten thousand copies—was all but sold out. Most important, the reviews were excellent and meaningful because they placed great emphasis on the significance of the Gullah Geechee language itself and its projected rebirth in society. The success of *De Nyew Testament* has prompted many scholars and authorities in the field of linguistics and languages to take a closer look at the importance of the Gullah language in the Sea Islands and society in general.

Dr. Robert Hodgson, dean of the Nida Institute for Biblical Scholarship at the American Bible Society, has said that the translation is one in which everyone can take pride because of its historical and cultural significance, and he points out that this is more than just an unusual translation success story. "The Gullah New Testament raises the Gullah language and culture to a new level by enshrining the Scriptures in a Creole language once denigrated as a second-class version of English.... African American churches around the country will celebrate this new translation for its lively tone and musical rhythms, reminiscent of today's hip-hop vernacular, but also for its recovery of an almost forgotten chapter in the history of African-Americans." A member of the translation team—a Gullah herself—put it more succinctly and to the point when she remarked, "That's the first time I heard God talk the way I talk!"[40]

OH YES, I KNOW HE WILL!

On a Sunday morning in a pray's house on a Sea Island, the preacher looks out over the small assembled congregation and intones words of hope that the Savior is coming. In a deep voice, as though from the tomb, he intones his assurance:

> *Oh yes! I know he will! All right! Yeah! Amen! Look on the mountain*
> *Beside the hill of Galilee my Lord!*
> *Watch his disciple*
> *Riding on the sea—Yeah. Uh huh!*
> *Tossing by the wind and rain—Yeah. Come up*
> *Going over the sea of temptation—Uh hum*
> *Brother, I don't know*
> *But I begin to think*
> *In this Christian life—Yes*
> *Sometimes you gone be toss—Yes, yeah*
> *By the wind of life—Yes, my Lord!*
> *The wind gonna blow you*
> *From one side to the other—Yes!*

CHAPTER SIX

HEALING AND FOLK MEDICINE

Enslaved Africans brought to America their rich memories of cultural folk beliefs and medicinal herbal remedies that proved invaluable for the treatment of diseases and other assaults on their physical, mental, and emotional beings within the brutal plantation system. The remarkable survival of these cultural practices in many Gullah Geechee communities can be attributed to the geographical locations of the coastal Carolinas and Georgia, which provided "a fertile environment for the survival of West African culture." They lived and worked "on moist and verdant ground, not entirely unlike the lands from which they had been taken," says author Roger Pinckney. Among them were men who had learned the healing arts in the lands of their births and continued these traditions despite risk of severe physical punishment from white overseers who regarded such practices as an "allegiance to the devil!"[1]

Studies have consistently shown a unique awareness by sea islanders of the world around them, particularly as it pertains to their health and wellness. After their arrival, enslaved Africans transplanted their knowledge of plants throughout the Gullah Geechee region, creating a rich repository of herbal remedies that only a precious few have been able to master. These specialists were by default the Black community's medical doctors, who helped wage a daily battle against illness and against a spiritual world of equal threat to the Gullah Geechee people.

The Conjurer

Historical narratives from interviews of formerly enslaved Africans often use the term *conjurer* for a witch doctor, hoodoo doctor, root doctor, two-facer, and wangateur. This person usually had a long apprenticeship period under a father or mother or from older relatives or friends. Easily identifiable within the Gullah community, "conjurers cultivated an aura of mystery which lent credibility to their reputations as men familiar with supernatural lore," writes theologian Albert Raboteau. "Distinctive features, such as 'red eyes' and 'blue gums,' unusual dress, and the accoutrements of his trade—crooked can, charms, and conjur bag—all were outward manifestations of the root worker's special expertise."[2] Looking upon the conjur bag was avoided for risk of death, and there were numerous stories of tragic endings for those unlucky enough to do so. A woman on Sandy Island remembered, "I heard tell bout a man ober de ribbah what jus looked on a conjur man bag, and he died."[3] Items commonly found in the conjur bag were "goopher dust" or graveyard dirt, charms, horse-hair, roots, and various assortments of herbs.

Although Gullahs embraced the teachings of Christianity, they still retained their ancestral beliefs in the power of magic or the supernatural to bring misfortune or healing to community members. They would consult with a conjurer when seeking retribution against an enemy or protection against someone who had placed a spell on them. But these mystical figures were equally adept at healing physical and mental maladies, and there are several accounts of them giving a person a root, herb, charm, or even liquor for various

OVERLEAF: Dr. Wilder, a "root doctor" in the Sea Islands in the early 1900s, displaying a snake. *Transparency No. 49363. (Photo by Julian Dimock.) Courtesy of the American Museum of Natural History Library.*

ailments. A Geechee man from Georgia attests to his recovery from a "puhcu-leyuh disease" when a female conjurer instructed him to "drink a haffuh pint uh wiskey and tro way duh udduh res uh duh pint. Attuh uh done dis, uh git well agen."[4]

During the late 1930s, the Works Progress Administration's Georgia Writ-er's Program under the supervision of Mary Granger conducted interviews of residents living in the community of Sandfly, some ten miles south of Sa-vannah, Georgia. Once described as a "scattered Negro community spreading through the hot pine barrens to the nearby Isle of Hope," it had a population of about three hundred inhabitants.[5] The history of Sandfly dates to the early 1700s, when enslaved people working on Wormsloe and another nearby plan-tation settled there. "After they were freed, they bought sizable parcels, built homes, and passed them down to the next generation. Why they would have named their settlement for a gnat is uncertain, but many believe they had in mind a song, "'Sandfly Bite Me' that boatmen would sing as they navigated the marshes."[6] When the Works Progress Administration (WPA) interview-ers arrived, they found, in fact, several men who were fishermen along the At-lantic coast.

The WPA's interest in this little buggy strip of coastal Georgia stemmed from the known reliance of the families and forebears in the ancient Gullah Geechee traditions of conjuring. During interviews, they readily described many of their experiences and the reasons why this was a distinct part of their spiritual, supernatural, and metaphysical lives. One Geechee resident said, "A woman that lived in Homestead Park jis couldn't seem to have nuthin but bad luck. She thought maybe an enemy had conjuhed uh, so she looked in the yahd an sho nough theah wuz a cunjuh bag. It wuz a queah lookin bundle with a lot of brown clay in it. She destroyed the bag an the bad luck stopped an the evil spirits didn't bothuh us none."[7]

As explained earlier, graveyard dirt was often found in conjure bags, but many believed it was only effective when taken from the grave of a murder victim, and a payment of a few coins was left at the graveside for the deceased to use in the other world. There were other examples where people believed that powerful charms (usually malicious rather than favorable) could be made from dust, such as dirt from a person's foot tracks. One woman, who feared this type of dust, carried a small rake and *down du road she would go, rakin' up uh footsteps in back of uh, so dat nobody could git dat dus an fix uh.*

In another case, a small boy in the Sandfly community was experiencing great mental anguish. When his parents tried to determine the cause, he kept repeating that he had "snakes sliding about in my head." When they called in a local doctor, he diagnosed the illness as ringworm, which causes patches and itchiness on the scalp, thus, giving the boy the sensation of something moving in his head. The physician gave the mother some fungus-killing cream to apply to the head with the assurance that the problem would soon be resolved. But such was not the case. The boy called out from his bed shortly after dark, screaming in terror that there were snakes in his hair. The mother applied more ointment, to no avail. But early the next morning, she looked out the window and saw a snake—an omen. She grabbed a stove shovel and killed it. And lo, within a few hours, her young son said the snakes had "gone away" from his head. He was cured.

A highly influential figure in Sandfly was Ophelia Baker, better known as Madam Truth, a self-professed fortune-teller and clairoyant—a conjurer. A WPA interviewer gave this description of Madam Truth:

> The woman's sober attire and her modern, attractive house give little evidence of her profession. When holding a séance, however, her whole appearance undergoes a change; her body becomes tense and jerks spasmodically; her dark eyes roll wildly. Of her ability in her chosen field, the medium says, "*I advise on business an love affeahs. I tell good an bad nooz comin tuh yuh. Deah's a remedy fuh ebry trouble and I hab dat remedy, fuh a spirit hab brung it tuh me.*"

Madam Truth, a member of the Holy Sanctified Church of Sandfly, said that all members must undergo a sanctifying process in order to be saved. After this has been accomplished members claim to be able to hear, from a great distance, singing, talking, and the sounding of drums. We were told that the beating of the drums has a special significance. . . . The plump, dark-skinned fortune teller said that she had spent her childhood on Skidaway Island. She remembered hearing the drums beaten to tell the people in the nearby settlements of an approaching dance or festival. Her father had been one of those who beat the drum and thumped out a regular message on it, a message that could be heard for miles and was clearly understood by all those who had heard it. Members of the church are forbidden to eat certain kinds of fish and also cabbage, lettuce, and other green vegetables. The reason they give is that they have received a warning from the spirits that it is unwise to eat these foods.

In her reflection of going to a wake service, Madam Truth states, "Coffee and sandwiches were served to the mourners, and each one poured some of the coffee on the ground for the spirit of the deceased." Superstition was a guiding force in Sandfly, often preempting their religious beliefs and sometimes simply intermeshing with them. For example, "a silver coin was frequently worn on the ankle to insure good luck. It would give warning by turning black if an enemy made any attempt to 'conjure' the wearer. To 'conjure' was to evoke the evil spirits to do harm to someone. It is recalled that one woman fell mysteriously ill as a result of a 'conjure' and felt snakes running up and down her left side under the skin."[9]

Healing Herbs and Common Roots

Before seeking the services of a conjurer to treat illnesses, Gullah Geechee families relied upon a core group of medicinal herbs. These included "life-everlasting" (*Gnaphalium polycephalum*), which was used to relieve cramps, cure colds, combat diseases of the bowels and pulmonary system, and relieve foot pain. Dog fennel (*Anthemis cotula L.*) and mullein (*Verbascum thapsus*) were popular for treating colds, stuffy noses, headaches, and nervous conditions. Bark from a red oak tree (*Quercus falcata*), when boiled and drank as a tea, was said by many elderly people to alleviate rheumatism, as well as dysentery and other intestinal complaints.

During the early 1970s, Daniel E. Moerman, a medical researcher, conducted extensive ethnographic interviews concerning medicinal plant use and indigenous systems of popular medicine and concluded that folk medical practices and belief systems persisted as an adaptive response to inadequate access to healthcare. Among those interviewed was Dr. York Bailey, the first Black medical doctor on St. Helena Island and graduate of Penn School, for whom one of the school's buildings is named. Besides completing extensive research and interviews, Moerman compiled *The St. Helena Popular Pharmacopeia*, a detailed presentation of plants and species with medical applications. He is also given credit for compiling extensive data about the structure of sea island households, the relationships of family members, situations regarding health, medicine, social services, and the availability of medical assistance and pharmaceuticals.

Other research in the 1970s was done by anthropologist Faith Mitchell, whose study of traditional folk beliefs and medicine on St. Helena Island resulted in her 1978 book *Hoodoo Medicine: Gullah Herbal Remedies*. Mitchell's work presents no fewer than fifty detailed drawings of botanical elements, and she examines medicinal plant practices and those enslaved people who were often by default the Black community's medical doctors. According to Mitchell, there were three types of Black medicine practitioners. First, there were those who practiced healing techniques using barks, berries, herbs, leaves, and roots to combat natural illness such as common colds, flu, or malaria. Second, there were specialists who dealt with "spiritual illness" by using the laying on of hands or verbal intonations. Third, there were those who really deserved the term *witch doctor* because they were concerned with persons who had occult disturbances that were supposedly caused when they were "hexed" by voodoo (sometimes called "hoodoo") beings who dealt in African mystic beliefs in the supernatural.

One of the most interesting and lucid accounts of Gullah Geechee medical and health practices was given by Vennie Deas-Moore, a field researcher and writer at the Medical University of South Carolina in Charleston. "During my mother's youth and well into my childhood," she wrote in an article titled "Home Remedies, Herb Doctors, and Granny Midwives," "my family relied on home remedies, herb doctors, and granny midwives. Home remedies were made mostly from dried plants and other materials that could be gathered from yards and from the woods, such as asafetida, Spanish moss, and milkweed. Many of these remedies have proven to be medically valid. Mama speaks of how her grandmother, Mulsey, doctored her when she was sick or injured. When she was too sick she was taken to the herb doctor of the village. The herb doctor had a cure for anything that ailed you. There were roots, barks, and herbs stored in the mason jars that lined the walls of his house. During those days, there were no doctors for at least twenty or thirty miles, but the old people knew the herbs. Dogwood tea was good for a fever.... For bad neck ache, pinetop tea was good. Get a pine the height of you. Get the limb, break off just the top, right at the level of your neck."

Deas-Moore further explained that the large variety of herbs and roots fell within three broad areas: (1) common ingredients that could be purchased at the general store, such as apple cider vinegar, alcohol, table salt, syrup, lard, sulfur, bluestone, and Epsom salts; (2) patent medicines such as witch hazel, saltpeter, ammonia, oil of wintergreen, pure spirits of gum, and turpentine; and (3) common roots and herbs such as bloodroot, snakeroot, pokeroot, muckle bush, and life-everlasting. "Gathering, mixing, and prescribing roots and herbs," she emphasized, "required a good knowledge of where to find them at what time of the year, how to prepare them, how much to use, and for which ailments, and so on."[10]

There were said to be almost one hundred plants in West and Central Africa for healing aches and pains, and many of them were available in the coastal corridors of America. Initially, Penn School founder Laura Towne was skeptical about the medical value of the islanders' herbal remedies. She was especially critical of a conjurer named "Doctor Jacobs," "a man who has poisoned enough people with his herbs and roots and magic, for his chief remedy with drugs is spells and incantations." She wanted no part of a voodoo man whose "pharmacopeia" included rat tea, dried frogs, nail clippings, graveyard dirt, and lizard legs. But she eventually discovered that many of the medications in common use by islander families actually contained elements that were medically viable. Eventually, she combined her knowledge of homeopathic medicine with what she garnered from the old-time residents to administer effective medical care to the entire Gullah Geechee community on St. Helena Island.

Towne's acceptance of the Gullahs' herbal remedies is shown by the numerous entries in her diary discussing the use of blackberry for diarrhea and dysentery, swamp grass for poultices, sassafras tea as a tonic for colds, galax (an evergreen) for high blood pressure, kidney weed as a diuretic, sassafras roots for colic, ironweed combined with mare's milk as an eyewash to improve sexual potency, acid from willow leaves to treat rheumatism, the juice of wild figs for skin lesions, nightshade to reduce fevers, jimson weed as a salve, chinaberry to purge intestinal worms, and basil for sore throats. Common, too, was the practice of applying a mash of stems, flowers, and leaves to rashes or applying a scrap of brown paper, licked lightly and placed at the center of a baby's forehead, to eliminate hiccups.

One form of medication that was of special interest, in part because of its unusual nature and substance, was the application of spider webs to the skin— most often to the face and neck—to alleviate sores and painful insect bites. Strange though this practice may have seemed, it apparently was effective. Was this a practice that was more effective mentally than medically? An article in the Associated Press on October 31, 2004, provides some credible insight. Headlined "Healing Power of Spider Silk Examined," it covered the work of Michael Ellison, a Clemson University materials science professor whose laboratory research indicated that spider's silk was proving to be effective in help-ing wounds heal more quickly.

The most popular herb throughout the Corridor was an annual known as life-everlasting, whose leaves, stems, and flowers were boiled and taken by pa-tients to ease a cold, cough, or congestion and fever. Often it was combined with mullein or sea myrtle to relieve cramps, pulmonary distress, and loose bowels. When dried and smoked, this plant was said to relieve asthma, and it could also be applied to sore feet and when chewed could ease the pain of a toothache. Cornelia Walker Bailey was a great supporter of the use of life-everlasting because of her family's long devotion to this herb.

> Grandma and Grandpa raised Mama on life everlasting tea, and Grandpa never gave it up, even when he could afford coffee. Papa drank life ever-lasting tea, and he drank it more than Mama did. That's probably be-cause Papa was practically raised by Uncle Nero. His uncle was the only relative left still around after Grandma Gibb left Sapelo and went off to Florida. Papa would come across life everlasting growing in the woods while he was driving his tractor, and he would bring home these huge bunches of it tied to his knapsack and hang them up outside in the corn house to dry. Life everlasting's got tiny little leaves that turn kinda silver-gray in the fall, when it's ready for you to pick it, and little white blos-soms on top. So when he wanted some tea, he'd go out back, break a piece off, and boil it up.[11]

Often, "several different herbs could be used to treat one illness, and many different ailments treated with the same plant. Tannin-rich astringents, like the leaves of sweet gum, myrtle, and blackberry, were invaluable in treating the all-too-common profuse diarrhea and dysentery; bitterness was prized in searching for a cure for ever-present malaria. More than a dozen plants were used to treat colds, a dozen more for fever; a half dozen were applied to sores, and as many again were taken as tonics, considered especially beneficial when whiskey was added."[12] Further remedies include the use of aloe leaves and the bark of the angelica tree, known to natives as "rattlesnake master" because of their use as an antidote to the bites of deadly snakes. An example of a lesser concoction is sassafras roots for brewing tea as a health tonic. Sassafras also earned a reputation as a cure for venereal disease and even blindness when combined with milk from a mare and applied as an eyewash. Another form of eyewash was made from roots of the heartleaf plant, which was said to treat bloodshot eyes effectively and clear the vision.

Roger Pinckney lists any number of home remedies that were not just hearsay but passed down in his own family. He recalls bloodroot tea for the skin, peppermint oil to ease stomach pains, wild grapevine sap for patients having difficulties urinating, and basil leaves in the bath to serve as a natural deodorant. As he further explains, the Gullah peoples "widely used turpentine as an emergency balm, antibiotic, and sealant for cuts, abrasions, and lacerations while working in the pinewoods. Gunpowder mixed with whiskey will calm the heart and give power. Benefits from turpentine and whiskey may be enthusiastically debated with less than certain conclusions, but smokeless gunpowder contains nitroglycerine, a common heart stimulant." If buzzard's carcass is available, you can extract a lard from its innards and apply it as a rub for joint stiffness. This was especially effective, it was said, if the stiffness had come about because the patient had walked over an evil root buried beneath the doorstep. Although it was admitted that the odor of a dead buzzard was pretty hard to take, it was definitely effective—so much so that if a person overdid the application on his legs, he could get "so limber that he could no longer walk!"[13]

Research conducted by the National Park Service found many of these folk remedies to be effective despite the skepticism of non-Gullah practitioners. This study notes that "a surprising number of food plants, especially fruits, also yielded products used to treat disease. "Fig, peach, pomegranate, persimmon, along with basil, okra, and pumpkin, found their way into the pharmacological lore of the sea islands. No line can be drawn between folk medicine and the scientific medicine of the time."[14] Comparative studies revealed that many of the species of plants common to Gullah application were actually mentioned independently in the *U.S. Pharmacopeia*, the *National Formulary*, or both, from as far back as 1820 to the present century.

Moreover, this study compared plants and natural substances traditionally used in Africa to similar species in the Americas and found at least fourteen plants containing healing properties existed in the Sea Islands as well as in West Africa. "Although most of the items are employed to treat more than one condition," said the report, "the same plant is often used in the same way on both sides of the Atlantic. Thus, wormseed and the chinaberry tree are taken as a vermifuge, especially against Necator americanus or hookworm. The crushed flowers of okra are applied to snake bites, and cotton is used for abortion or uterine contraction in the Old World and in the New. Nightshade, taken for fever in the Lowcountry and in Africa, has known antibacterial action. Jimson weed, used as a vermifuge, cold medicine, and salve in Carolina, is taken as a narcotic in West Africa.... Basil, taken for colds and other ailments, and pomegranate, used to stop diarrhea in South Carolina, are best known as anthelmintics in West Africa; pumpkin, taken for dropsy as a diuretic, is also used to treat worms there."[15] The conclusion was that there was evidence of a very strong link, medicinally, between where enslaved Africans came from and where they ended up, but even more conclusive was the fact that the art of healing, the natural substances, and the beliefs surrounding them were so strikingly similar.

There is no doubt that all along the Gullah Geechee Corridor, whether on the islands or within thirty or forty miles inland, there was, is, and always has been a surprising abundance of natural resources for healing the body and even the mind and spirit. Applications of these innumerable plants, herbs, roots, and other gatherings from forests, fields, marshes, and streams were largely in the hands of Gullah Geechee community members, who knew the sources, seasons, and methods of preparation. Among them were special herbalists known as conjurers or root doctors, whose physical actions and verbal communications played a vital part in the treatment and the cure.

The Infamous Dr. Buzzard

Root doctors traditionally had trade names or nicknames taken from the animal kingdom that set them apart from other kinds of practitioners. Thus, we find numerous stories about Dr. Lizard, Dr. Crow, Dr. Snake, Dr. Wasp, Dr. Eagle, and the like. According to Jack Montgomery, author of *American Shamans: Journeys with Traditional Healers*, there was usually a special quality responsible for the spiritual gifts of these root doctors:

> It is widely believed that a child who is born with a caul or membrane over the face at birth has been chosen by the spirit world for a special role in life. The survival from a dangerous accident or a miraculous recovery from a near-fatal illness can bestow such a spiritual mantle. In these cases, the living soul has passed temporarily into the spirit realm and returned to this existence, bringing back some of the otherworldly presence. Being born with a particularly dark complexion was thought to confer special powers for working magic or communicating with the spirit world.[16]

The birth of a child with a caul covering their face represented to the enslaved community a life destined to have strong connections to the spiritual realm. One example is James Washington, a root doctor who could tell the future because he was born with a double caul. Washington's special gift provided him keen insight into the supernatural world. "He said that some magic can guard you from harm, but evil magic can put you down sick; hair is the most powerful thing an enemy can get hold of because it is so close to the brain." Root doctors can be traced back to Africa, where the special power of those born with a caul is recognized in Dahomey (present-day Benin), and there is great reverence given to the diviner or fortune-teller among the Ashanti people in south-central Ghana; the place of hair in magic is widespread among many Africans from the Ewe to the Mpongwe; and the role of conjure and charms is universal.[17]

Arguably, the most well-known conjurer of the twentieth century was Dr. Buzzard, a resident on St. Helena Island. His real name was Stephany Robinson (1885–1947), and according to legend, his father was a "witch doctor" who had been brought directly from West Africa. Robinson, however, was the second Dr. Buzzard—the first was a white conjurer who died in the late nineteenth century. "Dr. Buzzard [Stephany Robinson] not only sold roots to a nationwide clientele that numbered in the thousands and predicted winning numbers in clandestine lotteries, but he was also reputed to have spirits at his command—various haunts and hags that flirted around the edges of island reality. If Dr. Buzzard put an evil root on a man, locals said, that man was as good as dead."[18] On the other hand, he was said to have been equally effective in banishing mental illness, bringing success to people in love, and protecting people from evil spirits who tried to do them bodily harm or destroy their businesses.

Dr. Buzzard enjoyed great wealth from local sales of his charms and potions and mail orders from Gullahs who had moved north. Like many in his profession, he was aware of the laws surrounding the sale and shipping of "homemade medicines" and on one occasion destroyed fifteen hundred dollars' worth of postal money orders when he learned that Beaufort Sheriff James McTeer was about to charge him with medical malpractice. Despite a lack of physical evidence, McTeer promised one of Dr. Buzzard's clients his protection if he testified to the purchase of home remedies from the famed root doctor in open court. Dr. Buzzard was known for "spreading powder in the courtroom before a criminal or civil trial to affect those who would come into contact with or see it, rendering them unable to give evidence as a witness."[19] McTeer, himself a root doctor, felt capable of thwarting any of Dr. Buzzard's spells and tricks, even the conjurer's "chewing the root" in court.

He would simply sit in the court, behind his purple sunglasses, staring at the proposed witness. The effect was devastating to a prosecuting attorney, who found he had a witness who had become completely in-capable of giving testimony. "Chewing the root" is a powerful form of spellcasting, which is witnessed by the intended victim and usually oth-ers nearby. "Chewing the root" demonstrates the two facets of the root doctor's spellcasting. The first concerns the personal magical power he or she can summon and the ability to focus that power externally with intention and tangibility. The second involves the public practice of that magical power, where it is witnessed and understood by the victim and the community. This action creates and enhances the personal reputa-tion of the root doctor.[20]

Despite McTeer's assurances, his witness was unable to give testimony against Dr. Buzzard. When he entered the courtroom and faced the great con-jurer, "he began to groan and 'beat himself' as if he were covered with stinging ants. After a few moments, the prisoner collapsed and began foaming at the mouth."[21] Dr. Buzzard had eliminated another would-be witness. By the 1930s, Dr. Buzzard was known as far away as Louisiana, Florida, and Virginia, and many found ways to capitalize on his fame. Mamie Garvin Fields, a teacher on Johns Island, South Carolina, recalled "a local hoodoo doctor, Jimmie Bris-bane, who was a higher type of witchdoctor, because he knew how to drive all the way to Beaufort and consult with Dr. Buzzard."[22] Cornelia Walker Bailey has much to say about another Doctor Buzzard on Sapelo:

The church was a huge part of our lives. We went there to worship and to settle disputes. People were called before the elders for adultery disputes, stealing disputes, fistfights, name calling, and to try to prove who was the rightful father of a child if a man denied he was or if any woman other than Grandma had the nerve not to tell.

But we had Dr. Buzzard too. Let's say I tried the church and that didn't work. I'm still angry so I need to do something a little more dras-tic. I'll try Dr. Buzzard. And *in come* Dr. Buzzard. Dr. Buzzard was the root doctor. The conjurer. The worker of *black magic*. He could put a spell on you and do you bodily harm. He could lift a spell off you. He could even turn a spell around and throw it back on the one that put it on you to begin with. Some places people call that voodoo or hoodoo, but over here we mostly said "root" or "mojo" to refer to the mysterious roots and herbs Dr. Buzzard used. No one was safe from root, absolutely no one, and the old people had a hard time believing in natural illness. It was hard for them to take the word of a doctor about anything. Even if someone persuaded them and said, "Take them to the doctor, take them to the doctor," if the doctor didn't find an instant cure, then the illness was blamed on something different. *Entirely different.* Root. Somebody "fixed" somebody.

When my aunt Della got breast cancer, Grandma refused to believe it was cancer. She said those doctors removed Della's breasts for nothing, that somebody worked root on her daughter. She went to Brunswick [Georgia] and got Aunt Della out of that hospital and brought her back over here. Aunt Della died at home, and after that Grandma didn't believe in hospitals any more.[23]

When Dr. Buzzard's son drowned in a car accident, he met with Sheriff McTeer and promised to give up homemade medicines but not spells. The two great rivals eventually became "friends of a sort." Upon his death, Dr. Buzzard's son-in-law, Buzzy, took over the business.

Hants, Hags, and Plat-Eyes

Enslaved people introduced to American culture West and Central African cosmological beings called hants, hags, and plat-eyes, who have appeared in literary works, songs, and of course ghost stories. While Black people held fast to their newly adopted Christian teachings, they revered the spiritual world's collection of supernatural creatures, who were blamed for unusual accidents, occurrences, and unexplained deaths. Hants or "haints" were the spirits of the dead who returned occasionally to trouble the living. West African religions taught that death "was not complete for up to five years," so a spirit could freely interact with the living during this time. The passing of a child over a casket was done to avoid such visitations by hants, who often possessed human and inhuman physical features and abilities.

During the 1930s, Murrells Inlet resident Zackie Knox described a hant with a face red "lak de brick en de chimbley" wearing a long white robe.[24] Maum Nellie, an elder within the same community, gave an even more graphic account of her sighting of a hant during a full moon: "It start way cross de fiel'. It bark lak fox. It howl lak dawg. It hoot lak squinch owl. It soun lak all de beas' ob de woods. En fuss news it hit de house. It circle. It prowl same lak stray dawg. En while she hol' she bref [breath], de door what she done bolt mube [move] open. De pot lid lif. De rockin chair rock."[25]

The color blue on buildings proved an effective deterrent against haints because these creatures thought it was water—a substance they could not cross over. According to author Alicia O'Brien, "the dregs of indigo dye from boiling pots were the first source of blue stain for window and door decorations. Application on house trim, especially windows and doorways, is a protection aimed at warding off bad luck or the evil spirits tempted to enter through the portals."[26] Throughout Charleston visitors will find blue ceilings over many of the porches, and doors, shutters, and sometimes entire houses are painted blue. This "haint blue" also appeared on Gullah graveside decorations.

Hags or "boo hags" were the disembodied spirits of witches who would shed their skin at night and "ride" people—that is give them nightmares. Hags would slip off their skin like clothing, storing it in drawers, closets, or under staircases for safekeeping as they searched for entry into someone's home. According to one Gullah informant, "Hag sperit can go troo de keyhole of de do' en ef dey lak you dey goes in sucks your blood troo yer nose."[27] Often, the very young were the favorite victims of these vampire-like creatures, says Johns Island singer and storyteller Janie Hunter:

> Hags come to your house and hag your children. Children can't sleep, or a hag take somebody child and put 'em under the bed. Sometime a hag sit on you and keep you from getting up, try to smother you. But you could tell a hag. I heard my old people say, if you want to tell a hag, put a broom 'cross your door. If that's a hag, he going to take up that broom, ain't going step across it. If a hag bother you, use salt and pepper. Sprinkle either on your bed or 'cross your door and they won't come in. The salt burn their skin.[28]

There are numerous accounts of Gullah men who suspected their wives of being hags. The advice often given to them was to wait until night when their wife had left and look under the staircase for her skin. "Ef ye fin' she skin, you salt en pepper it good same lak you salt en pepper fish what you goin fry. Ef she gone haggin, she sho lef' it, en if you salts it, she kain't git back in."[29] The only way to kill a hag was to put them in a barrel of tar and burn them up.

The most feared of the spirits was the plat-eye, a malicious shape-shifter, who could assume a human or animal form. Maum Addie, a formerly enslaved person in All-Saints Parrish, stated, "De ole folks is talk bout Plat-eye. Dey say dey takes shape ob all kind de critter—dawg, cat, hawg, mule, varmint, an I hear tell ob plat-eye takin form ob gator."[30] In the 1960s, Johns Islander James Mackey described his encounter with a plat-eye. "One almost knock me off my foot one night. I was coming out just about dusk-dark and something come around me like a long black snake—tie around me. It shoot up, and I ain't feel like I was onto the ground at all. Only way I came back in this world, a dog smell my scent and that dog bark. Didn't for that, I'd been gone."[31]

Plat-eyes tended to stay near graveyards or pathways where dead bodies had crossed, cleverly and calmly waiting for their victims to appear. Some even attest to their ability to "lure their victims into a seemingly safe situation, before robbing them of their senses."[32] The best protection against a plat-eye was to have on hand a mixture of gunpowder and sulfur because the strong odor repelled them. But plat-eyes liked the taste of whiskey, so the sea islanders knew if they poured a bit on the ground, it would distract the creature from harming them.

Attempts at Modernization

There were many well-meaning white missionaries and Black leaders who were successful in getting Gullahs to eliminate some of their superstitious practices. Penn School's second principal, Rossa Cooley, recognized the value, practical knowledge, and traditional community status of the granny midwives, but she deplored the unsanitary practices they often used in the birthing process. The use of cobwebs in the navel, for example, was cited as one of the practices that should be abandoned. Sociologist T. J. Woofter cited more graphic examples of the superstitions practiced by midwives during his stay on St. Helena Island in the 1920s:

> Sometimes the midwives would put a hoe or a plow point or an ax under the bed to cut the after pains attending childbirth. Gizzard tea, or tea made from the nest of the mud dauber, were also thought to reduce the after pains. Even more extreme, one practice involved standing the

woman in childbirth up in a corner and assisting the process by having several robust women beat, punch, and shake her. Often the midwife would tie a piece of the umbilical cord around the mother's toe for relief after birth, and some women thought it dangerous to bathe the baby before it was nine days old.[33]

In conjunction with the State Board of Health, licensed nurses began regular courses of training for the islander midwives at Penn School (later renamed Penn Center). The often elderly women received supplies and instruments, such as sterile dressings, medical scissors, and needles; were taught new procedures; and attended periodic health and medical meetings. Yet every attempt was made to show deep and abiding respect for the midwives who had given many years of service to the island's residents. This respect earned the midwives' trust and ensured their cooperation in spreading knowledge about hygiene and sanitation practices.

From the 1920s on, public health nurses, largely African Americans, traveled the Sea Islands and Lowcountry providing a compassionate link between modern clinical medicine and the old-time health practices. These women instructed the rural population about sanitary procedures and alerted families about signs of communicable diseases or other threats to their health and well-being. Many of these practitioners were well-educated nurse-midwives with a working knowledge of obstetrics. One outstanding example was Maude Cullen, who was born in Quincy, Florida, in 1898, educated at Florida A&M, and a graduate of a nursing course before moving to South Carolina. She was so successful in her calling as a nurse, dietician, midwife, and psychologist that *Life* magazine published an award-winning twelve-page photographic profile of her work in 1951, which generated great interest and some $27,000 in contributions that were used to construct a modern clinic in Pineville, South Carolina. Elderly residents in the more remote areas of the Lowcountry still clung to the healing practices of their forebears and looked sometimes with suspicion on modern medical technology.

The few licensed Black physicians faced formidable challenges, not the least of which were suspicion and lack of trust from local families because of their unfamiliar procedures and medications that differed completely from the traditional folk medicines. In some cases, these new-style doctors were accused of trying to usurp the authority of the root doctors or herb doctors who had been treating the local populations for generations. If they tried to oppose any of the methods or medications prescribed by the old-time practitioners, they risked losing much of their practice in the community. In some cases, they also risked losing their fees for services because patients who were cured of an illness ascribed the results to the herb doctor who was also treating them and not to the modern-age physician. Doctors who succeeded best were likely to be those who had the sense to acknowledge some of the ancient practices by working through a granny or midwife, thus achieving a kind of "seal of approval." It was essential, too, that doctors make house calls for the most part, seldom requiring patients to visit their offices.

However, the greatest opposition to conjuration came from African American Christians who considered this practice to be of the devil. Georgian Martha Colquitt remembered hearing about voodoo, but her grandmother and mother, devout Christians, "told us chillun voodoo wuz a no 'count doin of the devil, and Christians wuz never to pay it no 'tention. Us wuz to be happy in de Lord and let voodoo and de devil alone." However, there were often unclear dividing lines because Colquitt also maintained that to "hear scritch owls holler . . . meant somebody in dat house wuz goin' to die." She further confessed, "I sho' does b'livee in ha'nts 'cause I done heared one and I seed it too, leasewise I seed its light."[34]

Native American Herbal Remedies

Long before enslaved Africans were brought to the Sea Islands, Native Americans throughout the Carolinas, Georgia, and Florida possessed extensive knowledge of magical practices, talismans, omens, the use of drums, dancing, rituals, taboos, and other aspects of ethnology and folklore. Here, as examples, are representative Native American herbal remedies that are very similar to those used in the Gullah Geechee culture.

> Snakeweed: chewed up and applied to insect bites and stings, also as a
> tea for help with labor pains
> Skunk cabbage roots: to ease spells of asthma
> Wormwood leaves: boiled as a tea to cure bronchitis
> Horsemint leaves: crushed in cold water and imbibed to alleviate back
> pain
> Thistle blossoms: boiled into a thick liquid to apply to burns and skin
> lesions
> Chokeberry juice: swallowed to stop internal bleeding
> Cotton roots: boiled as a tea to relieve labor pains

Catnip leaf tea: to ease infants with colic

Wild cherry bark: ground, steeped in hot water, and gargled for coughs

Sarsaparilla: dried roots in warm water, used as a cough remedy

Dandelions: simmered into a broth to help heartburn and act as a tonic

Witch hazel leaves: boiled into a liquid and applied to aching backs and
bones

Pokeweed berries: pulverized and applied to ease pains of rheumatism
and gout

Dogwood bark: in hot water, for rectal distress, applied with a syringe
made from a rabbit's bladder or injected through a syringe made
from the hollow bone of a bird

Wild lettuce: chewed slowly for sedative purposes and nervousness

Persimmon bark: boiled in water to form a dark liquid used as a mouth
rinse, especially for infants with thrush

OLD TIME TREATMENTS LIVE ON

Root doctors are by no means extinct along the Gullah Corridor and in the Sea
Island and Lowcountry villages, where generations of families have relied on
them for treatment. Here, at random, are some of the old-time prescriptions
and treatments that are still being used for specific diseases, accidents, and
other physiological, psychological, and even spiritual ailments.

Bladder distress: Mix two tablespoons of flax seed with two tablespoons of cream of tartar in a glass of water and drink half in the
morning and half at night.

Rheumatism: Steep six leaves of wild Aaron's rod (mullein) in a quart
of water and drink half a glass of the liquid four times a day.

Temporary blindness: Mix slate dust with pulverized sugar and have
someone blow it in the eyes of the patient. Another remedy is the
juice from the gall bladder of a catfish, placed in the affected eyes
with an eye dropper.

Swelling of the skin or joints: Mix the oil from blending white roses,
lavender, and honeysuckle; apply this to the affected part and rub
well into the skin.

Stomachache: Make a gravy of bay leaves and parched rice, well
blended, and drink a cup of it very slowly.

Wounds: Especially for injuries from rusty nails or other metal objects piercing the skin and likely to cause lockjaw, mix a compound of bacon fat and tobacco leaves and squeeze it into the wound. The treatment is most effective if a copper penny is then taped against the sore.

Loss of memory: Mix bay leaves, sarsaparilla root, and sheep weed bark, ground well to a powder. Boil mixture in water as a tea and drink during the day until the memory improves.

CHAPTER SEVEN

THE GULLAH LANGUAGE

A famous Gullah Geechee proverb says, *"Ef oona ent kno weh oona da gwuine, oona should kno weh oona kum from."* Translated into English it means, "If you don't know where you are going, you should know where you come from."

Hearing the distinctive Gullah Geechee language for the first time in places such as Charleston, Beaufort, Savannah, St. Helena Island, and St. Simons Island often gives visitors the impression of being in a foreign country. John Bennett, a leading figure in the Charleston Renaissance, wrote "There is a patois spoken in the mainland and island regions, bordering the South Atlantic Seaboard, so singular in its sound as constantly to be mistaken for a foreign language."[1] The Gullahs' distinctive speech was the byproduct of the overwhelming Black majority existing in the Sea Islands, geographic isolation of Black communities, and cultural ties to West and Central Africa. Fortunately, there has been an impressive body of scholarship from experts from many different fields who study the Gullah Geechee language because of its remarkable ability to survive the most devastating period in American history—slavery.

The Gullah language, a Creole blend of English and the Ewe, Fante, Efik, Ibebio, Igobo, Yoruba, Twi, Kongo, and Mandinka West African languages, developed and thrived in the isolated plantations along the coastal South.[2] Even after the freeing of the enslaved people in the early 1860s, limited access to the islands helped to ensure the continuation of Gullah speech and customs until the middle of the next century. In effect, most of the Gullah peoples along the coast were as isolated as they had been before Emancipation. During the 1930s and 1940s, when white developers began building bridges to the Gullahs' scenic beaches, Black residents reminisced about the past and often used the phrase "before the bridge" or "after the bridge." Although conveniences on the mainland were now readily assessable, many of them preferred the "before the bridge" period when life was peaceful and the "entire village" raised the children.

Due to the encroachment of resort communities and pressure to assimilate into the "modern" world, Gullahs have lost many of their ancestral stories and traditions brought long ago to these shores. Yet they are resilient in their commitment to saving as much of their land and culture as possible. You will hear them talk of life before the *cumyas*, those who are recent arrivals to the area, and the problems experienced by the *binyas*, Gullah families whose domiciles can be traced back to plantation life. At local cultural festivals and celebrations, you can still listen to traditional spirituals such as *"Kumbaya"* ("Come By Here"), watch nimble hands weave gorgeous sweetgrass baskets, see beautiful Gullah artworks, and of course hear the unique Gullah language. According to a news reporter, "There are many interlocking parts to the whole. The Gullah culture of the Lowcountry is such a system. It has a language, history, economic system, and artistic vision found nowhere else. It is, indeed, a heritage so rich no price tag can measure its value."[3]

Lorenzo Dow Turner

If there is any single person who deserves credit for highlighting the significance of the Gullah Geechee language, it is Lorenzo Dow Turner (1890–1972),

OVERLEAF: Enslaved people with a donkey cart on Hopkinson's Plantation, Edisto Island, South Carolina. *Library of Congress, LC-DIG-ppmsca-11370.*

an African American linguist who conducted extensive studies of the islanders' speech in the 1930s. This was a remarkable feat, given the fact that Turner was head of the English Department at Howard University and editor and publisher of the *Washington Sun* newspaper. Through intensive research and singular purpose, he established Gullah as a new area of scholarship, despite the prevailing view of it as crude and unworthy of study.

Turner, a graduate of Howard University in 1910, worked his way through college as a Pullman car porter and waiter with the Commonwealth Steamboat Line. He was a rare person who could hold his own at the highest levels of academia yet was perfectly at ease with a farmhand in the cotton fields, a shrimp boat crew in Port Royal Sound, or a midwife in her shanty. Most importantly he learned to speak Gullah Geechee and distinguish its nuances so well that he could tell you whether the speaker was from an inland produce farm in the Lowcountry of South Carolina, Daufuskie Island off Savannah, Georgia, or the waterfront of Sapelo Island, Georgia.

In the field of linguistics, he was astonishingly gifted. During his early academic career, he studied Portuguese, Arabic, German, French, Italian, Kino, Igbo, Yoruba, Krio, Mende, and two Native American dialects and had a reading knowledge of Latin and Greek. He became eminently well qualified in documenting, analyzing, and comparing the Gullah dialect with African, Louisiana Creole, Afro-Brazilian Creole, Native American, and Arabic languages. His seminal work *Africanisms of the Gullah Dialect* proved convincingly that Gullah was strongly influenced by African languages, not only in the variety of sounds but also in vocabulary, grammar, sentence structure, and semantics. He identified, for example, more than three hundred "loan words" from African sources that are common in Gullah speech and some four thousand African personal names that are also used by the Gullah peoples in America.

Turner traveled to the remotest coastal communities of the Carolinas and Georgia, and he met people who readily recited tales and sang songs of African origin. For example, Rosina Cohen on Edisto Island, South Carolina, told him a story about "sikin" (seekin'); on Johns Island, Sanko Singleton told him about the supernatural creature "di hag" (hag); and in Harris Neck, Georgia, Amelia Dawley sang the famous "Mende Song" for him. Other informants could remember simple arithmetic in the Mende, Vai, or Fulani vernacular of West Africa:

> As regards numerals, I interviewed several older Gullahs, each of whom could count from one to nineteen in the Fula language. Usually, the Gul-

lahs did not know the name of the language in which they counted but said that they learned the numerals from older relatives or friends.... The Gullahs' pronunciation of the Fula numerals... is almost identical with that of my Fula informant, Sayid Ibrahim, of Sierra Leone.[4]

Turner accumulated an exhaustive amount of information from what at first seemed like a fairly simple study of an African-based language. It was said that he explored more than twenty African languages, including Wolof, spoken in Senegal; Malinke and Bambara, spoken in Guinea; Mandinka, spoken in Senegal and Guinea; Fula, spoken in Senegal, Gambia, and Guinea; Mende, spoken in Sierra Leone; Vai, spoken in Liberia; Twi and Fante, spoken in Ghana; Ga and Ewe, spoken in Togo; Fon, spoken in Benin; Yoruba, Bini, Hausa, Ibo, Ibibio, and Efik, spoken in Nigeria; and Kongo, Umbundu, and Kimbundu, spoken in Angola.

Despite being one of the few African American linguistics at a time when the majority of his peers were white upper crust, he not only held his own but dared to take issue with some of the top practitioners in his field. He particularly criticized Henry Mencken, George Krapp, and Ambrose Gonzalez, who termed the Gullahs' grammar and pronunciation as "incorrect English" and of little value as a language. He described all three as "shocking" in their lack of knowledge about, or interest in, the Gullah tongue as a language in its own right. He believed that their findings were partly due to the ability of Gullahs to "code switch" when speaking to someone outside of their community.

In the presence of strangers, they are "likely to use speech that is essentially English in vocabulary," says Turner. "When he talks to his friends, however, or to the members of the family, his language is different. My first recordings of the speech of the Gullahs contain fewer African words by far than those made when I was no longer a stranger to them." Turner benefited greatly from being African American because the islanders were more willing to trust someone who looked like them. On one occasion when he brought a white colleague along on an interview, his Gullah informant refused to speak and asked him "mek una fa brin de buckra," meaning "Why did you bring the white man?"[5]

Beginning in 1932, Turner was virtually a resident among Gullah communities in South Carolina and Georgia, and over a period of some fifteen years, he amassed an impressive body of phonetic transcriptions of the Gullahs' speech that he compared with West and Central African languages. Attesting to his thoroughness, those who knew him said that he did not rely on his own judgment alone but enlisted the help of twenty-seven researchers who between them had an accumulated knowledge of more than fifteen African languages. He also was in touch with more than fifty informants in a number of key Gullah communities in Georgia and South Carolina. He focused his investigations in four categories: distinctive figures of speech, the dynamics of language usage, the role of the language within the Gullah culture, and the origins and composition as a Creole language system.

His *Africanisms in the Gullah Dialect*, published in 1949 by Arno Press and the *New York Times* through the University of Chicago Press, is an unparalleled work responsible for Turner's universal acknowledgment as the "father of Gullah studies." In the preface of *Africanisms*, Turner summarizes his efforts:

> Gullah is a Creolized form of English revealing survivals from many of the African languages spoken by the slaves who were brought to South Carolina and Georgia during the eighteenth century and the first half of the nineteenth. These survivals are most numerous in the vocabulary of the dialect but can be observed also in its sounds, syntax, morphology, and intonation; and there are many striking similarities between Gullah and the African languages in the methods used to form words. The purpose of this study is to record the most important of these Africanisms and to list their equivalents in the West African languages. One chapter in the volume is devoted to Gullah texts, in phonetic notation, that show varying degrees of indebtedness to African sources.
>
> The present study is the result of an investigation of the dialect that has extended over a period of fifteen years. The communities in coastal South Carolina that furnished the most distinctive specimens of the dialect were Waccamaw (a peninsula near Georgetown) and James, John's, Wadmalaw, Edisto, St. Helena, and Hilton Head Islands. Those in Georgia were Darien, Harris Neck (a peninsula near Darien), Sapeloe Island, St. Simon Island, and St. Mary's. On the mainland of both South Carolina and Georgia many of the communities in which specimens of the dialect were recorded are situated twenty miles or further from the coast.[6]

Equally important, Turner devoted a large segment of his research time to the recording of sacred and secular spirituals that had their origins in West and Central Africa. These are available today in the Lorenzo Dow Turner audio recordings, held in university archival collections and some public libraries, most notably the Hog Hammock Public Library, Sapelo Island, Georgia. An example is "New Rice and Okra," sung by Julia Armstrong on St. Simons Island, Georgia:

> New rice and okra,
> I've come, I've come
> Eat some and leave some
> I've come, I've come.
> Beat rice, beat, bang, bang,
> I've come, I've come.[7]

Turner also recorded Sapelo Islander Katie Brown singing "Getting Religion":

> *An' I first got religion, that is,*
> *By goin' to church with my mother.*
> *Every night, I would beg her to let me go to church*
> *An' she carry me to church.*
> *An' then I heard the old people singing.*
> *It make me feel like I ought to been a Christian.*
> *An' I went to pray.*
>
> *An' I prayed an' I prayed*
> *Until I got my religion.*[8]

Turner found many common words in English that are almost directly related to their African counterparts. These include, for example, the following:

Animal names: Bambi, gorilla, zebra
Plant names and foods: banana, goober, okra, yam
Action words: bogus, booboo, boogie, dig, hippie, honkie, jamboree,
    juke, sock, tote
Religious and "otherworld" terms: bad eye, booger, boogie, mojo, voo-
    doo, zombie
Musical and dance terms: bamboula, banjo, bongo, jive, mambo, samba

According to Joseph E. Holloway, a linguist at California State University:

Many words associated with cowboy culture and originating from this relationship have found their way into American English. For example, *bronco* (probably of Efik/Ibibio and Spanish origins) was used centuries ago by the Spanish and by enslaved Africans working with cattle and horses. *Buckra*, also deriving from this relationship, comes from *mbakara*, the Efik/Ibibio word for "white man." *Buckaroo*, also from *mbakara*, was used to describe a class of whites who worked as bronco busters. *Dogies*, a word that even found its way into popular cowboy songs, as in "get along little dogies," originated from the Kimbundu *kidogo*, a little something, and *(ki) dodo*, small.[9]

The Gullah People and Their African Heritage

William S. Pollitzer (1923–2002), professor of anatomy and anthropology at the University of North Carolina at Chapel Hill, is best known for his book *The Gullah People and Their African Heritage*. In a section of his book titled "Historical Highlights," Pollitzer identifies an entry in the *South Carolina Gazette* on September 25, 1794, as the first effort to reproduce Gullah dialect. Later, Edgar Allan Poe tried to reproduce Gullah in his curious tale "The Gold Bug," published in 1843, whose setting was Sullivan's Island, just off the port of Charleston, South Carolina. There was more extensive use of Gullah language by Ambrose Gonzales, a wealthy newspaper publisher and son of a Cuban revolutionary leader, who wrote a series of books starting with *The Black Border: Gullah Stories of the Carolina Coast*, published first in 1922. Although Gonzales based his dialogues on his many conversations with formerly enslaved persons on his family's rice plantations, he tended to take almost a condescending view of the Gullahs. He has been cited as having stimulated a great deal of public interest in the Gullah culture, but he seldom used the kinds of true Africanisms that scholars such as Turner were later to pinpoint in their writings.

Pollitzer's study built on much of Turner's work, especially as he discusses the two kinds of given names for Gullahs: one used in school and with strangers, which was English, and the other a nickname, or "basket name," which was nearly always of African origin. "To the African," he wrote, "the power to name is the power to control. Even when the Gullah name is English, it follows African naming practices, like those of the Twi, Dahomeans, Mandingo, Yoruba, and Ibo tribes of northern Nigeria, and the Ovimbundu of Angola. Almost universally in Africa a child has at least two given names, bestowed by an intriguing array of circumstances. Widespread is the practice of naming the baby for the day of the week. . . . Also common is the month or season of its birth [or] birth order. . . . Conditions at birth, such as feet foremost, head presentation, born of a prolonged pregnancy, or with the cord or caul about the neck, are well-known sources of names among the Dahomeans.

"The list of reasons for naming a newborn child are endless: time and dates; appearance of the infant, such as skin color, small size, fat, or wide-lipped; parts of the body; animals and birds; feelings and emotions seemingly expressed at the start of life; kings, queens, and other rulers; and occupations. *Do-um*, suggesting 'Do it,'" says Pollitzer, "was earned for assiduous application to an endeavor and audacity in sexual adventure. *Cunjie*, with very broad cheekbones, may have come from the Hausa word for cheek. *Yaa* for a girl and *Yao* for a boy, meaning Thursday, keeps alive the Ewe practice for naming a baby for the day of the week on which it was born. Even an English-appearing name like *Joe* may be an abbreviation for *Cudjo*, a male born on Monday."[10]

Turner discovered that some of the names considered most impressive for an enslaved worker related to the place of birth or other location meaningful to the person so named. Thus, he gave as examples *Asante*, referring to the Gold Coast, *Loanda* in Angola, and *Wida* in Dahomey. *Nago* refers to southern Nigeria, and *Uzebu* relates to the home of a chief at Benin City. He found Islamic influences in a number of names, including *Aluwa* in Wolof, which is a wooden tablet containing verses of the Koran, and *Hadijata*, the name of Mohammed's first wife; legends and folklore also play a part with names like *Akiti*, a famous hunter, and other characters who were well known in the tales told by parents and storytellers.

Down by the Riverside

Inaccuracies regarding the spellings and pronunciations of African names were often due to the transition from the sound spoken by the enslaved to the script written by the white owner, says Charles Joyner (1935–2016), author of *Down by the Riverside*. What the planter thought a given spoken name to be and what the enslaved African thought a given spoken name to be were rarely the same. In many cases, owners wrote into their record books whatever English name sounded most like the pronunciation they heard. "If an [enslaved] couple named their son *Keta*, a common name among the Yoruba, Hausa, and Bambara, the [planter] might have understood the child's name to be *Cato*. Similarly, if an [enslaved] couple told a planter that they had named their daughter *Haga*, a Mandingo name, he might have written *Hagar* into his records."[11]

Joyner also analyzed Gullah grammar and found a lack of distinction between male and female pronouns. "In this regard, they retained a structure common to a number of African languages, such as Ibo, Ga, and Yoruba."

The initial all-purpose Gullah pronoun was *e*, as in "*After de war e come back and took into big drinking and was' em till e fall tru*" ("After the war he came back and took to big drinking and wasted it [his money] until it fell through [he lost it]"). *E* served as the masculine, feminine, and neuter pronoun. Later, under the influence of English, *he* became the all-purpose Gullah pronoun, although *e* was not completely replaced during slavery, when the last generation of slaves was learning to speak the language. The Gullah pronoun *he* was not the same, however, as the English pronoun *he* but served for masculine, feminine, and neuter gender. Interchangeable with *e*, *he* could serve as a subject or to indicate possession, as in "*He broke he whiskey jug*" ("He broke his whiskey jug") or "*Sam he husband name*" ("Sam was her husband's name"). The Gullah pronoun for objects in All Saints Parish was *em*, which served for masculine, feminine, and neuter gender, whether singular or plural, as in "*See em the one time*" ("I saw him once"); "*Grandfather took old Miss Sally on he back to hid em in the wood where Maussa*" ("Grandfather took old Miss Sally on his back to hide her in the woods where the master [was hiding]"); "*He couldn't believe em*" ("He couldn't believe it"); and "*Flat em all up to Marlboro*" ("They took them all on flatboats up to Marlboro District").[12]

Joyner, who with Mary Arnold Twining conducted extensive research in such Gullah strongholds as Waccamaw Neck and the islands of Wadmalaw, Yonges, Edisto, and St. Simons, explained two other features of the Gullah system that distinguish it from English. First, Gullah speakers marked possession by *juxtaposition* rather than by word forms, as in "*He people wuz always free*" ("His people were always free") or "*Joshuway been Cindy pa*" ("Joshua was Cindy's father"). The other distinctive feature was the practice of nonredundant plurals. If pluralization was otherwise indicated in a Gullah sentence, it was not also indicated by the noun, as in "*Dan'l and Summer two both my uncle*" ("Both Daniel and Summer were my uncles"). As Joyner concluded, "This practice was in sharp contrast to English, which required agreement in number between determiners and the nouns they modified."[13]

An important discussion offered by Joyner pertained to retentions and alterations made to African proverbs. Enslaved workers in All Saints Parish transformed these ancestral texts into "metaphors of their collective experience on the Waccamaw rice plantations. "The Hausa proverb—'Chattering doesn't cook the rice' continued in All Saints Parish as 'Promisin' talk don'

cook rice.' Another Hausa proverb 'Does dog eat dog?'—retained even its rhe-
torical question—'Does dog eat dog?'" The Gullah proverb 'Empty sack can't
stand upright alone' was a Waccamaw version of the Mandingo 'It is hard for
an empty sack to stand upright.'"[14]

Lastly, Joyner's most profound arguments address the negative stigma toward the Gullah Geechee language over the years by both Blacks and whites.
"In retrospect one should be more impressed with the success of the [en-
slaved], a people of diverse linguistic backgrounds and limited opportunities,
in creating a Creole language and culture than appalled at their 'failure' to
adopt *in toto* the language and culture of their [captors].... Since Gullah was
susceptible to individual manipulation, it was the shared property of everyone in the speech community, packed with the symbols of that community's
culture and its values.... As a moving force in the creation of Afro-American
culture in the crucible of slavery, the development of Gullah was comparable
to the development of English, German, or French in the creation of these re-
spective national cultures."[15]

When Roots Die

"She was beautiful. That was the first thing most people noticed about Patricia
Jones-Jackson (1946–1986). Those who knew her found her inner beauty—
her charm and kindness and intelligence—even more striking than her appearance. Hers was a very special grace." That was the beginning of the "In
Memoriam" to this fine scholar in her last and probably most important work,
When Roots Die: Endangered Traditions on the Sea Islands, written before she
died tragically in an accident while on an assignment for the National Geographic Society. Jones-Jackson, an associate professor of English at Howard
University, spent five years living among and studying the people she wrote
about—their work habits, their family lives, their communication methods,
and the stories they had to tell. And she had much to say about their language,
or, as she said in Gullah, "*The old-time talk we still de talkem here.*"

After extensive years of research, she made the important prediction that
the Gullah language would remain intact only as long as the families and communities themselves remained intact. It was vital, too, that those who spoke
Gullah be educated in the origins and roots of their language because when
the roots die, the language dies. She expressed it in the beginning of a key
chapter of her book:

The factors which nurtured the Sea Island culture also nurtured the development and perpetuation of the unusual Sea Island language called Gullah or Geechee. The geographical isolation, the marginal contact with speakers outside the Sea Island communities, and the social and economic independence contributed to creating an environment where a mixed language could thrive. Gullah is defined as a Creole, the language that results when a pidgin, which has no native speakers but comes into existence as the product of communication among speakers of different linguistic backgrounds, takes over as the only language of the community.

The Sea Island language, like the culture, is undergoing transformations. Several varieties of contemporary Gullah can be heard in day-to-day conversation on topics ranging from who is running for president to the best bogging place in the creek. With the exception of the unusual accent, some speakers show little deviation from standard English at all. The degree of standard English acquisition is a reflection of such factors as the level of education, the accessibility or inaccessibility of a given island to outside forces, and the extent of inside social mobility. Just as one hears a form of standard English, one also hears the "real Gullah" spoken by children and adults in all aspects of community life.[16]

Jones-Jackson concluded that the very isolation of so many communities and tiny pockets of isolated neighborhoods in the Sea Islands of the Carolinas and Georgia was fortunate as far as the Gullah language was concerned because there were so few mixtures with people speaking standard English or other vernaculars. She said, "It can be credited with achieving even more than that. Growing up as a black majority almost free from outside social influences, such as racial prejudice . . . undoubtedly affected the attitudes and perceptions of the islanders, to the extent that few of them wish to leave the islands today."

This was particularly true until the middle of the twentieth century when many of the islands were still without bridges and where some of the inhabitants had never even been to the mainland. Even during her research in the 1980s, she reported that "several of the elderly informants for this study reported that they had not left their island in at least forty years." And she added, "The islanders are very private people and will often guard the secrets of their culture just as they make attempts to guard their language."[17]

Jones-Jackson made another interesting observation that had been overlooked even by some of the most accomplished researchers. Very minor details of speech, such as a consistent use of certain letters or a distinctive "frizzing" sound on words beginning with *w*, subtle though they may be, permit Gullahs to determine which island the speaker is from. "During my first few years on the islands," she wrote, "I learned that I should not try to pass myself off as an islander by an attempt to imitate the local language. While I may have had the syntax right, I was never able to perfect the accent, and it is the stress and intonation that give one away. When I asked the islanders how they were able to detect such small differences, I was often told, '*I ain't know how I de know, but I de know.*'"[18]

As was pointed out in her sampling of characteristic "interpretations" of Gullah talk, a number of idioms were found to be common in the speech of elderly islanders. She gives the following examples:

> *dark the light*: the sun was set
> *out the light*: turn the light out
> *hot the water*: bring the water to a boil
> *ugly too much*: very ugly
> *the old man bury*: the old man is dead
> *this side*: this island
> *do the feet to you*: cause harm to come to you
> *can't bring the word right now*: I can't remember at the moment,
>   or I will not speak of it at this time
> *pull off my hat*: I had to run
> *de fix for you*: lie in wait for you
> *watchitsir!*: watch your step!
> *dayclean*: daybreak
> *clean skin*: a person with light skin color
> *one day mong all!*: finally!
> *nothing for dead*: nothing dying
> *the sun de red for down*: sunset
> *knock em*: hit
> *sweetmouth*: flatter
> *rest you mouth!*: shut up!
> *long eye*: envy

Jones-Jackson explained, too, that many characteristic features of grammar and syntax differ from those of other African American forms of speech and writing. "Unlike standard English," she says, "which relies heavily on subordination to convey relationships between ideas, contemporary Gullah relies on coordination, or the combination of sentences that are short, abrupt, and loosely strung together."[19] In Gullah we see few of the parts of speech—verbs, adjectives, adverbs, conjunctions, and participles—that tie together complex English sentences. What results is a language that emphasizes the more vivid words and dispenses with the "joining" words. When Gullahs speak, they tend to use a single verb stem whether to refer to a present, past, or future action that is taking place, was taking place, or might take place. The time is not as important as the mood or tone of the action, and there is little or no passive construction. Neither are there plurals on nouns in the same sense that they are used in other languages. For example, *tu baskit* is "two baskets" and *dem boi* is "those boys." To say in English "I heard he knows some old stories" would translate into "*I hear tell e know sum old story.*"

The Little Gullah Geechee Book

Jessica Berry, author of *The Little Gullah Geechee Book,* is a Gullah educator, linguist, and musical performer. As a teenager, she recalled her problems in the classroom when white teachers would ask her to present work or read aloud. "Often times, I was asked to repeat myself or slow down because my class-mates and teachers did not understand me. After this occurred several times, I learned how to speak Mainstream American English (MAE) at school." For Berry and her Gullah classmates, "It was understood that it was our respon-sibility to change our language and not the responsibility of our teachers to learn Gullah."[20] Her experiences have influenced her passion in advocating for the acceptance of the Gullah Geechee language within the public schools and society as a whole.

Berry represents the younger generation of Gullahs who feels it is important to educate the general public and even their own community about the impor-tance of the language. Berry points to Public Law 109-338, signed by Congress in 2006, which established the Gullah Geechee Cultural Heritage Corridor, as one of the reasons this new generation (those ages thirteen to thirty) now takes pride in their culture and is not hesitant in "openly acknowledging their use of the Gullah language." This law also created the Gullah Geechee Cul-tural Heritage Commission, whose mission is to recognize, assist, identify, and preserve sites and historical data for the public's benefit and education. His-torically, the older generation (ages thirty-five to fifty-five) was less likely to speak the language because "they were punished for speaking Gullah in school and were told that their speech was bad or that it reflected broken English."[21]

Berry's training as a linguist helps her to identify and analyze contemporary Gullah speech commonly found in postings by young Gullahs on social media platforms like Facebook. These communications show the continuance of the Gullah language as well as new alterations to it:

a. If Geechee been dead somebody musee wake em up. Een goings no way. Ee ya fa stay. (If Geechee WAS dead someone must have woken it up. It's not going anywhere. It's here to stay.)

b. I say self. My self say huh. I say, boi ee hot out cha ya know. Myself say I know init ee musbe bout a hundred outcha. (I said, self, and my self said, huh? I said, boy it's hot out here, you know. My self said, I know right. It must be about one hundred out here.)

c. Eee is two coll out ya da be wurkin. (It is too cold out here to be working.)

These Facebook postings reveal important deviations from the Gullah Geechee spoken by the older generation and those residents Turner interviewed some ninety years ago. These differences are explored in Berry's dissertation, "Use of Copula and Auxiliary BE by African American Children with Gullah Geechee Heritage." In instances where Turner uses də for *be* (*is*, *are*), modern-day speakers tend to use *be* instead. She says, "Although də is a form that I have heard, the speakers who produce this form are typically Gullah adults who are over 65 years." In examples where Turner uses də for *be* (*was*), Berry indicates *been* as the preferred choice today. An example is the first Facebook posting "Geechee been dead somebody musee wake em up" (If Geechee was dead someone must have woken it up).

According to Berry, speakers from Turner's study in the 1940s preferred the use of də in place of *be* forms, whereas modern-day Gullah speakers prefer to use *be* or *been*. She calls Gullah an enclave language that experiences evolution and change across time as its speakers become less isolated. In her words, "this change manifests in my perception that the Gullah I speak is different from what is spoken by my grandparents."[23]

Gullah and the Poetic Tradition

Gullah by its very nature is an ebullient and exuberant language, and so it is only natural that many well-recognized poets—and quite a few lost in obscurity—have found a place in their creative works for its use. Many compositions express the emotions of the Black and enslaved populations of Africa and America, with themes relating to oppression, loss, hard work, and lifestyles.

There is little doubt that one of the most talented poets of his time regardless of race, was Paul Laurence Dunbar (1872–1906), whose parents were formerly enslaved workers. Unfortunately, he suffered not only from the general bias against Black people but also from the prejudices of the literary establishment, which refused to believe that uneducated people of color could possibly forge the English language into readable text, let alone poetic expression. One of his most memorable poems was "A Death Song," which in its extraordinarily eloquent Gullah speech, captures the heartfelt wishes of the enslaved to find earthly or heavenly rest for their weary souls.

> Lay me down beneaf de willers in de grass,
> Whah de branch 'll go a-singin' as it pass.
>> An' w'en I's a-layin' low,
>> I kin hyeah it as it go
> Singin', "Sleep, my honey, tek yo' res' at las."
>
> Lay me nigh to whah hit meks a little pool,
> An' de watah stan's so quiet lak an' cool,
>> Whah de little birds in spring,
>> Ust to come an' drink an' sing,
> An' de chillen waded on dey way to school.
>
> Let me settle w'en my shouldahs draps dey load
> Nigh enough to hyeah de noises in de road;
>> Fu' I t'ink de las' long res'
>> Gwine to soothe my sperrit bes'
> Ef I's layin' 'mong de t'ings I's allus knowed.

James Weldon Johnson (1871–1938), poet, diplomat, and civil rights activist, was one of the leading voices of the Harlem Renaissance. He is most known for penning the lyrics to "Lift Every Voice and Sing," also known as "The Negro National Anthem," a song that for more than a century has signified unity and justice within the Black community. Johnson's poetry is of equal importance as he demonstrates, in his poem "Sence You Went Away," his familiarity with Gullah words he undoubt-

edly heard as a child growing up in Jacksonville, Florida, located in the
southern portion of the Gullah Geechee Cultural Heritage Corridor.

> Seems lak to me de stars don't shine so bright,
> Seems lak to me de sun done loss his light,
> Seems lak to me der's nothin' goin' right,
>> Sence you went away.
>
> Seems lak to me de sky ain't half so blue,
> Seems lak to me dat eve'ything wants you,
> Seems lak to me I don't know what to do,
>> Sence you went away.
>
> Seems lak to me dat eve'ything is wrong,
> Seems lak to me de day's jes twice ez long,
> Seems lak to me de bird's forgot his song,
>> Sence you went away.
>
> Seems lak to me I jes can't he'p but sigh,
> Seems lak to me ma th'oat keeps gittin' dry,
> Seems lak to me a tear stays in ma eye,
>> Sence you went away.

A SAMPLING OF GULLAH PROVERBS

Dog got four feet but can't walk but one road.
No matter how many things you'd like to do, you can do only one at a
  time.

E teet da dig e grave.
He (or she) is overeating.

New broom sweeps clean but old broom gets corners.
To get the job done, use someone familiar with it.

Li'l pitcher got big ears.
Be careful what you say around children.

Evry sick ain't fa tell de doctor.
Don't tell the doctor all your ailments.

Mus tek cyear a de root fa heal de tree.
Take care of the roots in order to heal the tree.

BODY LANGUAGE

The Gullah Geechee Creole language, like almost every other language, is often accompanied by motions and gestures to emphasize what is being said verbally, whether with or without grunts, groans, or other variations of emphasis. The following examples are typical.

If a conversation between two men becomes heated, one of them is likely to cross his arms over his chest to signal the end of the conversation. Among the Congo people, this was called *tuluwa lwa luumba* and was considered to be more emphatic than the spoken word.

A simple left or right movement of the head by a person listening to a conversation can signal yes or no but is so subtle that only people who are familiar with each other can interpret which is which.

Children who are being rebuked by a parent and who feel that the reprimand is not justified will often turn their heads and purse their lips to avert a direct gaze. Known as a gesture of *nunsa*, this is sometimes captured in sculpture to add emotion to the piece of art.

When people stand with their arms akimbo, the pose is referred to as *pakalala* and proclaims that they are ready to accept a challenge.

SPIRITUAL OF UNKNOWN ORIGIN

This spiritual was said to have been composed shortly after Lincoln's Emancipation Proclamation of January 1, 1863.

Slavery chain done broke at last, broke at last, broke at last,
Slavery chain done broke at last,
Going to praise God till I die.
Way down in-a dat valley
Praying on my knees
Told God about my troubles,
And to help me ef-a He please.
I did tell him how I suffer,
In de dungeon and de chain,
And de days were with head bowed down,

And my broken flesh and pain.
I did know my Jesus heard me,
'Cause de spirit spoke to me
And said, "Rise my child, your chillun
And you shall be free.
I done 'p'int one mighty captain
For to marshal all my hosts
And to bring my bleeding ones to me
And not one shall be lost."
Slavery chain done broke at last, broke at last, broke at last,
Slavery chain done broke at last,
Going to praise God till I die.

BUH LION AND BUH GOAT

This tale, entitled *"Buh Lion and Buh Goat,"* was first published in 1888 by Charles Colcock Jones, who was an avid collector of Gullah stories.

Buh lion bin a hunt, an eh spy Buh Goat duh leddown topper er big rock duh wuk eh mout an der chaw. Eh creep up fuh ketch um. Wen eh git close ter um eh notus um good. Buh Goat keep on chaw. Buh Lion try fuh fine out wuh Buh Goat duh eat. Eh yent see nuttne nigh um ceptin de nekked rock wuh eh duh leddown on. Buh Lion stonish. Eh wait topper Buh Goat. Buh Goat keep on chaw, an chaw, an chaw. Buh Lion cant mek de ting out, an eh come close, an eh say: "Hay! Buh Goat, wuh you duh eat?" Buh Goat skade wen Buh Lion rise up befo um, but eh keep er bole harte, an eh mek ansur: "Me duh chaw dis rock, an ef you dont leff, wen me done long um me guine eat you." Dis big wud sabe Buh Goat. Bole man git outer diffikelty way coward man lose eh life.

Translation

Brother Lion was out hunting when he spotted Brother Goat lying down on top of a big rock working his mouth and chewing. He crept up to catch him. When he got close to him, he watched him good. Brother Goat kept on chewing. Brother Lion tried to find out what the goat was eating. He didn't see anything near him except the naked rock, which he was lying down on. The lion was astonished. He waited for Brother Goat. But Brother Goat just kept on chewing, and chewing, and chewing. When the lion couldn't make the thing out, he came close, and he said, "Hey! Brother Goat, what are you eating?" The goat was scared when the lion rose up before him, but he kept a bold heart, and he answered: "I am chewing this rock, and if you don't leave me in peace, when I am done with my eating, I will eat you." This big word saved Brother Goat. The message: A bold man gets out of difficulty where a cowardly man loses his life.

SPOKEN GULLAH

These sample sentences show how Gullah was spoken in the Sea Islands in the nineteenth century.

> *Uh gwine gone dey tomorruh.*
> I will go there tomorrow.

> *We blan ketch 'nuf cootuh dey.*
> We always catch a lot of turtles there.

> *Dem yent yeddy wuh oonuh say.*
> They did not hear what you said.

> *Dem chillun binnuh nyam all we rice.*
> Those children were eating all our rice.

> *E tell um say e haffuh do um.*
> He told him that he had to do it.

> *Duh him tell we say dem duh faa'muh.*
> He's the one who told us that they are farmers.

> *De buckruh dey duh 'ood duh hunt tuckrey.*
> The white man is in the woods hunting turkeys.

> *Alltwo dem 'ooman done fuh smaa't.*
> Both those women are really smart.

> *Enty duh dem shum dey?*
> Aren't they the ones who saw him there?

> *Dem dey duh wait fuh we.*
> They are there waiting for us.

A VERSION OF THE LORD'S PRAYER IN GULLAH

We Fada wa dey een heaben
Leb ebrybody hona ya nyame
Cause ya holy.
We pray dat soonya
Gwine rule oba de wol.
Wasoneba ting ya wahn
Let urŋ be so een dis wol
Same like e da dey een heaben.
Gii we de food wa we need
Dis day yah, an ebry day.
Fagibe we de bad ting we da do,
Same like we fagibe dem people
Wa do bad ta we.
Leh we down habe haad test
Wen Satan try we.
Keep we fom ebil.

A SAMPLE OF A TYPICAL GULLAH FOLK TALE WITH ANIMAL CHARACTERS

Why Bro Cat na da wash e face fo e eat e brekwas

Once upon a tim fo day was clean, one monin Bro Rat bina wanda roun de rim ob barril wuh bin half ful wid watuh an bin slip an fal een.

E binah tri fa gjt out, but ebry tim e fa grab de wal e slip and fal bac in da watuh. Wen e bin dun bout gib up e yeddy a nise.

Da nise binab Bro Cat who bim saach fa brekwas. Bro Cat cock e yez and yeddy de watuh da splas. E clim up de side de barril and lok een and bi see Bro Cat. E sae, "How yu git down en da, Bro Rat?" Bro Rat sae, "Maan, a bina wak roun de edge ob de barril fa lok een an a slip an a fall een. Eef you hep me fa git outa ya, I let you eat me fa brekwas." Bro Cat say, "Fa tru?" Bro Rat say, "Yeah fa true."

Bro Cat gon an clim up tuh de top ob de barril an bi rech down an grab Bro Rat by e tail.

E bi lay Bro Rat on de broad sid de barril an bi staat fa eat Bro Rat. Bro Rat hol- luh, "Oh no Bro Cat. Yu baffa leh me dri fus fo you choke yourself tu det. Go wush you face wile a dry."

Bro Cat gon fa wush e face an wen e bi git bac e brekwas bin gon. Bro Cat nebuh wush e face fo brekwas from dat dae tuh dis.

The English Translation: Why Bro Cat Does Not Wash His Face before Breakfast

Once upon a time, Bro Rat was wandering around the rim of a barrel half filled with water and slipped and fell in. He was futilely trying to climb up the slippery side of the barrel when Bro Cat, looking for breakfast, heard Bro Rat splashing in the barrel.

Bro Cat climbed up the side of the barrel to see who was in there and saw Bro Rat.

"How did you get yourself in such a fix?" asked Bro Cat.

Bro Rat answered, "Man, I was curious about what was inside the barrel and slipped and fell in. If you help me get out, I'll let you eat me."

"Would you really?" asked Bro Cat.

"Sure, I'll let you eat me," answered Bro Rat.

"That's a deal," said Bro Cat. Then he reached down with his two front paws and grabbed Bro Rat by the tail and laid him on a nearby board.

As Bro Rat lay there soggy, Bro Cat approached to begin his meal.

"Oh, no!" screamed Bro Rat. "You don't want to eat me like this. Man, my wet hair will choke you to death. You'd better let me dry so you can take my hair off. Why don't you go and wash your face while I dry here in this sun."

Bro Cat went and washed his face, but when he returned, Bro Rat had disappeared. From that day to this, Bro Cat has never washed his face before he eats breakfast.

—CHAPTER EIGHT—

PRESERVING THE CORRIDOR

I n October 2006, President George W. Bush signed a bill that formally recognized the historic and cultural contributions of the Gullah Geechee people and provided federal support for the preservation and interpretation of
"a coastal area running from southern North Carolina to northern Florida."
Although the news caused jubilation and pride for the approximately five hundred thousand people of Gullah descent who live in this region, it went unnoticed by most Americans, even some in the Southeast who had never heard
of the words *Gullah* or *Geechee* and knew little about the extensive African
retentions found in the designated states within the Corridor.

To increase public awareness of the unique Gullah culture within the
Corridor, a special Gullah Geechee Cultural Heritage Corridor Commission
conducts four quarterly public meetings each year that are designed to develop
partnerships with organizations focused on Gullah Geechee preservation and

interpretation; provide public educational programs at schools, libraries, and festivals; and offer much-needed assistance to local Gullah communities fighting to hold on to their land and culture. On October 29, 2007, the National Park Service officially announced the fifteen-member commission, and Congressman James Clyburn, the author of the legislation that created the Corridor, gave the keynote address. Since its inception, the appointed chairs of the Commission have been Emory Campbell, Ron Daise, Althea Sumpter, and Dionne Hoskins-Brown, current chair. Executive directors have been J. Herman Blake, Heather Hodges, and, most recently, Victoria Smalls.

The National Park Service (NPS) also initiated projects aimed at increasing awareness about the Gullah Geechee culture. Once such program provided public access to Tibwin Plantation, Hampton Plantation State Historic Site, and Snee Farm at the Charles Pinckney National Historic Site, all of which are located near U.S. Highway 17 in upper Charleston County. The NPS reported the following:

> Tibwin, Hampton, and Snee Farm (Charles Pinckney National Historic Site) each has an important story to tell. Each of the sites was owned by founding families of South Carolina. Each had numerous enslaved Africans who cleared the land, constructed the homes, planted the crops, and made other significant contributions to the infrastructure and wealth of the state and nation. Together, these sites have a synergistic relationship that enhances interpretation of South Carolina from the earliest colonial beginnings to the signing of the Declaration of Independence, the Revolutionary War, the framing and signing of the Constitution, the growth of the new nation, the Civil War, and beyond. The three sites represent a 300-year continuum of coastal history intertwined with the story of the Gullah Geechee people, their language, their skills, and their historic ties to Africa, their unique New World culture, and their contributions to the American story.

The Gullah Geechee Cultural Heritage Corridor encompasses the coastal regions of North Carolina, South Carolina, Georgia, and Florida and stretches

OVERLEAF: Before its destruction in the 1860s, Haig Point Plantation had the largest tabby domestic buildings in coastal South Carolina. Today, these ruins at Daufuskie Landing are the best-preserved tabby slave dwellings in the country. *Library of Congress, Prints & Photographs Division, HABS SC-867.*

some thirty miles to inland communities. This National Heritage area contains the greatest concentration of African culture in the Americas, based, in part, on the numbers of people and families who show familiarity with the Gullah language, art, music, foods, and crafts. These retentions can be attributed partially to the fact that more than 40 percent of the enslaved Africans who came to North America arrived through Charleston (then called Charles Town), causing South Carolina and Georgia to have the highest numbers of enslaved people in the Lower South by the end of the antebellum period.[1] Another well-known factor was the geographical isolation of the island and inland Gullah Geechee communities, which can still be seen today. Despite the effects of the Civil War, Reconstruction, the World Wars, and Jim Crowism, many Gullah families chose to remain on or near the land of their enslaved ancestors, and even when some left for better job opportunities on the mainland or in the North, they often returned home.

Charleston: The Beginning Point

The historic city of Charleston, South Carolina, known as the "Holy City," speaks volumes about the journey of enslaved Africans from their arrival as cargo to be sold at auction to their final destinations as enslaved workers on southern plantations. Whether it is the distinctive Gullah Geechee culture, historic architecture, or vestiges of a painful past, African Americans who visit this beautiful city feel a closeness to their ancestors who were forcibly taken from Africa. On Broad Street in the heart of downtown Charleston lies the office that served from 1869 to 1874 as the Freedman's Saving and Trust Company, a national bank for Black people. This bank provided "a safe depository, basic financial education, and employment for newly freed Blacks, "giving them hands-on training and experience in the banker's skills."[2] The Freedman's Banks also served to give legal title for Field Order 15 or "forty acres and a mule" until it was overturned by President Andrew Johnson, an avowed slaveholder.

On East Bay Street lies the huge Old Exchange and Provost Dungeon built in the 1771 as a customhouse. On the north side of the building was an open lot where a popular public auction of enslaved Africans occurred, but an 1856 city ordinance banning public sales forced slave auctions inside to other locations such as Ryan's Mart, the current Old Slave Mart Museum at 6 Chalmers Street. Established in 1852, this building had rooms for the enslaved persons and an auction block purposely hidden from public view. The city's Sullivan's Island, across the Ashley River, has been compared to Ellis Island because enslaved Africans, like many European immigrants, were checked for diseases before being allowed further entry into the country. The one difference, and a big one at that, was the obvious lack of choice for African Americans who had no illusions of a land of freedom, only the reality of a life in bondage.

Among the many Gullah-related locations in Charleston is the noted Emanuel African Methodist Episcopal Church, the oldest AME church in the South and the second oldest in the world. The original church was destroyed by fire in 1832, and its replacement was destroyed by the earthquake of 1886, but the current building, erected in 1892, has survived despite several large storms, severe floods, and a horrific hate crime. On June 17, 2015, Emanuel AME Church was the sight of the racially motivated shootings of nine church members, among them senior pastor and South Carolina State Senator Clementa C. Pinckney. In the seven years since this tragedy, the church has become a pilgrimage site as visitors from around the world come to offer their support to church members and their unity against such acts of terrorism. However, such well-meaning attention can be painful.

During one tour of Emanuel AME Church, Pastor Eric Manning addressed the guests by saying, "It gets weary" having to tell the story again and again, he said, and the steady stream of visitors forces some members to relive the tragedy over and over.[3] Rev. Anthony Thompson, who lost his wife Myra in the shooting, offers these sobering words about Charleston: "We are a very hospitable city. You know where we smile and we laugh, but there was always an undertone of racism which we would never talk about. And none of this came to focus until the Emanuel nine tragedy."[4]

There are also other buildings in Charleston, such as the slave quarters, that serve as symbols of the struggles African Americans historically experienced in the "Holy City." These often-forgotten structures were formerly servants' quarters, carriage houses, or "dependencies" in the eighteenth and nineteenth centuries. Behind the stately homes located in the downtown area "are smaller ones made of stone or wood, utilitarian, without verandas, elegant furniture, sweeping staircases or laughing men in fancy suits," says CNN travel writer Dartinia Hull. These were the living quarters for the enslaved workers who tended to the in-town homes of white owners. Now many of these, attached to the finest homes in the city, are noted as "some of the most expensive real estate properties in the area." Only a few of them, however, are on any of the many Gullah tours of this old city.[5]

In recent years, there has been a discovery of an Underground Railroad network that operated in and around Charleston County. Officially recognized as a National Park Service Underground Railroad Network to Freedom site, Four Holes Swamp, within the Audubon Center at Francis Beidler Forest, was a place of safety for runaways seeking freedom from slavery. Although northern destinations are usually associated with the Underground Railroad, which was "a system of secret locations where runaway slaves could hide out and later be moved, either up north or south into Florida," scholars now recognize the important resistance among Maroon communities living in geographically secluded areas like swamps. "An enslaved man named James Matthews hid in Four Holes Swamp on his way to Charleston in 1838, where he gained passage on a ship that took him to freedom in Boston," says author Herb Frazier. Frazier further writes of an enslaved man named Team, "who sometimes lived with maroon communities throughout Four Holes Swamp." This swamp's vast ecosystem of virgin cypress and tupelo trees made it "an ideal hideaway for freedom-seekers more than two centuries ago."[6]

Hilton Head: Arrival of the Resorts

Charles Fraser's transformation of Hilton Head Island, South Carolina, in the mid-1950s, served as the blueprint for golf and real estate development throughout the country. After Charles and his father, Joseph Fraser, persuaded the state of South Carolina to build a two-lane bridge to the island, and Charles assumed control of the southern third of the island, he launched the groundbreaking five-thousand-acre Sea Pines Plantation on Hilton Head. In a series of firsts, Charles Fraser (1929–2002) was "the first to combine golf and real estate development in a planned community, one of the first to use covenants and deed restrictions to protect the environment, and one of the first to promote intergenerational recreation in the same enterprise."[7] Before long,

> Other developers joined in, and resorts sprang up all over the island.
> Only about 20 percent of the island was actually owned by Gullah
> Geechee residents, much of the remaining land was owned by absentee

landlords who allowed free access to their property. The absentee landlords quickly sold out to developers. Between 1950 and 2000, the population of South Carolina Lowcountry counties increased by 151 percent,
while the national population as a whole increased by only 86 percent....

Before construction of Sea Pines Plantation, Gullah Geechee residents had been free to hunt and fish all over Hilton Head Island. Suddenly, fences and gates blocked much of the land. Residents were cut off
from their hunting and fishing grounds as well as their traditional burial
grounds. Fences meant that Gullah/Geechee islanders could no longer
"*go in duh creek*" to get supper.[8]

The loss of land and easy access to fishing and hunting resulted in the loss
of Geechee self-sufficiency and autonomy. Displaced and landless, Gullah
people increasingly turned to hourly labor, out-migration, or both. "Although
some islanders chose to remain in the vicinity to work in the resort industry,
they soon found that only minimum wage service sector jobs were available
to them. Low wages have forced these landless resort workers to face ever-
increasing commuting distances in order to find affordable housing."[9]

Today there are only about a dozen protected Gullah neighborhoods on
Hilton Head that can be reached by visitors on tours. Among these are Stoney,
called "the gateway to Hilton Head" but once a "downtown" area with a post
office, grocery store, and even a juke joint; Jonesville, known for its wheel-
wrights, shoemakers, and a small church; Spanish Wells, where Spanish explorers were said to have dug wells to replenish their freshwater supplies;
Simmons Fishing Camp, where boats carrying supplies from Savannah and
other mainland towns docked; Union Cemetery, established during the Civil
War for Union soldiers and later turned into farmlands; and Mitchellville, the
first self-governed town of formerly enslaved people in America.

Daufuskie Island: Defiant to Change

Daufuskie Island, just a few miles from Hilton Head and accessible only by
boat, also experienced resort development, but resistance from residents and
the natural environment has proven formidable. Up until the 1970s, the community only had an elementary school, church, and general store, and it was,
with few exceptions, free of white people. Historian Andrew Kahrl further
notes:

African Americans claimed ownership of roughly half of Daufuskie Island's total acreage; the rest belonged to absentee white landowners, who occasionally used it for hunting expeditions. But much of the island, including the white-owned lands and all of its shoreline, functionally served as a commons. Black families' cattle and hogs roamed and grazed freely, islanders fished its shores and hunted its wildlife without restrictions. The only fences on the island served to protect small garden plots from foraging animals.[10]

In the 1980s, the Melrose Company fenced and cleared four hundred acres of forestland for construction of a Jack Nicklaus–designed golf course, eliminating land the islanders used for grazing their cattle, fishing, and hunting. According to Kahrl, the Melrose Company "secured the approval of the state's Coastal Council (of which Melrose's CEO and attorney were both members) to close off access to public roads leading to the shore, thereby preventing islanders from enjoying access to places where they had fished and harvested shellfish for generations." Yet there were even more destructive actions to come.

Behind these newly built fences, developers leveled natural storm barriers, stripped the land of trees and vegetation, and stripped its inhabitants of their dignity and ancestry. In what amounted to an act of "cultural genocide," as attorneys for the NAACP Legal Defense Fund later charged, the Melrose Company built a real estate office and welcome center on top of a cemetery; during the construction, work crews (which included native Black Daufuskians hired as day laborers) dumped the bones of islanders' ancestors into the Cooper River, where they washed out to sea.[11]

In response, the islanders, represented by Christic Institute lawyers and organizers, filed a class-action lawsuit against the Melrose Company for illegal removal and desecration of graves. Daufuskie Island became the focus of a national civil rights campaign that resulted in extensive news coverage, culminating in a scathing report on the CBS news program *60 Minutes* in 1991. Amid mounting legal and labor problems, a 2006 report by the state's Office of Ocean and Coastal Resource Management singled out the Melrose tract as suffering the highest rates of erosion on an island (in one section, up to eleven feet per year). This was the result of measures taken by developers, beachfront owners, and the state to stabilize the shoreline and protect beachfront real estate from being washed out to sea. In 2008, the owners of the resort filed for bankruptcy and laid off its remaining staff. "In the years that followed, a series of investors sold and resold the property, and tested out various profit-making schemes, each more dubious than the last."[12]

Many of the problems developers experienced on Daufuskie can be attributed to the island's lack of a bridge. In comparison, the Frasers' success on Hilton Head was the direct result of their successful lobbying for a bridge. Without a bridge, the Daufuskie resort owners were forced to deal with crossing the unpredictable Calibogue Sound.

> There are 45,000 people on Hilton Head and upwards of a quarter million in Savannah and you can see both places from Daufuskie. Little wonder developers want Daufuskie for condos and gated communities—plantations, they call them—where you can't go unless you belong. Twenty years ago, developers came like Pharaoh's host in the old Gullah spiritual, two hundred million dollars strong. But the waters came together, rolling over Gucci shoes, and they all went down in a Red Sea of ink—International Paper, Haliburton Oil, and Club Corp. of America, chief among a great drowning of lesser corporations. Some say marine transportation did them in. Daufuskie is damned inconvenient. Every screw, every nail, every golf ball, T-bone, jug of whiskey, employee, and customer had to be hauled across Calibogue Sound, deep and wide and dangerous as a woman. And then the garbage and customers and employees and money had to be hauled back.[13]

In 2022, the failed Melrose Resort has a new buyer in Redfish Holdings of Chicago, Illinois. It remains to be seen if these developers will be able to succeed where so many have failed.

Saving Sandy Island

On the other side of the coin, there are a few Gullah communities that have been preserved because of measures taken by the government, interested individuals, and citizen groups. One such community is Sandy Island, which is located between the Waccamaw and the Great Pee Dee Rivers north of Charleston, South Carolina, and remains one of the few Gullah islands accessible only by boat. In 1989, wealthy businessmen Roger Milliken and E. Craig

Wall formed Sandy Island Associates and requested a permit to build a bridge to transport timber harvested from their significant land holdings in the north of the island. Together, the two men owned nine thousand acres—the lion's share of the island's approximately twelve thousand acres—but the cost of the bridge exceeded the value of the timber, and the islanders began to question Miliken and Wall's actual motives. Reverend George Weathers, the community's leader, argued, "Nearly $2 million to build that bridge for just a little amount of timber...why are you spending that kind of money...? Something else must be behind it. They also tried to get the permit in the absence of the community.... No one ever came to get our opinion on it."[14]

The residents eventually learned that the bridge would only be accessible to them in the event of an emergency; furthermore, Milliken and Wall's ultimate goal was to develop Sandy Island into an "exclusive and elite" resort community of "9,500 houses and condos and two golf courses."[15] Weathers quickly mobilized the community to stop the proposed bridge construction. In his words, "everyone was against it because we couldn't use it on our own terms."[16]

The islanders, through the help of the Coastal Conservation League, met with the Penn Center staff on St. Helena Island and received training on the history and tactics in land conservation. The community also held a long series of community meetings to discuss the bridge permit and what action to take, forming a formal organization called the Sandy Island Community Action Club. They were later joined by the Sierra Club and Georgetown League of Women Voters, who conducted meetings at the historic Sandy Island School. Through this collaborative action, the Sandy Islanders were able to garner a preservation easement over their property as part of the wetland mitigation of the Department of Transportation. Sandy Island was of particular value as a retreat for nature lovers because of its rare plants, aged longleaf pines, turkey oaks, wildlife, and unusual species of birds, including the red-cockaded woodpecker.

The land, now known as the Waccamaw Wildlife Conservancy, is owned by the Nature Conservancy and managed by the U.S. Department of Fish and Wildlife Services. When the transfer of the land went through, Reverend Weathers reflected on the land preservation: "This will keep the island from being developed too rapidly. And I hope it will give us a greater voice in what happens on the island in the future."[17] The Sandy Island community's battle for its land gained interest from local media as well as national newspapers such as the *New York Times*, *Los Angeles Times*, and the *Washington Post*. In

2006, South Carolina Educational Television's Betsy Newman chronicled this story in a documentary titled *Saving Sandy Island*. The preservation of Sandy Island saved the island's cultural landscape as well as its natural landscape.

Over the past few decades, two organizations on St. Helena Island have led efforts throughout the Corridor to preserve the Gullah Geechee people's lands. One is Penn Center, which continues its long-standing advocacy on behalf of the Gullah culture. Another is the organization known as the Gullah / Geechee Nation, founded in 1996 by Marquetta L. Goodwine, who lives on St. Helena. In 1996, Goodwine also known as Queen Quet, formed the Gullah/ Geechee Sea Island Coalition to "promote and participate in the preservation of Gullah and Geechee history, heritage, culture, and language; work toward Sea Island land reacquisition and maintenance; and celebrate Gullah/ Geechee culture through artistic and educational means electronically and via 'grassroots scholarship.'"[18]

Goodwine has been working for many years with local land planning groups—both civilian and governmental—to establish zones of protection for Gullah lands and, in some instances, to actually retrieve lands that were questionably, or in many cases illegally, taken away from inhabitants without cause. She has also gone to court, as well as to state, county, and city institutions on many occasions—and even to Washington—to speak out on behalf of Gullah and Geechee rights and the means to being self-sustaining.

Navassa: Restoring Its Farmland

Nestled on the west bank at the junction of the Brunswick and Northeast Cape Fear rivers lies the historic town of Navassa, which was the location of the Navassa Guano Company, a highly profitable fertilizer company founded in 1869. A group of wealthy Wilmington, North Carolina, businessmen built the company five miles north of Wilmington to keep the "guano acrid aroma out of the city and take advantage of a new rail line that crossed the river at that point. They built their factory upriver on a marshy peninsula where the Brunswick River emptied into the Cape Fear River." Although the Civil War had been over for four years, life for African Americans in Navassa had changed very little. The company's Black workers, who were freed formerly enslaved African Americans from nearby plantations, lived in the old slave quarters and even continued backbreaking work in rice fields owned by Navassa Guano. In 1879, when rice was no longer the cash crop it had been, the *Wilmington Morning Star* reported that "the prospects for the rice crop in this section are represented as very fine.... The Navassa Guano Company has some 200 acres that promise a very large yield."[19]

Since the eighteenth century, there were between seventy-five and eighty rice plantations with such names as Belvedere, Mulberry, Green Banks, Clarendon, Dalrymple, Old Town, Asperne, Orton, and The Bluffs along the banks of the Cape Fear in Brunswick County. In 1860 alone, The Bluffs and Asperne each produced an impressive 864,000 pounds of rice, or nearly 20,000 bushels, due in large part to the skills of their enslaved workforce.[20] Being the only deep-water port in early North Carolina, Brunswick County was the landing point for large ships like the transatlantic slave trading vessels that brought thousands of enslaved workers to the region. However, on July 1, 1857, the discovery by Baltimore ship captain Peter Duncan of a bed of guano, a natural fertilizer composed chiefly of dead sea fowl, on Navassa Island eventually led to fertilizer being the town's major industry.

After the closure of the Navassa Guano Company in 1927, several fertilizer businesses followed before a woodworking company named Kerr-McGee Chemical Corporation operated in Navassa from 1937–1974. When it was dismantled in 1980, workers irresponsibly mixed creosote, a carcinogenic form of tar used at the plant, with clean soil before putting it out to seed, causing an environmental disaster. Since then, it has had a devastating impact on the environment as the creosote penetrated up to "88ft into the soil, killing plants and damaging wildlife, making a return to the town's farming roots all but impossible."[21] But other companies in the area had also acted without regard for the environment—natural or human.

At the former Estech General Chemical and ExxonMobil site in Navassa, government officials found lead and arsenic contamination in the soil, sediment, and even groundwater. And in 2009, the Environmental Protection Agency responded to a waste spill at the former site of P&W Waste Oil, where a number of contaminated oil tanks had ruptured. Activist Veronica Carter says, "Companies exploit communities such as Navassa, thinking that if they dangle jobs in front of poor people, they'll look the other way when the environment is threatened. I don't know of many towns that have less than 2,000 people and have had this many brownfield and Superfund sites."[22]

Currently, there is an eighteen-year cleanup effort underway in Navassa coordinated by a group of federal and state environmental officials called the Natural Resources Trustee Council, who are responsible for spending $23 million to restore the town's natural resources. However, many of the Gullah Geechee residents question the council's primary objective. "Right now we're concentrating on the fish and the bugs and the birds, and all of that is good, but we are concerned about the humans that have been affected by this contaminant," says resident Ella Beatty. "Many of the residents, who are mostly poor, also want first dibs on cleanup and restoration jobs and [wondered] if the process would be transparent." Longtime Navassa mayor, Eulis Willis, a seventh-generation Navassa resident, gets emotional when asked about the cultural importance of the creosote-ridden marsh. "That's our livelihood. We are the results of the rice plantations planted along the Cape Fear River that border the [wood treatment plant] property. Rice plantations produced our culture.... We're trying to save some of that heritage."[23]

The Multistate Environmental Response Trust was given the task of reversing the environmental damage at the Kerr-McGee Chemical Superfund site and preparing the 154-acre property for sale or beneficial reuse. Superfund sites are areas nationwide, like those in Navassa, containing hazardous waste the federal government is remediating. After several years of environmental cleanup, the Multistate Trust felt that a "beneficial reuse" of the land would be a donation of twenty acres for the town of Navassa's proposed Moze Heritage Center and Nature Park. The Moze center will include an interactive museum that spans more than three hundred years of the town's history. Patrons will also be able to enjoy a kayak launch, fishing sites, and walking trails with posted signs telling the town's rich Gullah history.

The Golden Isles of Georgia

Heading south along Interstate 95 about halfway between Savannah, Georgia, and Jacksonville, Florida, are the Golden Isles in Glynn County, Georgia. Authors Amy Roberts and Patrick Holladay describe this area as a "mosaic of coastal mainland, four barrier islands, marshlands, rivers, creeks, and sandy beaches."

> Glynn County's constituents are the naturally beautiful Jekyll Island, which is the southernmost island; the picturesque tourist destination of St. Simons Island, slightly north of Jekyll Island; Sea Island, a private luxury resort; Little St. Simons Island, another private island rich in natural resources; and historic Brunswick, the important port city.[24]

The title "Golden Isles" is attributed to American poet Sidney Lanier's work "The Marshes of Glynn," although "golden" is not actually used in the poem. Lanier, a former Confederate soldier, contracted tuberculosis while a prisoner at the dreaded Union prison Point Lookup in Maryland, and he sought relief from the cold in Baltimore by visiting his brother-in-law in Brunswick. As the story goes, Lanier sat under an oak tree (now located in the median of U.S. Highway 17) and penned descriptions of the sparkling waters and scenic marshes.

Glooms of the live-oaks, beautiful-braided and woven
With intricate shades of the vines that myriad-cloven
Clamber the forks of the multiform boughs,—
Emerald twilights,—
Virginal shy lights,
Wrought of the leaves to allure to the whisper of vows,
When lovers pace timidly down through the green colonnades
Of the dim sweet woods, of the dear dark woods,
Of the heavenly woods and glades,
That run to the radiant marginal sand-beach within
The wide sea-marshes of Glynn;—
. . .
Beautiful glooms, soft dusks in the noon-day fire,—
Wildwood privacies, closets of lone desire,
Chamber from chamber parted with wavering arras of leaves,—
Cells for the passionate pleasure of prayer to the soul that grieves,
Pure with a sense of the passing of saints through the wood,
Cool for the dutiful weighing of ill with good;—
. . .
O braided dusks of the oak and woven shades of the vine,
While the riotous noon-day sun of the June-day long did shine
Ye held me fast in your heart and I held you fast in mine;
But now when the noon is no more, and riot is rest,
And the sun is a-wait at the ponderous gate of the West,
And the slant yellow beam down the wood-aisle doth seem
Like a lane into heaven that leads from a dream,—
Ay, now, when my soul all day hath drunken the soul of the oak,
And my heart is at ease from men, and the wearisome sound of the stroke
Of the scythe of time and the trowel of trade is low,

And belief overmasters doubt, and I know that I know,
And my spirit is grown to a lordly great compass within,
That the length and the breadth and the sweep of the marshes of Glynn
Will work me no fear like the fear they have wrought me of yore
When length was fatigue, and when breadth was but bitterness sore,
And when terror and shrinking and dreary un-namable pain
Drew over me out of the merciless miles of the plain . . .
By a world of marsh that borders a world of sea.[25]

Ossabaw Island, the northernmost outpost of the Golden Isles, has a history of occupation and settlement going back more than four thousand years. Noted for its ancient maritime forests, freshwater ponds, abundant salt marshes, and stretches of white sand beaches, it is "shaped like a wishbone" and is approximately twenty-five thousand acres—twice the size of Bermuda—with marshes in the center. Classified as a barrier island, it is the third largest of its type on the Georgia coast and is known for its abundance of floral species. In 1760, John Morel and his father-in-law bought Ossabaw from a land speculator, and with the help of thirty enslaved Africans purchased from an Augusta, Georgia estate, Morel turned his plantation into one of the largest producers of indigo in Georgia. The fertile soil was ideally suited for the planting and harvesting of indigo, which was a highly valued crop at this time.

Indigo had long been used in West Africa for the blue dyes in their cotton industries, so enslaved Africans were familiar with its cultivation. During his visit to the West African country of Dahomey (present-day Benin) in the eighteenth century, the Dutch merchant David van Nyendael wrote, "The inhabitants are very well skill'd in making several sorts of Dyes, as Green, Blue, Black, Red, and Yellow; the Blue they prepare from Indigo, which grows here."[26] The skilled enslaved workers knew exactly when to cut the plants at daybreak before the hot sun could dry the leaves, when to immerse them in vats and boil the sediment, and when to press them into molds for shipment to Savannah. Although many decades have passed since the very last crop of indigo went to market, the Ossabaw Island Foundation offers hands-on indigo dyeing workshops that inform guests of the expertise Gullah Geechee people had in cultivating indigo.

A popular destination in Georgia's Golden Isles is St. Simons Island, which lies off the coast not far from Brunswick, where many large plantations as well as small settlements flourished. Of the fourteen plantations on the island, the largest were Cannon's Point, Hamilton, Hampton, and Retreat. Here the planters developed and produced a fine, long-staple Sea Island cotton, which thrived in the Georgia soil under the right climatic conditions and was greatly prized in English cotton markets. St. Simons was a key site visited by researchers and interviewers during the Works Progress Administration's *Drums and Shadows* project in the 1930s, when access to the island was a small causeway and when almost all of the residents were descendants of freed formerly enslaved workers.

As recently as the 1960s, the African American population of St. Simons Island was almost three thousand, but gradually it dwindled to less than half that number, prompting St. Simons native Amy Roberts and other dedicated residents to take action for the preservation of their culture. Together they formed the St. Simons African-American Heritage Coalition "to maintain a vibrant presence where island ancestors first tasted freedom." Since 2004, this organization, in partnership with the St. Simons Land Trust, has been active in fundraising efforts to restore the Harrington Graded School, which was built in 1924 "as the main educational structure for three African American communities on St. Simons Island."[27] In August 2017, the former all-Black school officially reopened as the Historic Harrington School Cultural Center. The center's three main goals are (1) historical preservation and education, (2) heritage and cultural tourism, and (3) conservation, to include habitat protection and interpretation.[28]

St. Simons Island is also the location of one of the most dramatic acts of resistance ever recorded—the Igbo Landing at Dunbar Creek.

A rebellion and freedom march at the creek site took place in May 1803, involving a group of Igbo from the ancient West African civilization.... The Igbo had been captured in late 1802... by a notorious underworld clan from the Arochukwu community. Through arrangements made by a broker at a Gulf of Guinea seaport, they were delivered to a waiting sea vessel which brought them to Skidaway Island, just south of Savannah, Ga. A Savannah slave importer sold about 75 of the Igbo arrivals to two well-known coastal planters, Thomas Spalding of Sapelo and John Couper of Cannon's Point on St. Simons Island. When the schooner *York* carrying the Igbo reached its landing place on the bluff of Dunbar Creek in mid May 1803, the Igbo rebelled. Under the direction of a high Igbo official who was among them, the Igbo went ashore, singing an Igbo hymn ("The Water Spirit brought. The Water Spirit will take us home") and walked in unison into the creek. At least 10 of them drowned, accepting the protection of their God, Chukwu, and death over an alternative of slavery.[29]

One of the few contemporary accounts of the event was provided by Roswell King, a white overseer on nearby Pierce Butler plantation. King states that as soon as the Igbo landed on St. Simons Island, they "took to the swamp" dying by suicide by walking into Dunbar Creek. A separate account of the event names King as the person who recovered the bodies of the drowned Igbo.[30] In May 2022, more than two hundred years after the Igbo Landing occurred, the Coastal Georgia Historical Society finally dedicated a historic marker titled "Ibo Landing: The Legacy of Resisting Enslavement."

Cumberland Island National Seashore

One of the most cherished historic sites in Georgia is Cumberland Island, located off the coast near the mouth of the St. Marys River. Evidence shows that human occupation of the island occurred as early as four thousand years ago. Some of the earliest records were those provided by the Spanish Navy after they constructed the Fort of San Pedro on the island in 1569. Later a Franciscan monastery was established to convert the Timucuan Indians to Christianity. But the relationship with the Gullah peoples did not occur until sometime after General James Oglethorpe, founder of the British colony of Georgia in 1736, named the island Cumberland in honor of Prince William Augustus, the Duke of Cumberland. Plantations were then established, and shortly thereafter, enslaved Africans were brought to the island.

Following the general evacuation of white plantation owners and families after the Civil War, freed formerly enslaved people established Half Moon Bluff, a simple village of basic wood frame dwellings and animal shelters. During the following decades, African Americans purchased more parcels of land and maintained small farms and fishing docks. During this period, many of the homes and religious buildings were constructed of tabby, a cement made of lime, water, and crushed oyster shell, which were common building materials throughout the Gullah Corridor. Currently, much of Cumberland Island is managed as a government wilderness area, and many of the acres that are privately owned were purchased with funds provided by the Mellon Institute and Congress, to preserve the rights of families whose forebears were enslaved. The First African Baptist Church, constructed in 1937, is a center of religious and educational life for the community.

Most visitors to Cumberland reach the island through the docks at St. Marys, a village which in itself is a joy to behold and is sometimes referred to as "the jewel in the crown of the Colonial coast." Hundreds of years ago, the Creek, Guale, and Timucuan Indians, from what is now Florida a few miles to the south, saw it as a land of bountiful fish and game and soil on which crops could grow in abundance all year long. Sixteenth-century French explorers described an abundant land full of havens, rivers, and islands. Visitors today find St. Marys a charming place with canopies of centuries-old live oaks draped in Spanish moss and wisteria, magnolias, and white picket fences. For many years, it was the dwelling place for African American farmers and fishermen. By the 1930s, however, most African American residents were in their seventies and eighties, and few young people had interest in the old traditions. An excerpt from *Drums and Shadows* predicted a bleak future for the culture, as reported in an interview with Aunt Hettie Campbell, then seventy-two and living in a small house near the waterfront amid a surrounding arbor of flowers and shrubbery. Campbell reminisced about the olden days:

> *I do remembuh the big times we use tuh have wen I wuz young. We does plenty uh dances in does days. Dance roun in a ring.... We shouts an sings all night and wen he sun rise, we stahts ta dance. It ain so long since hey stop that back in the woods, but these young people hey does new kines uh dances.... Music? They mosly have guitah now, an we use to but we make em frum goad an we beats drums too. We make em frum coon hide stretched ovah hoops.*

Hettie has long since gone, and visitors to St. Marys are not likely to run into any African Americans performing the ring shout on the island. But the Gullah influence lingers and can be found in the town's history, in monuments of the past, in many of the older homes that are sometimes hidden behind clusters of wisteria, draping Spanish moss, and palm, and always in the atmosphere and fragrance of the surroundings along the shore at the fishing docks up and down the rivers and the inlets.

MAJOR SEA ISLANDS

South Carolina

Sea Islands in Charleston County, South Carolina

Bear Island
Bull Island
Daniel Island
Dewees Island
Edisto Island
Folly Island
Isle of Palms
James Island
Johns Island
Kiawah Island
Monis Island
Seabrook Island
Sullivan's Island
Wadmalaw Island

Sea Islands in Beaufort County, South Carolina

Cane Island
Cat Island
Coosaw Island
Dataw Island
Daufuskie Island
Distant Island
Fripp Island
Gibbes Island
Hilton Head Island
Hunting Island
Lady's Island
Morgan Island
Parris Island
Port Royal Island
Pritchards Island

St. Helena Island

St. Phillips Island

Georgia

The Golden Isles of Georgia

Cumberland Island

Jekyll Island

Little St. Simons Island

Ossabaw Island

Sapelo Island

Sea Island

St. Catherines Island

St. Simons Island

Tybee Island

Florida

Amelia Island and Fernandina Beach

THE GREENBOOK OF SOUTH CAROLINA

Throughout the Sea Islands and the Lowcountry, increasing attention is being paid to preserving knowledge of the Gullah culture and history through tours and historical journeys. One such example is *The Greenbook of South Carolina*, which provides the first mobile travel guide to African American cultural sites across South Carolina. A creation of the South Carolina African American Heritage Commission, *The Greenbook* showcases more than three hundred attractions found on the National Register of Historic Places or designated with the state's historic markers and includes all of the forty-six counties in South Carolina.

The name *Greenbook* pays homage to the original *Green Book* first published in 1936 by New York postman Victor Green. Green's travel guide informed African Americans of the safe harbors and welcoming environments across the United States where they could eat or find temporary lodging.

The purpose of *The Greenbook of South Carolina* is to increase awareness of the state's African American tourism destinations and encourage travelers to become immersed in the compelling story of African Americans in South Carolina.

THE GOLDEN ISLES OF GEORGIA

Sidney Lanier, the noted Georgia-born poet, described the Golden Isles of Georgia as "a world of marsh that borders a world of sea." He was also cognizant of the local color and patois of the Gullah peoples in the Sea Islands, as noted in this poem, written in 1876, echoing the language of a favorite Baptist preacher.

SOLO: Sin's rooster's crowed, Ole Mahster's riz,
De sleepin'-time is pas';
Wake up dem lazy Baptissis,

CHORUS: Dey's mightily in de grass, grass,
Dey's mightily in de grass.

Ole Mahster's blowed de mornin' horn,
He's blowed a powerful blas';
O Baptis' come, come hoe de corn,
You's mightily in de grass, grass,
You's mightily in de grass.

De Meth'dis team's done hitched; O fool,
De day's a-breakin' fas';
Gear up dat lean ole Baptis' mule,
Dey's mightily in de grass, grass,
Dey's mightily in de grass.

De workmen's few an' mons'rous slow,
De cotton's sheddin' fas';
Whoop, look, jes' look at de Baptis' row,
Hit's mightily in de grass, grass,
Hit's mightily in de grass.

Dey jay-bird squeal to de mockin'-bird: "Stop!
Don' gimme none o' yo' sass;
Better sing one song for de Baptis' crop,
Dey's mightily in de grass, grass,
Dey's mightily in de grass."

And de ole crow croak: "Don' work, no, no";
But de fiel'-lark say, "Yaas, yaas,

An' I spec' you mighty glad, you debblish crow,
Dat de Baptissis's in de grass, grass,
Dat de Baptissis's in de grass!"

Lord, thunder us up to de plowin'-match,
Lord, peerten de hoein' fas',
Yea, Lord, hab mussy on de Baptis' patch,
Dey's mightily in de grass, grass,
Dey's mightily in de grass.

—CHAPTER NINE—

GULLAH GEECHEE CUISINE

"Love is one of the best kept secrets and main ingredients in Gullah food," writes Veronica Davis Gerald in *The Ultimate Gullah Cookbook*. "However, of all the ingredients, it is most difficult to explain and to pass on in a recipe. For this reason, few books on this food culture attempt to include it. Some call it 'cooking from the heart'; others just call it *luv*. Whatever the preference, it is a spiritual exchange between the hands and heart of the preparer and the food itself, a spiritual transfer of love from the cook to those who will eat the food prepared."

Gerald knows of what she speaks. Of Gullah Geechee descent herself, she is a distinguished professor emeritus of English at Coastal Carolina University, served on the Gullah Geechee Cultural Heritage Corridor Commission, and has spent the better part of her life studying and preserving the culture of her people. "Around the Gullah table," she explains, "it is common to hear someone say, '*E put e fot en um dis time*' or '*Dey's a lot of luv in dis food.*' This is an expression of appreciation for the care, energy, and spirit communicated through the food from the cook to the recipient."[1]

Any understanding of the Gullah Geechee people would be limited without learning about the foods and recipes that are inherent in their culture, past and present, and in all the regions which they have frequented. "Gullah food is older than the South and as ancient as the world," says Gerald. "It is one of the oldest African American traditions being practiced today." Many of the foods that are familiar in the South and generally thought of as "American," originally arrived on slave ships from Africa. Among these are not only the various types of rice, but okra, yams, peas, sorghum, sesame seeds, peanuts, certain kinds of berries, peppers, watermelon, certain teas, various blends of coffee, and kola nuts, which were originally a stimulant and then used in recipes for cola drinks. The enslaved Africans fused similar and different ingredients and food practices between the Lowcountry and the West Coast of Africa to "create a food culture that would come to characterize the region."[2] Anthropologist William Pollitzer notes:

> In West and Central Africa, the starchy main dish of millet or rice or maize (after 1500) is usually boiled in a large jar; a vegetable relish with a little meat or fish added is cooked in a smaller one. The main dish is then served in a large bowl, the relish in smaller ones. Sitting on the ground in a group, native Africans take a ball of the starchy main dish in their hands and dip it into the relish.... The communal African style of cooking, eating, and drinking, learned by children from their parents, survived in America. Such techniques may have furnished antecedents for the stewed hominy, potages, pileus, and "Hoppin' John" that sea-island [enslaved workers] cooked in iron pots and served in ceramic bowls.[3]

Benjamin "BJ" Dennis, a native of Charleston, represents a new wave of Gullah chefs who are opening doors in the culinary world for their culture's

OVERLEAF: Baskets like those shown with this street vendor were the ancestors of the famous sweetgrass baskets still seen in coastal areas of South Carolina and Georgia. *From the George Johnson photograph collection (# VM 43/297) at the South Carolina Historical Society.*

food. Dennis pays homage to his grandparents who "kept him in touch with the old ways of the Sea Islands with their stories and by cooking him a traditional seafood-based diet (including shark and deviled crab) as well as other Gullah classics." Chef Dennis speaks about the current popularity of "one pot" Gullah dishes like Hoppin' John, a staple of Lowcountry cooking.

> Right now we have a renaissance. The appeal of Gullah cuisine is really spreading throughout the country. People are really interested in this culture. Food is the best way to show a culture sometimes. Get it in your belly. Get a taste of it. Hoppin' John is part of the Gullah culture. It came through the African Diaspora. You see peas and rice in so many cultures, but the roots of it go back to West Africa. It's become synonymous with New Year's Eve because of good luck. Peas and rice represent good luck. You have a bit of greens that represent money. You got good luck and you got money. You can't beat that.[4]

In 2018, the South Carolina Department of Parks, Recreation, and Tourism's *Discover South Carolina* videotaped Chef Dennis cooking his version of Hoppin' John:

1. If you are using smoked meat (ham hock), get it in the pot and boiling, so you can get it nice and tender. Cook it with lid on 30–40 minutes until tender. Do a nice dice on a white onion to add sweetness. Small dice on a green bell pepper. Mince two cloves of garlic. Go through the peas to ensure uniformity.

2. When the ham hock is halfway cooked and starting to separate, add a cup to a cup and a half of peas, the onion, bell pepper, and garlic. Add homemade pepper vinegar for aromatic flavor, sweetness, heat, and acidity. Give it a quick stir. Watch your water because peas soak up water.

3. Now add your dry spices. A pinch of salt, pinch of onion powder, good pinch of garlic powder, pinch of paprika, pinch of cayenne pepper, pinch of seasoning salt, and a little bit of garlic salt. Give it a stir and add a little water if needed. Cover and let it cook.

4. Take your rice and wash it in a bowl until the water is clear. You want the grains to be separate and dry (Dry meaning every grain is separate but moist). You will probably wash it 4–6 times. Gullah rice would need more washing than store-bought rice in order to neutralize the starches and avoid it being sticky.

5. Check peas to see if they are tender. Then add rice and add enough water to cover rice. Let it cook for 30 min. Fluff rice with fork to make sure grains are nice and separate.[5]

The limited number of utensils and cooking facilities available to the enslaved Africans resulted in these single-pot dishes that are favorites among Gullahs today. The first ingredient, of course, is always rice—whether white, brown, or otherwise—hence the tradition known as "the rice pot," for that treasured (and often antique) vessel in which just about everything is cooked. Following that, almost anything, fresh or otherwise, can follow, such as vegetables, seafood, chicken, ham, bacon, nuts, and of course a variety of spices.

Gerald finds it ironic that rice, the grain that was a staple in Africa for thousands of years, was also responsible for the enslavement of the people from Africa. They were brought to America for the simple reason that they were the world's greatest specialists in the growing of rice and would thus be valuable to those plantations in the Carolinas and Georgia that came to be known as the "rice plantations." A descendant of the owner of one such plantation went so far as to say that the enslaved workers were trapped by their own ability and ingenuity. In the seventeenth and eighteenth centuries, rice was planted, cultivated, and harvested entirely by hand, involving a crop cycle of one full year, starting each spring with the plowing of the fields by mules and oxen, the digging of trenches for the seeds, and the preparation of the seeds, which had to remain firmly embedded so they would not float to the surface when the fields were flooded.

Rice planting was a tricky business—more so than for most crops—because it necessitated many steps. Flooding, for example, required a "sprout flood" shortly after the seeds were planted, then another for the "first hoeing" (*da fus hoe*), and then the most permanent, the "long water" (*da long waduh*), which drenched the fields and eliminated insects, weeds, and any other infestations that might later harm the budding crops. In late spring, the remaining water was drained off in order to start "dry cultivation," extensive hoeing, and another period of complete flooding that supported new plants, now heavy with emerging rice kernels. All along the way, this process required great personal attention on the part of the workers and constant supervision by the Black overseer, who was a highly respected enslaved worker. Near the end of the year, essential tasks included chopping and drying the rice, sheaving, threshing, winnowing, fanning, pounding, and husking—resulting in rice often called in the Lowcountry "Carolina gold" because of the gold color of its unhulled grains and great value. For generations of enslaved African Americans, rice was their work; rice was their sustenance; rice was their goal—or as the Geechee saying went, "*Es da Geeche got a peck ah rice, dey'll outlive Methusla.*"

Although enslaved workers endured unimaginable hardships in the production of rice, it was also an important mainstay in their diet. And one of the favorite preparations still popular among Gullahs today is red rice, which connects to West African jollof, especially when served with a "gumbo containing okra, fish, tomatoes, and hot peppers."[6] Emily Meggett, author of *Gullah Geechee Home Cooking: Recipes from the Matriarch of Edisto Island*, remembers such a dish: "On Edisto, Wednesdays and Fridays were seafood days. We had shrimp or fish with red rice, so it was something to look forward to. Back in the day, you didn't use tomato paste and sauce, you used the tomatoes you'd planted in your garden. The tomato paste works just as good, though, and Gullah Geechee red rice is one of the best dishes you can enjoy. . . . Red rice goes back to the old, old days—the days before me, my momma, and hers."

Meggett, 89, has lived on Edisto for her entire life and counts fifty grandchildren and great-grandchildren among her heirs. In her cookbook she offers insight into the beautiful, earthy one-pot red rice dish that borrows from the traditions of her African ancestors. According to Meggett, "Charleston red rice owes a great debt to the enslaved Africans who brought their knowledge of rice and vegetable farming to the United States."

Red Rice

Active time: 45 minutes | Total time: 1 hour, 5 minutes
4 servings

INGREDIENTS
3 thick slices bacon or about 3 ounces salt pork, cut into ½-inch pieces
1 medium yellow onion (8 ounces), diced
1 bell pepper (any color), diced
2 stalks celery, chopped (about ½ cup)
8 ounces smoked pork sausage, sliced into ¼-inch thick rounds
  or chopped into bite-size pieces
6 tablespoons tomato paste
2½ cups water
½ teaspoon crushed red pepper flakes
¾ teaspoon Nature's Seasons, sazon, powdered adobo, or other similar
  salted seasoning blend, plus more to taste
1 cup (about 6 ounces) long-grain rice, unrinsed

DIRECTIONS

In a large pot over medium heat, fry the bacon or salt pork, stirring occasionally, until browned on all sides, about 5 minutes. Add the onion, bell pepper, and celery, and cook, stirring occasionally, until tender, 5 to 7 minutes. Stir in the sausage, and cook until lightly browned, stirring as needed, about 5 minutes. Stir in the tomato paste, letting it coat all of the vegetables and meat, and then add the water. Increase the heat to high and bring to a boil.

Stir in the crushed red pepper flakes and Nature's Seasons or other spice mix. Taste, and adjust the seasoning, if needed. Add the rice and cook, stirring frequently to keep the rice from sticking, until most of the liquid has been absorbed and the rice is tender, about 10 minutes. Decrease the heat to the lowest possible setting, cover the pot, and cook, stirring occasionally, with a wooden spatula or fork to help fluff the grains, for 25 to 30 minutes, or until the rice has absorbed all the liquid and is tender and fluffy. Remove from the heat and serve family-style.[7]

Josephine Beoku-Betts, author of "We Got Our Way of Cooking Things: Women, Food, and Preservation of Cultural Identity Among the Gullah," cites one sea islander's words: "Rice is security. If you have some rice, you'll never starve. It is a bellyful. You should never find a cupboard without it."[8]

In the early days, pots were difficult to clean because rice had a tendency to cake and resist even the strongest soaps, says Veronica Gerald; thus, they had to be scraped and scrubbed with a lot of elbow grease. The pot itself was considered more important than the recipes for which it was used, and in between the preparation of more solid foods this vessel was equally effective in simmering soups, which were often made from partial leftovers of the main meal. In fact, it was considered poor taste to leave an empty but scummy rice pot soaking on the stove between meals. Rather, "the pot should always have a fitted lid and be washed and ready for use at all times." As a consequence, she says, "stories about the rice pot are a part of Gullah families around the world."[9] A few of these include strong family disputes over which child in a family was to be bequeathed a certain pot after the death of a parent in whose possession it had been.

Over the years, the Gullah cuisine has of course been influenced by other cultures along the Gullah Corridor of the Carolinas and Georgia. Chiefly, these have been English, French, and Spanish influences, and in some regions the foods and cooking of Native American Indian tribes. In this respect we see chili peppers and hot sauces from Spanish-speaking peoples who arrived on American shores from the Caribbean; grits from southern cooks in cities such as Charleston and Savannah; corn bread from New Englanders who have escaped from cold winters to migrate southward; shellfish delicacies from cooks who have moved eastward from New Orleans; teas from visiting Asians; pastries from French expatriates; pastas from Italian newcomers; and roasts from the British. Despite these influences, nothing can match the unique Gullah ingredients in the cooked pot because there was very, very little that ever went to waste, whether the sources were field, forest, stream, ocean, or just plain backyard. In this respect, we see recipes that call for what to many are rather unappetizing ingredients, such as ox tails, fish bones, fins, snake livers, and frogs' eggs, in addition to various parts of the pig, including neck bones, hog maws, pigs' feet, jowls, ears, chitlins (intestines), and eyeballs.

Gullah dishes such as Limpin' Susan, Hoppin' John, sweet potato pone, Gullah sunrise, and Sat'day monin pancakes often have backstories as colorful as the titles themselves. For example, Hoppin' John was supposedly a crippled street vendor in Charleston who hawked peas and rice while Limpin' Susan, a dish of okra and rice, was Hoppin' John's wife, mistress, or even cousin.[10] Another creative title for a dish is neck bones 'n' gravy, sometimes called "neck bones divine," made with pork neck bones, bell peppers, onions, rice, and almost anything else the cook wants to throw in the pot. Neck bones, which are almost never on the shopping list of non-Gullah cooks, are best if soaked in water for thirty minutes or so to remove salt and then simmered for an hour and a half along with the other ingredients. Despite the inclusion of recipes in this chapter, most Gullah cooks prefer to cook according to personal taste, adding or changing by instinct, governed in many ways by what their mothers and grandmothers did before them.

An unexpected Gullah favorite is chitlins or chits, the primary ingredients of which are chitterlings (small intestines from hogs), a chunk of hog maw, celery, onions, peppers, and various spices according to the cook's taste. Only the best of cooks, however, can handle this recipe properly, since the chitterlings and maw are processed and cooked separately at the beginning, washed, and refrigerated overnight before they can even get to the mixing and cooking stage. Further boiling, simmering, combining, and flavoring make this dish a complicated one, not to be undertaken lightly by inexperienced chefs.

"The tradition of eating chitlins is one that developed in America," writes Gerald. It originated during plantation days when the slave families were given those parts of hogs and other domestic animals that the white families did not want, including not only the intestines but also feet, jowls, ears, tails, maws, and heads. Gerald states, "Adaptive and creative cooks learned to clean them and prepare them in the most delectable way so that the desire for the meat crossed into freedom and remains today an expected and anticipated dish at all big celebrations and occasions." Her comments did not come from a history book but from personal experience in the Sea Islands. "On hog killing days, when we were children, the steam from the chitterlings could be seen like fog in the cold air when they were taken out of the warm bellies of the hogs. Before they made it to the Gullah table, however, there was the long, arduous process of cleaning and preparing them to be cooked." As can be imagined, the initial task of removing, cutting, separating, and cleaning alone was one that few people—even slaves—could face. "Even today," says Gerald, "great respect is given to those who 'kin clean chitlins.' Most Gullah will not eat chitlins from 'jis anybody.'"[11]

Transplanted Food Sources

Where did the many foods and food substances associated with the Gullah culture originate? According to William Pollitzer,

Africa is home to many life-sustaining crops, including nine cereals, half a dozen root crops, five oil producing plants, a dozen forage crops, a dozen vegetables, three fruits and nuts, coffee, sesame, and the ancient and ubiquitous bottle gourd or calabash useful as a drinking cup, float for fishnet, or sound box for music. West Africa alone is the locus of origin of cereals such as Guinea millet, fonio, African rice, pearl millet, and sorghum; cowpeas, okra, some species of yam, oil palm, and the akee apple, as well as varieties of cotton.... Best known from West Africa is that tasty mucilaginous vegetable, okra or gumbo (*Abelmoschus esculentus*). First domesticated in tropical Africa, it spread widely along the Guinea coast and into the Cameroons by the time of the slave trade and was brought to the Americas in the 1600s....

The black-eyed or cow pea (*Vigna unguiculata*) is an import from West and Central Africa that found its way to the West Indies and the Lowcountry. First domesticated at the margin of the forest and savannah in tropical West Africa, its seeds are known from Kintampo in central Ghana as early as 1800 B.C. and at Zimbabwe in southeast Africa by 1000 A.D....

The circular route of the peanut (*Arachis hypogaea*) is unique. Taken from Brazil to Africa around 1500 by the Portuguese, it established a secondary center in the Congo [and] was widespread in West Africa by 1600. Fed to slaves on ships to Virginia, peanuts spread to South Carolina. Eggplant, originally cultivated in India, was brought by Arabs into Spain and by Persians into Africa before the arrival of Europeans. Widespread from Senegal to Cameroon, it is known not only as a food but also as a medicine and as a symbol of fertility. Watermelon (*Citrullus lanatus*), a native of the dry savannah of east and south Africa, was grown in the Nile valley by 2000 B.C., and brought to Florida by Spanish colonists in the middle of the sixteenth century.[12]

Gullahs and Their Natural Environment

Josephine Beoku-Betts's interviews of twenty-two Gullah women revealed how these mothers and grandmothers transferred to the younger generation a respect for the environment as a food source and vital contributor to the harmonic balance of life.

The value of self-sufficiency in food supply is an integral aspect of the Gullah food system. Men and women of all ages are conversant with hunting, fishing, and gardening as ways to provide food. From an early age, both men and women are socialized into the concept and the practice of self-sufficiency as a primary goal of the food system and are encouraged to participate in the outdoor food-procuring activities of parents and other kin or community members. Velma Moore, a woman in her mid-40s, became sensitive to environmental causes when, as a child, she accompanied both her parents on daily walks in the woods. This experience taught her a variety of survival skills involving the use of the island's natural resources for subsistence and medicine. Now married and the mother of five children, Velma pointed out that she encourages the practice of these traditions among her sons and daughters.

Grandparents also play an important role in developing children's skills in food self-sufficiency. A typical example was Maisie Gables, a lively and active woman about 70 years of age. When I interviewed Miss Maisie, as she was called, I did not know that our scheduled appointments conflicted with her plans to go fishing with her five-year-old granddaughter, whom she was teaching to fish. Miss Maisie explained later that her granddaughter liked fishing from an early age, so she had decided to cultivate this interest by teaching her the necessary skills, as she had once been taught by her mother. By transmitting these skills, which are part of collective memory, the senior generation of Gullah women fosters and sustains cultural identity intergenerationally, thus broadening the base of cultural knowledge in the community.

While the Gullah depend on their natural surroundings as a reliable source of food, they also have a deep understanding of their coexistence with other living things and believe that the use of these resources should be moderate and nonexploitative. This sense of shared membership in the natural environment stems from Gullah belief systems, which emphasize harmony and social exchange between the human and the natural world. Such a view is influenced by African spiritual beliefs, which are community centered and involve a set of relationships involving God, the ancestors, other human beings (including those yet unborn), and other living and nonliving things. In this complex system of relationships, the well-being of the whole is paramount; individual existence is woven into the whole.

Some aspects of this world view are reflected in my interview with Velma Moore. She describes herself as a self-taught woman, although "self-taught" does not adequately describe her intelligence, strong will, and vast knowledge of Gullah history and culture. During one interview, she revealed that she, like many Gullah women, had been taught to hunt and would do so if necessary. Even so, she considered herself a keen environmentalist, with concern for the protection of nature, and would not engage in such activities for recreation because "it is not sporting to go up and kill animals that can't shoot you back." In other words, although she would rely on these resources for survival, anything beyond that purpose would threaten the harmony with nature.[13]

Delicious Miss Brown

Kardea Brown's Food Network show *Delicious Miss Brown* is the biggest stage Gullah food has ever been given. Debuting on July 28, 2019, Brown presents southern-inspired dishes from her family's home on Edisto Island and reaches an estimated one million viewers per episode. Brown, who was raised by her mother and grandmother, spent much of her childhood surrounded by her extended Gullah family on Wadmalaw Island. It was during these formative years that Brown's grandmother Josephine "insisted on teaching her about Gullah foodways. For that generation, keeping the culture alive involves cooking.... That's how Brown learned to prepare okra stew, shrimp and grits, stewed lima beans, and pimiento cheese dishes that are often associated with Charleston's distinct brand of Lowcountry cuisine but aren't credited to the Gullah people." According to Brown, "It's a Gullah tradition to make okra stew on Fridays, so everyone can gather around and eat a hearty meal after a long week."[14]

Brown understands the huge responsibilities of being the host of a popular show and being Gullah Geechee and embraces opportunities to have in-depth conversations that recognize the centrality of Gullah cuisine. "Gullah people laid the foundation for Southern cooking. Before farm-to-table was a fad, it was what Gullah people did, so I wanted to show the world that African American people don't just fry chicken and eat collard greens swimming in meat. It's very intentional on my part, to show a different part of the South."[15]

She also wants to use her national platform to "show viewers that we are more alike than we are different, which is so important at a time when racial tensions are high. Family and love are the center of my life. I hope my show encourages viewers to make love the center of their lives, too."[16]

Brown disagrees with those who believe the Gullah Geechee culture is disappearing due to climate change and the lack of interest by the younger generation. She insists that her generation is committed to keeping these traditions alive because chefs like BJ Dennis are championing this cuisine on a national level. Brown proudly states, "Gullah cuisine is food of survival.... The food is at the center of it all, like little branches that connect everything else."[17]

The Gullah dish most visitors to the Lowcountry want to try is Frogmore Stew, also known as Lowcountry Boil or Beaufort Boil. Frogmore was named for the fishing community and commercial center on St. Helena Island, where seafood restaurants, a post office, and historic Penn Center are located. As the story goes, Richard Gay, owner of Gay Fish Company on the island, coined the title in the 1960s when he prepared a cookout of leftovers for his fellow guardsmen, and after it appeared on the cover of *Gourmet Magazine* in the 1980s, this one-pot dish gained national attention. In her cookbook, Veronica Gerald includes a recipe for Frogmore Stew (Seafood B'ile), which is inspired by her dear friend Emory Campbell.

Seafood B'ile

(aka Gullah Bowl/Frogmore Stew/Lowcountry Boil)
5 lbs small medium unpeeled red potatoes cut in quarters
10 ears 4-inch yellow corn, shucked and brushed
5 lbs shrimp (leave shells on)
4 lbs smoked sausage cut into quarter inches
pre-cooked seasoned crawfish (optional)
2 large onions (diced)
2 large green peppers (cored and diced)
4 carrots (sliced)
4 stalks celery (sliced)
3 quarts water
1/2 cup seafood/Accent/Gullah Luv Seasoning mixture (or salt and pep-
    per mixture)
3 bay leaves (preferably freshly picked)

Wash and prepare vegetables and meats.
    Fill 12-quart pot with water. Add 1/2 cup seasoning mixture.
    Bring to a boil. Add red potatoes and corn.
    Once water starts to boil again, add smoked sausage, diced onion, bell
peppers, carrots, and celery.
    Bring to a boil again. Add shrimp (and precooked seasoned crawfish,
if desired).
    Bring to another boil. When done, shrimp will be reddish pink. Serve
in bowls.[18]

The importance of seafood in Gullah cooking is perhaps best described by
Emily Meggett: "Seafood isn't just part of Gullah Geechee culture and food,
it's the foundation of eating... because you can't talk about Gullah Geechee
cooking without talking about seafood first.... Gullah people refused to let
slavery's cruelty destroy our ancestral connection with the waters."[19]

A GULLAH COOK'S POINT OF VIEW

If you would like to view the situation from the standpoint of a Gullah cook, here is an enslaved African's recipe for rice as recommended by a formerly enslaved person from Brookgreen Plantation:

Fus ting yo roll up yo sleeves es high es yo kin, en yo tak soap en yo wash yo han clean. Den yo wash yo pot clean. Fill um wid col wata en put on da fia. Now wile yo wait de wata de bile, yo put yo rice een a piggin en yo wash well. Den wen yo dun put salt een yo pot, en bile high. Yo put yo rice een en le um bile till e swell, den yo pour off de wata en yo pot back o de stove, fo steam.

—CHAPTER TEN—

GULLAH CELEBRATIONS

The numbers of festivals, feasts, holidays, and other events recognizing the Gullah Geechee culture have increased noticeably over just the past two decades in the Sea Islands and Lowcountry. In addition, there has been immense growth in the number of businesses and organizations devoted exclusively to this culture, including dress and gift boutiques, art galleries and museums, specialized grocery markets, bookstores, visitor centers, and institutions of higher education. Penn Center, the former school for freed enslaved persons that was founded in 1862, is responsible for much of this growth because of its early leadership in highlighting the Gullah Geechee culture through summer Gullah institutes, the York W. Bailey Museum, exhibits of Gullah arts and artifacts, and annual Heritage Days Celebration.

When Emory Campbell became executive director of Penn Center in 1980, two of his main goals were to restore Penn Center's historical importance and broaden the appreciation for Gullah culture. Campbell accomplished both of these objectives with one single event—Penn Center's Heritage Days Celebration. However, Heritage Days may never have occurred without Campbell's slow acceptance of his own Gullah identity through what he termed his "unmasking journey." He credits scholars J. Herman Blake, Patricia Guthrie, and John Gadson with leading him to a "sense of place and self as a Gullah Geechee person."[1] Blake's extensive work on Daufuskie Island in the 1970s, particularly his oral history project, informed Campbell of the immense value of the "Gullah story" and aided his own efforts to help Daufuskie's families cope with their isolation from the mainland.

Guthrie's study of pray's houses on St. Helena Island in the mid-1970s (cited in chapter 5 of this book), revealed to Campbell the West and Central African retentions in these storied institutions and the effective system by which pray's house elders settled disputes among members. In his words, "her work quickened my memory of similar [pray's] house activities when I was growing up on Hilton Head Island."[2] But Gadson, who was then executive director of Penn Center, may have had the greatest impact on Campbell's journey with the Sea Island Language Project, sponsored by a grant from the U.S. Department of Labor. This project's goal was to teach English to Gullah-speaking high school graduates, so they would have a better chance at employment at resorts on Hilton Head Island. Many among Campbell's generation were often ashamed to speak Gullah publicly and recognize its significance as a language, but he gradually became aware of the connections between Gullah grammar and West African languages. Campbell's efforts to promote Gullah Geechee culture through the Heritage Days Celebration coincided with his own journey of self-discovery and self-acceptance. In his book *Gullah Cultural Legacies*, Campbell discusses the popular parade held on the Saturday of Heritage Days:

> In addition to giving the audience a reference for the final day's beginning, the parade reflects the culture of the region. Participating units perform in accordance with Gullah cultural traditions, displaying art forms ranging from that which depicts the role of community elders to "jump (picnic) band music." Participating groups include fraternities and sororities, farmers groups, daycare centers, the military bands, fire departments, and others, resulting in a parade of about 100 units. Be-

OVERLEAF: *The Old Plantation* was painted circa 1790. The two female figures are playing the shegureh, an instrument used by women of the Mende and neighboring tribes in Sierra Leone. *The Colonial Williamsburg Foundation. Gift of Abby Aldrich Rockefeller.*

ginning at the St. Helena Elementary School on U.S. Highway 21 East (the only route to and from the mainland) West to Martin Luther King Drive, then South to Penn Center Historical Landmark District.

. . .

All bands, except the military band, give performances of their music and movements. These bands may render previously rehearsed historical musical numbers that include jazz, blues, or contemporary musical numbers. . . . These performances prepare the cheering crowds for a day of fine Gullah cuisine, a variety of Gullah cultural forms from center stage whence the prizes are awarded. It embodies the Gullah culture in a convincing art form—the family depicted by the elders and youth, food ways (rice, sweet potatoes, etc.), spirituality (gospel choir), visual art (baskets), performance art (bands and music) are all presented artfully in an hour and a half to a diverse and appreciative audience. The Penn Center Heritage Days Celebration Parade is indeed a cultural art form where one has the rare opportunity to thoroughly immerse oneself in the Gullah culture.[3]

Along with the parade, Heritage Days features an old-fashioned prayer service at either Brick Baptist Church, Ebenezer Baptist Church, or Bethesda Christian Fellowship, which are the churches nearest to Penn Center. On the grounds of Penn are authentic presentations of basketry, storytelling, netmaking, Gullah food and music, as well as educational seminars, and cultural symposiums. Occurring during three days in the second week of November, it draws thousands of people annually from around the country and is one of Campbell's greatest gifts to the Gullah Geechee people. This event proved Campbell to be correct when he said, "The foods we ate, the songs we sang, the spirits we embraced, the noble families in which we were loved, and the language we spoke, were eminently worthy of study and preservation."[4]

Five years after the inaugural Heritage Days Celebration, residents of Beaufort County were treated to a second African American cultural event known as the Gullah Festival when five women envisioned a celebration similar to the popular Decoration Day or Memorial Day events the Black community had enjoyed for many years. Although often used interchangeably today, Decoration Day and Memorial Day were historically segregated events held on two different days. Historian Bruce Baker writes, "In the South the name Memorial Day came to refer to Confederate Memorial Day celebrated on May 10th in the Carolinas, while Decoration Day celebrated three weeks later was given but cursory attention by most southern whites. Union veterans, though White and Black, gathered from far and wide to decorate the graves."[5]

Decoration Day featured a parade, picnics, and other festivities that attracted thousands of African Americans who came to honor the many soldiers (Union and Confederate) buried at Beaufort National Cemetery. The five organizers of the Gullah Festival—Rosalie Pazant and her daughters, Charlotte Pazant Brown, Lolita Pazant Harris, and Reba Pazant, and family friend Dr. Marlena McGhee Smalls—wanted an event with the same old-time flavor as Decoration Day but with entertainment. "They tossed around several names and finally came up with a name representative of the area and decided to call their new venture 'The Gullah Festival.' Under the helm of Mrs. Pazant, their dream became a reality and the first year of the festival was 1986."[6]

Under the current leadership of Thomas Roy Hicks, president and CEO, the Gullah Festival, now known as the Original Gullah Festival, offers guests Gullah food, African-inspired vendors, various styles of live music, drumming, dancing, storytelling, and a *Decoration Day* play performed by Aunt Pearlie Sue (Anita Singleton Prather) and the Gullah Kinfolk. This musical stage play uses interactive storytelling, dancing, and foot-stomping music to "tell the story of just how Decoration Day 'usta be' and how it grew into what we know today as Memorial Day."[7] The Original Gullah Festival draws thousands of visitors over a three-day period in celebration of the Gullah culture.

One of the oldest and most fascinating events along the Corridor is the annual Georgia Sea Islands Festival, which is sponsored by the St. Simons African American Heritage Coalition on the first Saturday in June on St. Simons Island. Bessie Jones and Mabel Hillery, members of the famed Georgia Sea Island Singers, began the festival on August 20–21, 1977, to showcase Gullah crafts, choral singing, blues, and children's games.[8] After the deaths of Hillery and Jones, another Georgia Sea Island member, Frankie Quimby, carried on the festival until 1998. The Georgia Sea Island Festival was revived in August 2002, when the St. Simons African American Heritage Coalition hosted the event as part of an educational effort to inform the community about the value of their property and their Gullah Geechee culture. Emory Rooks, a festival organizer and leader of the St. Simons African American Heritage Coalition, says, "This is a way to celebrate African Americans and the Gullah Geechee heritage through our food, dancing, entertainment, and arts and crafts."[9]

Since 2011, the Jacksonville Gullah Geechee Nation Community Development Corporation (CDC), under the leadership of President and CEO

Saundra Morene, has sponsored the Gullah Fest in Jacksonville, Florida, on the last Saturday in October. Held in the vicinity of Black-owned restaurants, boutiques, and shops along Pearl Street, this event is "designed to educate patrons of all ages on the historical footprint of Jacksonville's African American influences." Gullah Fest features performances by local artists, schools, poets, and an annual appearance by the Geechee Gullah Ring Shouters of Darien, Georgia. The Jacksonville Gullah Geechee Nation CDC is "dedicated to the education, development, and preservation of Gullah Geechee culture, history, and communities throughout the city of Jacksonville, Florida."[10]

Since 1995, the Sapelo Island Cultural and Revitalization Society has presented its Sapelo Island Cultural Arts Festival on the third Saturday in October. This event features ring shouters, storytellers, local food vendors, gospel choirs, Geechee Gullah arts and crafts, African dancers, and children's activities. In addition, guests can attend a traditional church service and a guided tour of this beautiful island. The Sapelo Island Cultural and Revitalization Society was founded in 1993 by "Hogg Hummock resident and non-resident descendants who wanted to enhance the future of their community by educating all visitors to the island about the history."[11] One of the main goals for many of the Black residents is to have a better ferry or a bridge to improve access to the community and more job opportunities to truly achieve an "enhanced future."

Since 1996, the Native Island Business and Community Affairs Association (NIBCAA) has hosted the annual Native Islander Gullah Celebration, now known as the Hilton Head Island Gullah Celebration. Held throughout the month of February, a "slow month" for tourism, this event helps visitors and the local population better understand and appreciate the rich heritage that exists on Hilton Head Island and to help preserve as many aspects of the old Gullah culture as possible. A popular feature on the first Saturday in February is the Taste of Gullah Festival, which takes place on the grounds of the Arts Center of Coastal Carolina. Taste, in this context, applies to music, art, and food, as festival organizers attempt to "give people a taste of what the island was like before it transitioned into a popular tourist destination."[12] Popular performers are the El Shaddai Gospel Choir, Natalie Daise, and storyteller Louis Cohen. An important feature of this festival is a symposium where panelists and audiences of people from the Sea Islands, the Caribbean, and Africa gather to learn about and share the history of the Gullah culture as it relates to their unique life experiences.

Eric Turpin, executive director of NIBCAA, views the celebration as helping tell part of the larger African American story on Hilton Head Island. "Everything on the island is connected; the historic Mitchelville, the Gullah Museum, the Gullah Tours and the Gullah Celebration. Each of them is separate, but we're working together on the same theme of maintaining the island's cultural preservation and tourism to improve the economic, social, and living conditions of low-income residents of Hilton Head Island and neighboring communities and to raise awareness of Hilton Head's indigenous African American community's arts, crafts, and food culture."[13]

One of the newest Gullah events is the North Carolina Rice Festival in Leland, North Carolina. Sponsored by the Leland Tourism Development Authority (LTD Authority) on the first weekend in March, this annual festival attracts "families, history enthusiasts, educators, tourists and residents alike who learn about the region's rich and diverse cultural history of rice farming."[14] W. C. Lanier, a local promoter, founded the festival in 2014 as a one-day fall event taking place in Belville, North Carolina. Upon his death, the LTD Authority bought the rights from Lanier's heirs and transitioned the festival from a fall to a spring event and expanded it to three days. Visitors to the North Carolina Rice Festival can expect to experience Gullah food, music, vendors, films, and lectures that highlight the rice contributions of the enslaved Africans in Brunswick County, North Carolina.

All of these festivals and celebrations include a growing number of performers of traditional and contemporary Gullah Geechee music. A National Park Service study reports, "Many of these groups reach out to their audience and create an instinctive performance that enables those in attendance to share in the singing, clapping, and rhythms of the music." Among the most notable of the traditional artists are the McIntosh County Shouters, the Georgia Sea Island Singers, the Moving Star Hall Singers, the Brotherhood Gospel Singers of Mount Pleasant, and the Plantation Singers of Charleston. Popular musical ensembles who present traditional as well as contemporary Gullah arrangements include Dr. Marlena Smalls and the Hallelujah Singers, Aunt Pearlie Sue and the Gullah Kinfolk, and Ron and Natalie Daise, all with roots in Beaufort, South Carolina.[15]

Gullah Arts and Crafts

One of the most distinctive crafts associated with African Americans and particularly those with strong Gullah backgrounds, is coiled sweetgrass basketry. A fine example of a celebration of this art form is the Sweetgrass Festival held at the Waterfront Park in Mount Pleasant, South Carolina. Thomasena Stokes-Marshall, the first African American to serve on Mount Pleasant's town council, founded the Annual Sweetgrass Cultural Arts Festival Association in 2004 to bring awareness of the threat to the sweetgrass basket tradition posed by the increasing amount of residential and commercial development on Gullah Geechee lands.[16] In 2005, Stokes-Marshall spearheaded the first Sweetgrass Festival to showcase the artistry of the basket makers, whose legacy is traced back to West and Central Africa, where the technique was developed over many generations.

Basketmaking in America began in the seventeenth and eighteenth centuries when enslaved Africans on southern plantations needed a means to carry foods and household supplies. Back in their homeland in West and Central Africa, they made baskets for these very purposes and discovered ideal sewing materials in grasses growing in the marshlands of the Carolinas. Not only were they of utilitarian value in the enslaved quarters and fields, but one type, known as the "fanner basket," became an essential tool in the processing of rice at that stage of its cultivation when it was necessary to separate the ripe kernel from the husk. The workers in the field, equipped with the proper size and shape of sweetgrass basket, simply tossed the rice into the air and caught it cleanly in a basket as the chaff blew away. This was known as "fanning the rice." Some of the baskets, because of their relatively large size, were also conveniently used by mothers for carrying their infants.

Although sweetgrass baskets over the past few decades or so have become increasingly more elaborate and intricate—some to such a degree that they are more ornamental than utilitarian—they are still used in Gullah households and kitchens for serving or storage containers or handbags. One of the current problems in the production of these baskets, however, is the steady disappearance of marshlands and seashore grasslands due to excessive commercial development. As a result, many basket makers (referred to commonly as "sewers") are forced to use long leaf pine needles or bulrush on St. Helena Island, which is a darker, more brittle marsh grass that is "rougher on the hands and more difficult to bind tightly."[17] Because sewers are being forced to find materials in farther regions of South Carolina, there is a concern for the future of this art form.

At the end of the nineteenth century, Charleston, South Carolina, was a training center for a wide variety of crafts and occupations, including basketmaking. Yet the city's reputation for basketry really started around 1916, when a white entrepreneur, Clarence Legerton, formed the Sea Grass Basket Company on King Street and sold the baskets not only in local shops but also in a growing mail-order business. Among the many talented basket makers today is Jery Bennett-Taylor, who was born and raised in the town of Mount Pleasant, South Carolina, and learned the weaving art at her grandmother's knee. Although she studied medical administration and could have had a successful career in that area, her skills and real interests were in basket weaving, and she is represented in a display at the Smithsonian in Washington, D.C.

Although baskets and basket makers can be found throughout the Sea Islands, the Mount Pleasant area, to the northwest of Charleston, is the center of the art in America. Few people—even the basket makers themselves—can explain to lay persons how these intricate baskets are designed and woven. The basic patterns begin with a knot or long row, which is gradually extended round and round and upward until the basket reaches its desired size. The intricate shapes and styles of the baskets require skills that the weavers have developed over many years and etched into their memories, bit by bit, as they move from basic steps to more advanced ones. The Sweetgrass Cultural Arts Festival is traditionally held in July and includes not only arts and crafts but also music, food, dancing, and other traditional performances.

Often, the most popular areas in many of these festivals are the vendor spaces where Gullah woodworkers and quilters display and sell their artwork. Their works are called traditional and fall into the "folk art" category because the artists are largely self-taught, adapting their personal skills and ingenuity to their particular art form. In the past, male enslaved workers had to undertake some of the more laborious jobs like repairing plantation homes, building their own family shanties from the crudest wood supplies, chair-making, and constructing small boats for fishing along the bays, creeks, and tidal inlets. As a result, these men became highly skilled carpenters and cabinetmakers and could do wonders with nothing more than a pocketknife and a chunk of yellow pine. In some regions, the whittling of canes became something of a specialty. Along with boatbuilding, many men—and boys as well—became specialists in the knotting and weaving of fishnets and ropes.

Quilting was one of the most common handicrafts of Gullah women, who transformed assortments of old rags, torn clothing, and sometimes even the more flexible marsh grasses into objects of beauty as well as utility on southern plantations. Charles Joyner discusses how enslaved women "gathered together at night, after a day's work in the rice fields, to make warm and often beautiful quilts to supplement the supply of blankets," usually making one quilt to supplement their allotment of one new blanket every three years. "They made quilting an occasion for social interaction as well as an occasion for work, thus helping to ease the burden of bondage." The most common quilt was the patchwork, in which the design was created like a mosaic from numerous patches of cloth. Other types were pieced, appliqued, ubiquitous strip, and string quilts.[18]

Fine Arts

Several art galleries and institutions in South Carolina, such as Penn Center on St. Helena Island, the Colleton Museum and Farmers Market in Walterboro, Gallery Chuma in Charleston and Red Piano Art Gallery Too on St. Helena Island have strongly supported Gullah Geechee artists. The Red Piano Art Galley Too, under the leadership of Mary Inabinett Mack, is of particular importance because of its longevity and role in legitimizing Gullah Geechee art in the Lowcountry. In recognition of her achievements, Mack became a member of the Penn Center 1862 Circle and received the Elizabeth O'Neill Verner Governor's Award for the Arts, South Carolina's highest award for achievement in the arts.

For nearly thirty years, Mack's Red Piano Too Art Galley was the launching pad for more than twenty emerging artists and gave self-taught folk artists a venue to display their work. Notable names include James Denmark, Diane Britton Dunham, Sonja Griffin Evans, and Saundra Renee Smith. Victoria Smalls, executive director of the Gullah Geechee Cultural Heritage Corridor Commission and herself an artist, recalls Mack's support of her pastel paintings early in her career. Mack allowed her to sell them on consignment at the Red Piano Too, and Smalls was surprised when her work sold out and Mack personally requested more. Not long afterward, she started working at the gallery—"curating exhibits, learning fine framing, and getting to know the artists on an individual level"—which resulted in what she calls "the most perfect arts education." "Simply being surrounded by people who expressed their love for all things Gullah through fine arts."[19] In 2020, Mary Mack closed the doors on her Red Piano Too Art Gallery on St. Helena Island, ending one of the South's most important galleries for Gullah art.

Although many know of Jonathan Green's exquisite art, there were earlier Gullah artists, such as William Henry Johnson, who are equally deserving of recognition. Born in Florence, South Carolina, in 1901, Johnson grew up in poverty and with little formal education. As a youngster, he began copying comics in the dirt with such skill that one of his teachers gave him supplies and encouraged him to study art, which resulted in his decision to go to New York to attend the National Academy of Design. With financial support and great determination, he did well and received a number of awards for his work.

Despite his reputation as a landscape painter, he began to devote more and more time in the 1930s to what he termed a "primitive" style, using bright and contrasting colors and two-dimensional figures to depict African Americans and everyday figures, often of a religious nature. But Johnson was destined to be plagued by misfortune in the 1940s. A fire destroyed much of his work and possessions; his wife died of breast cancer; the beginning of World War II saw a lessening of public interest in his field of art; and worst of all, his untreated syphilis resulted in an ever-worsening mental illness that gradually destroyed his ability to paint. After being found wandering and lost in the streets of Oslo, Norway, he was brought back to the states and institutionalized at New York City's Central Islip State Hospital on December 1, 1947. He spent the remaining twenty-three years of his life there. He has been acclaimed as one of America's most important artists.

Sam Doyle (1906–1985) is considered to have been one of the best artists from the Gullah Geechee Corridor. He attended Penn School, where the teachers recognized and encouraged his artistic talent, but he dropped out of school in the ninth grade to support his family, turning down an opportunity to go to New York City to study. He worked as a stock clerk, then a porter in a warehouse for twenty years, and finally at a small laundromat near the Marine Corps Recruit Depot at Parris Island. As a self-taught artist, Doyle began painting not on the typical artist's canvas but on wood, sheet metal, cloth, and almost anything handy that would hold paint. Against the backdrop of St. Helena Island's rural scenery, Doyle created eclectic works representing historical events, community members, and religious scenes. Examples range from *Dr. Buzz*, a portrait of a voodoo practitioner, to *The First Football Game on St. Helena Island*.

He had a deep commitment to the local community and displayed his art outside in his yard, a space he called the "Nationwide Outdoor Art Gallery." "Doyle used his yard as a vehicle for grassroots education and for encouraging memory, cultural pride, and humor, says art expert William F. Brooks. Doyle found inspiration from cast-off materials, such as roofing tin and enamel house paint, to "create portraits characterized by bold juxtapositions of bright colors, expressive gestures, and a frequent use of text to convey the identity of each subject." [20]

In 2008, Richard Dennis White, a self-taught artist and musician, received the Sam Doyle Award for artistic excellence, and he is also the recipient of the May Kourtrolakis and Beaufort Art Association awards of excellence. White, a native of Beaufort, South Carolina, attended college at Ohio University Southern, in Ironton, Ohio, and, upon graduation, joined the U.S. Navy. Later, he became a truck driver to pay the rent, but an accident left him unable to do physical work and uninspired to continue his lifelong interest in painting. It so happened that his career took a turn for the better when one day, while tossing out some pieces of wood, he spotted a pattern of sorts in the grain. He glued two chunks together, started whittling away, and lo and behold, he discovered his artistic path. This was his first wood carving, titled *Cerebral Island*, showing a mask in the foreground and a painted island, palm tree, and full moon in the background. His wood carvings, including the popular *Old Man Playing the Guitar*, have received further awards for their authentic representations of Gullah culture.

Joe Pinckney (1930–2005) came to his art late in life. He did not complete his first Gullah painting until 1970, when he became interested in the subject in discussions with some fellow native islanders. "It was an extraordinary kind of art," explains Emory Campbell about his longtime friend, "because Joe did such a great job of portraying Gullah life and people and all of the traditions of the Gullah culture." Pinckney, a South Carolinian, was always one of the favorite exhibit artists during Heritage Days, the Gullah celebration on Penn Center's campus each November. His paintings, such as the one titled *Daufuskie Island Road*, tend to have more detail and fewer bright colors than some of the other characteristic Gullah palettes. Typical of Pinckney's style is his depiction of a single-room Gullah house of the early twentieth century, on short pilings, with a simple porch, tin roof, and crooked steps, a curving mud road, crude fences, two women working, a live oak, and a background of bushes and smaller trees.

James Denmark was born in Winter Haven, Florida, into a family of artists and later came under the influence of Samella Lewis, who exposed him to the traditions of the African American art movement. Other influences include Norman Lewis (1909–1979), Romare Bearden (1911–1988), and Ernest Crichlow (1914–2005), who helped to organize what is thought to be the earliest gallery exhibition of Black artists. Denmark is best known for his collages that feature bright hand-colored fabrics and objects. Byrma Braham, a New York art director, says of him, "James Denmark has plunged himself heart and soul into his craft, and as a technician he has mastered the difficult medium of collages. However, his importance as an artist reaches far beyond that. His work reveals deep commitment to restoring us to our dignity as human beings and as a race."[21] He exhibited a special skill with collages, watercolors, and woodcuts, and is particularly identified by his improvisational style, brightly handcrafted fabrics, and intermingled objects. He has had more than sixty one-man exhibitions.

Sonja Griffin Evans is an international Gullah artist born and raised in Beaufort, South Carolina. Evans credits her Gullah culture with infusing the purest representations of the island's beauty and spirituality into her artwork. As a prolific mixed-media artist, she incorporates items such as tin and wood but is equally adept at "painting the vibrantly textured colored art on canvas that is acknowledged as the traditional Gullah style. In both mediums, Sonja is careful to express her culture in its purest form." Evans sees beauty and purpose in all of God's creations and feels nothing should be wasted. In her approach to her craft, she says, "I merely hold the paint brush, but God ultimately creates the art." Evans recalls a poignant moment when she truly understood the power of letting God control her creative process:

> Creating and presenting one of my *Freedom Doors* to Congressman John Lewis in Washington, D.C., was my favorite and most memorable experience. After presenting my painting, *Freedom's Door*, to honor him, he wept on my shoulders. He then looked me in the eyes and said, "You made me cry. I will never forget you." It was a moment in time that allowed me and my art the opportunity to connect and honor a man, who sacrificed so much for so many. *Freedom's Door* will always be my favorite and most memorable piece of art.[22]

Deeper Insights into the Gullah Culture

For those who want to know more about the subject than can be found at festivals and celebrations, there are an increasing number of educational programs and institutes open to the public that are led by scholars who are well qualified to teach this subject. In the past, there was the Penn Center's Gullah Studies Summer Institute, a two-week program designed to introduce a broad and diverse audience to the Gullah culture with offerings in history, language, music, religion, traditions, and heritage. Subjects covered included the origins of slavery in West Africa, cultural legacies, the Gullah language, religious practices, civil rights, music, dance, culinary arts, medicines and healing, oral traditions, genealogy, theater, photography, crafts, art, and the environment.

For more extensive training, the University of South Carolina Beaufort hosts a Sea Island Institute focused on interdisciplinary research, outreach, and education services to support the needs of the local community. The Institute has the following programs: Center for Events Management and Hospitality Training, which provides training of hospitality workers in local history, culture, and ecology; Water Quality Laboratory, which allows analyses of stormwater runoff and health of the local estuarine system; and Institute for the Study of the Reconstruction Era, where researchers study local history, with an emphasis on the Reconstruction era, and run a summer institute to train K–12 teachers.[23]

In 2016, Coastal Carolina University, in Conway, South Carolina, established the Charles W. Joyner Institute for Gullah and African Diaspora Studies. Named in honor of the groundbreaking historian and anthropologist, the Institute is "dedicated to a critical understanding of the experiences of Gullah Geechee people and other descendants within the global African diaspora."[24] As the first interdisciplinary institute dedicated to a critical study of the experiences of the Gullah Geechee people and other descendants within the global African diaspora, it has been at the forefront of scholarship through its annual International Gullah Geechee and African Diaspora Conference, which brings together national and international scholars and community practitioners in serious discussions, performances, roundtables, and its many community-based initiatives.

In partnership with Coastal Carolina University's Athenaeum Press, under the leadership of Alli Crandell, the Institute produced several student-based grant projects focused on the cultural preservation of Gullah culture. In 2014, *Gullah: The Voice of an Island* captured the singing of four elderly singers on St. Helena Island, who continue a song tradition dating back to the nineteenth century. These singers received the Jean Laney Folk Heritage Award for South Carolina, the state's highest honor for a folk artist, and continue to educate audiences about the central role of Gullah music in America. And in 2017, the Institute and Athenaeum Press collaborated on the Sandy Island project *At Low Tide: The Voices of Sandy Island*, which consists of a virtual reality documentary and book offering a glimpse into this community, whose self-sufficiency and self-governance bolster it against its uncertain future.

This project resulted in two larger, grant-funded projects: The Sandy Island Cultural Initiative (National Park Service) and the Gullah Geechee Digital Project (National Archives, Gaylord Donnelley, Horry County Higher Education Commission). Crandell states, "The Sandy Island Cultural Initiative is working on documenting and preserving the Sandy Island school house while The Gullah Geechee Digital Project is a collaboration between the South Carolina Historical Society, the American Folklife Institute at the Library of Congress, and the Association for Cultural Equity to digitize thousands of photographs, interviews and historical records."[25]

In 2021, Georgia Southern University established the Gullah Geechee Cultural Heritage Center to increase awareness about the Gullah Geechee culture and to celebrate it while allowing a space for the Gullah Geechee community to come together and problem solve. The origins of the Center stem from director Maxine Bryant's growing interest in Gullah Geechee culture after local tours with Georgia Southern professor and cultural historian Amir Jamal Touré, J.D., who is also the resident scholar for Geechee Kunda Cultural Center and Museum in Riceboro, Georgia. These scholars were concerned that few within the Gullah community could still speak the language and that the stories of the elders would be lost. When asked to become director, Bryant enlisted the aid of Touré, and together they helm the Center with assistance from a nine-person advisory council that includes master storyteller and Gullah Geechee advocate Pat Gunn, as well as various university members.

The Center hosts monthly community meetings to allow the Gullah Geechee community to discuss pertinent topics such as land inheritance and preservation of public space considered sacred ground by the Gullah Geechee. Bryant is also excited about new oral history projects that will capture rich cultural memories from local Gullah Geechee community elders. Carl L. Reiber, Ph.D., Georgia Southern's provost and vice president for academic affairs is confident that Bryant's "expertise, enthusiasm, and strong community connections will be tremendous assets as she establishes the Center and Georgia Southern University as leaders in the preservation, education, and promotion of Gullah Geechee culture and heritage."[26]

CHAPTER ELEVEN

MUSIC, SONG, AND DANCE

"Music, which arrived in the New World with the [enslaved] Africans, survived with them the trauma of exile, forced labor, and alienation," states musicologist Dena Epstein. "Wherever the Africans were taken, the music went with them, merging to a degree with the white man's culture, but never losing its distinctive qualities. How it was modified by its new surroundings and how it modifies the music of the whites is a fascinating aspect of music in the Americas."[1] As the Gullah culture emerged, there were two areas that most fascinated white observers: language and music. As mentioned in chapter 7, visitors to the Sea Islands during the nineteenth century commented on the strange patois of the Gullah's speech and tried, often in vain, to transcribe this Creole language into standard English. At this same time, white missionaries, who worked in this region, published numerous song collections and articles containing the islanders' music, usually referred to as "slave songs." Later these "slave songs" would be known as Negro spirituals.

Gullah Geechee Song Collections

The Gullah Geechee people contributed the earliest and most studied body of Negro spirituals in America, but few are aware that songs such as "Nobody Knows de Trouble I've Seen," "Roll Jordon Roll," "Down by the Riverside," "Come by Here," and thousands of others emanated from the Sea Islands region. Willis Laurence James, folklorist at Spelman College for three decades, convincingly argued, in the 1960s, that more spirituals were written in the Sea Islands than in any other part of the country, reflecting the "tremendous creative forces active in the so-called Gullah country."[2] As Epstein suggests, aspects of the West and Central African musical culture assimilated the surroundings of the southern plantation, the white planter's church, and especially the camp meetings during the Great Awakening, but the characteristic rhythmic complexity, improvisation, blues notes, and call and response never lost its hold on enslaved Africans.

The starting point for serious study of Negro spirituals is the landmark collection *Slave Songs of the United States*, published in 1867 by white missionaries William Allen, Charles Ware, and Lucy McKim Garrison from their experiences on St. Helena Island. Another major contributor to this collection was Thomas Wentworth Higginson, a white abolitionist who was a colonel in the First South Carolina Volunteers, the first regiment of African Americans to be formed in the Union Army. Writing an article in June 1867 for the *Atlantic Monthly*, he described his experiences one night while returning on horseback to his army camp. He heard groups of freedmen "chanting, often harshly, but always in the most perfect time." He was so impressed that, when he reached his tent, he wrote down the words to thirty-seven songs and later shared them with Allen, Ware, and Garrison.[3] The *Slave Songs* collection is of vital importance because it sheds light on the melodies and musical performances of seventy-seven St. Helena spirituals, gives a critical analysis of the Gullah language, and provides a lengthy discussion of the uses of songs for work (agricultural, rowing) and religious services (shouting, baptism, seekin', the Lord's supper).

OVERLEAF: A typical group of native Sea Island musicians at the end of the nineteenth century. *From the John Bennett papers (#1176.00) at the South Carolina Historical Society.*

The demand for boats to transport people and goods to and from island communities in the Sea Islands region resulted in the unique genre known as rowing songs. During trips that could last several days, a song leader, called a patroon, would lead crews of "stout" Black men in the singing of spirituals to synchronize their rowing strokes and entertain white passengers. As part of their forced labor, these men had to perform upbeat, happy songs regardless of unfavorable conditions such as bad weather, a heavy load, or in some cases a disagreeable passenger. Bartholomew Carroll, a Charlestonian editor, describes a boat ride to Edisto Island in 1842 involving a rather drunk passenger, his uncle Ralph. Once the passengers and their belongings are onboard, "each oarsman takes his place, releases himself of his jacket, and seems to wonder in his mind, if uncle Ralph goes on drinking, whether his cheeks will not surpass in color said oarsmen's red flannel shirt. . . . " "Big-Mouth Joe," the leading oarsman, announces his departure from the city with a song in whose chorus everyone joins.

> Now we gwine leab Charlestown city,
>
> Pull boys, pull!
> The gals we leab it is a pity,
> Pull boys, pull!
> Mass Ralph 'e take a big strong toddy,
> Pull boys, pull!
> Mass Ralph 'e aint gwine let us noddy,
> Pull boys, pull[4]

The most well-known rowing song is the popular "Michael, Row the Boat Ashore," which was a number one hit in 1960 by the Highwaymen after Tony Saletan discovered a copy of *Slave Songs* in the Widener Library at Harvard University. Later, this spiritual became a freedom song during the civil rights movement with the new verses "Mississippi next to go, Alleluia" and "Christian brothers don't be slow, Alleluia."

Throughout the Corridor there is a small repertoire of Gullah songs performed exclusively for Communion or the Lord's Supper, the most important religious service in most churches. The monthly observance of Communion, usually on the first Sunday, has ensured that century-old spirituals like "De Blood Done Sign My Name," "Let Us Break Bread Togeda," and "Drinkin' ob de Wine" are still being sung. A Gullah text version of "Drinkin' ob de Wine":

> Drinkin' ob de wine, wine, wine
> Drinkin' ob de wine, oh yea my Lawd
> Ought duh been dere ten tousan yeah
> Drinkin' ob de wine[5]

Other major song collections derived from St. Helena Island include *Thirty-Six South Carolina Spirituals* (Carl Diton), *Saint Helena Island Spirituals* (Nicholas Ballanta-Taylor), *The Carolina Low Country* (Society for the Preservation of Spirituals), *Folk Culture on St. Helena Island* (Guy Johnson), and *The Religious Life of South Carolina Coastal and Sea Island Negroes* (Samuel Lawton).

In the 1940s, Lydia Parrish published sixty songs from St. Simons Island in the collection *Slave Songs of the Georgia Sea Islands*. Parrish discusses specific uses of each spiritual among the island's residents and presents songs like "I Wok Om A-Mona," also known as the "Mende Song," with remarkable retentions of original West African texts. As mentioned in chapter 1, Joe Opala and Cynthia Schmidt traced this song to a village in Sierra Leone in the 1990s. Their journey of discovery was captured in the documentary *The Language You Cry In*. Yet there was another song Parrish transcribed titled "Rockah Mh Moomba" that also contained many West African words. James Rogers, born in Liberty County, Georgia, learned this song from Dublin Scribben, a formerly enslaved person who could still "talk de ole African talk," and sang it for Parrish. According to Rogers, "When de ole man Dublin and his daughter Bessie get togedder she shouted; when she say 'quank' de ole woman jump way over, and den de ole man jump, and den turn back again. Do de same t'ing ober, ebery time":

> Rockah mh moomba
> Cum bo-ba yonda
> Lil-aye tambe
> I rocka mh mooba
> (Cum) bo-ba yonda
> Lil-aye tambe
> Ashawilligo homasha banga
> L'ashawilligo homasha quank!
> Ashawilligo homasha banga
> L'ashawilligo homasha quank![6]

Parrish's concern for the survival of the St. Simons song tradition led her to organize the Spiritual Singers Society of Coastal Georgia, later renamed the Georgia Sea Island Singers by Bessie Jones.

Another important source of Gullah spirituals is Guy and Candie Carawan's song collection *Ain't You Got a Right to the Tree of Life? The People
of Johns Island, South Carolina—Their Faces, Their Words, and Their Song.*
Originally published in 1964 at the height of the civil rights movement, these
songs reveal the immense West African musical elements in the John Islanders' music as well as this community's aspirations for a better quality of life.
Septima Clark, Esau Jenkins, and Bernice Robinson held Citizenship School
classes to help the island's residents pass the literacy requirements for voting
registration, and they used the powerful words in their spirituals to reinforce
reading and further motivate the adult learners. Guy Carawan recalls a poignant moment when an elderly woman at class one night said, "We had been
swallerin' bitter pills and chewing dry bones for a long time. Then the local
preacher, who had just had a cross burned in his front yard the night before
for organizing the class, said, Yes, and it's made us tough. I can remember the
days when they'd only feed us cornbread and sweet potatoes and still we'd
plow the hell out of their mules. That's why today we can take anything, them
burning crosses in our yards and knocking on our doors late at night." Carawan says, "It is a touching sight to see some of these old people with hands
roughened and calloused from a lifetime of plowing and swinging axes and
picks, struggling to hold a pencil steady and slowly laboring to write their
a-b-c's."[7] Carawan's initial role was to use the community's music to assist in
the adult instruction, but he realized even greater value beyond the island's
shores when Gullah spirituals like "Keep Your Eyes on the Prize" became key
nonviolent songs in the fight for equal access to healthcare, education, and
jobs in the South.

> Paul and Silas, bound in jail,
> Had no money for to go their bail,
> Keep your eyes on the prize, hold on, hold on.
> Hold on, Hold on,
> Keep your eyes on the prize, hold on, hold on.[8]

For nearly a century, Gullah Geechee songs that had previously been passed
along only from mouth to mouth and ear to ear became recorded on paper
and later in print. It was evident that "white folk" were increasingly interested
in African American music in the Sea Islands region. However, lost in translation were the complex clapping patterns, groans, and falsetto moans, thud
of the feet, and melodic improvisation in Black music—impossible to write
down.

Gullah Legacy of Musical Instruments

Among the enslaved Africans forcibly brought to the New World were professional musicians, singers, and instrumentalists, known as griots. From his travels to West Africa in 1834, John Howison made observations about these musicians:

> They have professional and itinerant musicians called Guiriots.... Their musical instruments are drums, flutes, and horns, and a kind of rude guitar. These people hire themselves by the day and month to anyone that is disposed to entertain them, and their business is to accompany him wherever he goes, and to sing his praises and proclaim his virtues.[9]

These guiriots, the French word for griots, traditionally performed on African lutes in their homeland, but as enslaved people on southern plantations, they constructed similar instruments called banjars made out of a dried calabash gourd covered with a swatch of sheep or goat skin and with strings made out of animal gut—the forerunner of the modern-day banjo. "This symbol of Appalachia is heard around the world, but Africans brought the banjar with them to America," states scholar Cecilia Conway. "The banjo that developed from it eventually helped create the sounds used in American minstrel, ragtime, blues, jazz, old-time, country, bluegrass, and other musical styles. The banjo retained the short drone African thumb string of the banjar but replaced the gourd body with a cheese-box (or sometimes inset-rim) wooden sound chamber."[10]

An image of the banjar being played in Charleston, South Carolina, is captured in the popular painting *The Old Plantation*, attributed to John Rose, an owner of a plantation in Beaufort County, South Carolina. Rose presents a rare city scene involving the playing of the banjar, which was thought exclusive to the more rural settings of a plantation. According to historian Nic Butler, this banjar performer may have been a patroon (boatmen song leader) who, "after docking at the crowded capital and unloading his owner's cargo . . . , might have found a spot near the wharves to serenade his neighbors and perhaps kick up the dust."[11]

The availability of an enslaved fiddler for dances was a necessity for white plantation owners, and rare was the plantation without one. A formerly enslaved musician remembers: "I was a good fiddler, used to be a fiddler for the white girls to dance. Just picked it up, it was a natural gift. I could still play if I had a fiddle.... Played all those old-time songs ... 'Soldier's Joy,' 'Jimmy Long Josey,' 'Arkansas Traveler,' and 'Black-eyed Susie.'" This unknown fiddler also provides a vivid account of Old John Dayton, a famed fiddler who played for all of the major dances on the plantation. "Yes sir, that man could play. When he saw down on the fiddle and pull out that tune, 'Oh, the Monkey Marry to the Baboon Sister,' he make a parson dance."[12] An Englishman traveling from Augusta, Georgia, to Charleston, South Carolina, references an enslaved fiddler he encountered while lodging at a home overnight. "In the evening a Black fiddler amused us for a while, and I danced four reels in company with the girls and their brother. The country people of Georgia and Carolina are alike fond of the violin and the dance."[13]

Enslaved Africans knew that if they could play a violin well enough, their lives would be easier. Solomon Northup, a kidnapped freedman from the North, states, "Alas! had it not been for my beloved violin, I scarcely can conceive how I could have endured the long years of bondage. It introduced me to great houses—relieved me of many days' labor in the field—supplied me with conveniences for my cabin—with pipes and tobacco, and extra pairs of shoes."[14]

By all accounts, Gullahs were without peer in their ability to create highly complex musical accompaniments and communicative codes with drums. In fact, the state of South Carolina banned drums following the Stono Rebellion in 1730, in which enslaved Africans seized a store containing firearms and marched off on a trail of destruction with two drums and banners flying. Having reached more than sixty in number, they paused at a large field and "set to dancing, singing, and beating drums to draw more Negroes to them."[15] Now known as "telegraphic drumming," whites realized the threat of the Gullahs' advanced communication system and passed South Carolina's Slave Act of 1740, banning "drums, horns, or other loud instruments, which may call together, or give sign or notice to one another of their wicked designs or purposes."

The Slave Act, however, may have been only enforced within city limits, leaving Gullahs in the more rural areas free to continue their drumming tradition. In 1805, a visitor to a plantation in Georgetown, South Carolina, cites a serenade by enslaved Black people playing "violins and drums" during a Christmas celebration.[16] There were apparently fewer restrictions in Georgia as evidenced by the Works Progress Administration's Writer's Program interview of a Gullah drum maker near Savannah in the 1930s:

In Brownville we found a man who knew how to make the old-time drums. He made one for us out of a hollow log, across the end of which he tightly stretched a goat skin. He fastened the skin to the log by means of a number of wooden pegs. Unlike modern drums, this one was taller than it was wide, measuring about eighteen inches in length and ten inches in diameter. The drum maker, James Collier, a middle-aged, intelligent, well-educated Negro, said he had made a number of drums in this primitive manner. Collier told us that he had heard of drums having been used during funeral ceremonies in former years. The mourners beat the drum while on the way to the cemetery; after arriving they marched around the grave in a ring and beat the drum and shouted. "They call it the dead march," explained the man.[17]

Gullah Geechee Songs on the Concert Stage

Shortly after the Civil War, religious organizations, northern white philanthropists, and the Freedmen's Bureau began establishing institutions of higher learning in the South for newly freed Black people. Among these were Atlanta University (now Clark Atlanta University), Brown Theological Institute (now Edward Waters College), Claflin University, the Fisk Freed Colored School (now Fisk University), and Hampton Normal and Agricultural Institute (now Hampton University). Despite early financial support, these institutions often lacked the necessary funds to afford new buildings, educational materials, and, at times, teacher salaries, but Fisk and Hampton were the earliest schools to realize that concert tours featuring Europeanized versions of the Negro spiritual could provide the financial security they so desperately needed.

On October 6, 1871, the Fisk Jubilee Singers, under the direction of George White, began their historic first tour with nine singers, which included two quartets and Ella Sheppard alternating between singing soprano and playing piano. Since most of these singers were formerly enslaved persons, the term *jubilee* was most appropriate. The naming of jubilee was based on Leviticus 25:10: "And ye shall hallow the fiftieth year, and proclaim liberty throughout all the land unto all the inhabitants thereof: it shall be a jubilee unto you." At first, the Jubilee Singers sang ballads and patriotic anthems, but George White, hoping for more of an impact on white audiences, eventually featured a program mostly consisting of spirituals. When he did so, it was reported that the music was not only well received but "often moved audiences to tears."

Between 1871 and 1873, the Jubilee Singers toured most of the northern states and made an appearance at the White House, and their European tour featured a performance for Queen Victoria and Prime Minister William Gladstone. The funds from their many tours greatly assisted the struggling school and paid for the construction of the first permanent building at Fisk, Jubilee Hall.

Among the nine original members of the Fisk Jubilee Singers was Benjamin Holmes, a tenor who grew up in and around Charleston, South Carolina. These Gullah Geechee roots may point to Homes as a source for four songs from the *Slave Songs* collection—"Roll, Jordan Roll," "Many Thousand Go," "Nobody Knows the Trouble I've Had," and "Lay This Body Down (I'm Traveling to the Grave)"—included in the Fisk Jubilee's 1872 song collection titled *Jubilee Songs: As Sung by the Jubilee Singers of Fisk University*. E. M. Cravath, field secretary of the American Missionary Association, which helped found Fisk, admits that many of the singers learned these songs "in childhood," but Cravath also describes how the school altered the students' performance of these spirituals:

> By the severe discipline to which the Jubilee Singers have been subjected in the school-room, they have been educated out of the peculiarities of the Negro dialect, and they do not attempt to imitate the peculiar pronunciation of their race.... They do not attempt to imitate the grotesque bodily motions or the drawling intonations that often characterize the singing of great congregations of the colored people in their excited religious meetings.[18]

This purging away of the more distinctive African aspects of Black music gained the approval of white audiences who celebrated African American music on the concert stage for the first time. Such a blueprint for success was quickly followed by the Fisk Jubilee Singers' great rival, the Hampton Singers.

Under the leadership of choir director Thomas Fenner, and later R. Nathaniel Dett, the Hampton Singers, numbering seventeen, took extensive fundraising concert tours from 1873–1875, contributing greatly to Hampton's endowment, the construction of Virginia Hall on its campus, and the dissemination of an impressive number of Gullah Geechee songs. To meet the demands of his concert tours, Thomas Fenner, who helped to establish the New England Conservatory of Music, arranged fifty Negro spirituals in 1874 in a collection titled *Cabin and Plantation Songs as Sung by the Hampton Students*.

Fenner, in comparison to George White, was more conscious of doing "justice to the music" of the enslaved Africans and avoided alterations that might destroy the songs' "original characteristics."[19] He consulted the *Slave Songs* collection and arranged choral versions of the Gullah songs "Nobody Knows the Trouble I've Had," "Go in the Wilderness," "Praise Member," "The Golden Altar," and "King Emanuel." In fact, he copied verbatim the citation given in *Slave Songs* of the performance of "Nobody Knows the Trouble I've Had" in Charleston. The only major difference between the two versions is Fenner's change to the opening two notes from an ascending perfect fourth interval ("Here Comes the Bride") to its now signature descending major sixth interval.

> Oh, nobody knows de trouble I've seen,
> Nobody knows but Jesus,
> Nobody knows de trouble I've seen.
> Glory Hallelujah!
> Sometimes I'm up, sometimes I'm down;
> Oh, yes, Lord;
> Sometimes I'm almost to de groun',
> Oh, yes, Lord.
> Although you see me goin' 'long so
> Oh, yes, Lord;
> I have my trials here below,
> Oh, yes, Lord.[20]

As a result of the success of Fisk and Hampton, "other struggling Negro colleges were inspired to send out spiritual-singing fundraisers," says Eileen Southern in her seminal work *The Music of Black Americans*, "and a tradition was established that lasted through the twentieth century. Perhaps equally important, a large part of the Western world was introduced to the folksongs of Black America."[21] These folksongs, many of which were from the Sea Islands, were disseminated into far-flung lands. In the end, few places in the world had not heard of the Negro spiritual.

More St. Helena Island songs made it northward when Hampton Institute teacher Natalie Curtis Burlin traveled to the island during World War I and brought back the Gullah spirituals "Ride On, Jedus" and "God's A-Gwineter Move All de Troubles Away." These songs eventually became patriotic songs with new words especially designed for the war effort. The original chorus and first verse of "Ride On, Jedus" contains these lyrics:

O ride on Jedus, ride on Jedus,
Ride on conquerin' King
I want t' go t' hebben in de mornin'
Ef you see my mother, O yes
Jis tell her for me, O yes
For t' meet me t' morrow in Galilee
Want t' go t' hebben in de mornin'.[22]

To raise support for World War I, Burlin retitled "Ride on Jesus" as "Hymn of Freedom" with these new words:

O march on, Freedom, march on Freedom
March on, conquering hosts
Liberty is calling
To martyred Belgium, Freedom!
To wounded France, Freedom!
Tis God who summons our advance!
Liberty is calling![23]

As choral groups, song leaders, and soldiers sang the "Hymn of Freedom," they probably never knew of this song's Gullah Geechee roots. Similar to the laudable efforts of Fisk and Hampton, the musical contributions of the Sea Islands regions were overlooked and eventually forgotten.

Early Black Arrangers of Gullah Spirituals

Following the work of George White and Thomas Fenner, there was a core group of Black composers who were the first to truly assimilate the unique African elements of the Negro spiritual into a body of composed music. Eileen Southern states, "Unlike the White composers of so-called Negro music who proceeded and followed them, these men did not have to understand first the 'exotic' music before employing it in their composition; to them this music was not exotic but natural."[24] Among composers of note were Harry Burleigh, John Rosamond Johnson, James Weldon Johnson, Hall Johnson, Edward Boatner, and William Levi Dawson, who developed an extensive repertoire of Gullah-infused compositions, many of which are still popular today.

Harry Thacker Burleigh (1866–1949) grew up hearing spirituals from his grandfather, a formerly enslaved man who had been blinded by a savage beating before escaping to the North. He was a graduate of the National Conservatory of Music, under the direction of the Czech composer Antonin Dvořák, who was fascinated with Burleigh's knowledge and singing of Negro spirituals. Dvořák proclaimed these songs of the enslaved to be "the real foundation of any serious and original school of composition to be developed in the United States."[25] The second movement of Dvořák's Symphony No. 9 entitled "Largo" is believed to be based on a Negro spiritual melody.

Among Burleigh's most recognized works are his solo arrangements of Negro spirituals that were performed by such musical luminaries as Roland Hayes, Marian Anderson, and Paul Robeson and nearly every African American classical singer ever since. Burleigh's most popular solo pieces include "Deep River," "Steal Away to Jesus," and "Sometimes I Feel Like a Motherless Child," and the Gullah Geechee spirituals "Ain't Goin' to Study War No Mo' (Down by the Riverside)," "Nobody Knows de Trouble I've Seen," "I Got a Home in A-Dat Rock," "Go Down in the Lonesome Valley," and "Ev'ry Time I Feel the Spirit." Through all these songs there breathes a hope, says Burleigh, "a faith in the ultimate justice and brotherhood of man. The cadences of sorrow invariably turn to joy, and the message is ever manifest that eventually deliverance from all that hinders and oppresses the soul will come, and man—every man—will be free."[26] During his career, Burleigh performed internationally before thousands of people from many cultures, including King Edward VII and President Theodore Roosevelt.

John Rosamond Johnson (1873–1954) was born in Jacksonville, Florida, and began playing the piano at the age of four. He studied at the New England Conservatory of Music and later with the Black composer Samuel Coleridge-Taylor in London. Many of J. Rosamond Johnson's best-known works were written along with his brother James Weldon Johnson, such as "Lift Every Voice and Sing," often referred to as the "Black National Anthem." This song's words tell of the struggles of African Americans following Reconstruction. The Johnson brothers further collaborated with Lawrence Brown (1893–1972), composer, pianist, and tenor, on two volumes of *The Book of American Negro Spirituals*. Among the Gullah songs in these collections are "Roll Jordon, Roll," "I Couldn't Hear Nobody Pray," "I Got a Home In-A-Dat Rock," "I Done Done What Ya' Tol' Me to Do," "Ev'ry Time I Feel de Spirit," and "Too Late," a ring shout song.

James Weldon Johnson (1871–1938), writer and civil rights leader, provided many of the texts for the spirituals in *The Book of American Negro Spirituals* and wrote the collection's thought-provoking preface. In it, he connects the rhythms, dance (ring shout), and the call and response singing style of the enslaved Black people to Africa and cites *Slave Songs of the United States* as well as Thomas Higginson, but he fails to recognize any African influences in the Gullah language.

> Something should be said to give a general idea about the "language" in which these songs were written. Negro dialect in America is the result of the effort of the [enslaved] to establish a medium of communication between himself and his [owner]. This he did by dropping his original language and formulating a phonologically and grammatically simplified English; that is, an English in which the harsh and difficult sounds were elided, and the secondary moods and tenses were eliminated . . . , so the original African languages became absolutely lost.

> The dialect spoken in the Sea Islands off the coast of Georgia and South Carolina remains closer to African form than the dialect of any other section, and still contains some African words. It is, at any rate, farther from English than the speech of American Negroes anywhere else. But it is remarkable how few words of known African origin there are in the Negro dialect generally spoken throughout the United States.[27]

Johnson expressed the views of many Black and white people who understood Gullah Geechee to be simply a corruption of standard English. Had he lived longer, Johnson would have learned of the work done by Lorenzo Dow Turner and discovered the West and Central African linguistic base of Gullah. Surprisingly, Johnson is quick to recognize the enslaved persons living in Louisiana who created a "distinct language." "This language is known as Creole. Creole is an Africanized French, but it is neither African nor French. It is a language in itself."[28]

Hall Johnson (1888–1970) was born in Athens, Georgia, and as a boy, he taught himself how to play the violin after hearing a violin recital by Joseph Henry Douglass, grandson of noted Black leader Frederick Douglass. He was also influenced by his grandmother, who often sang spirituals to him. He earned a degree at Allen University in Columbia, South Carolina, and received further training at Atlanta University, the Juilliard School, Hahn School of Music, and the University of Pennsylvania. Johnson was acclaimed along with Harry Burleigh as "one of the two American composers who elevated the African American spiritual to an art form, comparable in its musical sophistication to the compositions of European Classical composers."[29]

Johnson's most popular works are his choral and solo arrangements of Negro spirituals that often contain a more authentic representation of the Gullah language than his contemporaries. Some of the Gullah songs he arranged are "In Bright Mansions Above," "Give Me Jesus," and "Roll, Jerd'n, Roll." Johnson formed the Hall Johnson Choir, which made many sound recordings, and took extensive tours, including a trip to Berlin, Germany, in 1951, representing the United States at the International Festival of Fine Arts.

Edward Boatner traveled with his father, an itinerant minister, when he was a young boy, and thus at an early age, he came into contact with rural church choirs and the old hymns. He studied at Western University and Boston Conservatory and received his degree in music at Chicago Music College. At this point, Boatner began his career as a concert singer and was for a time associated with Nathaniel Dett, who encouraged him and assisted him in his work. He sang leading roles with the National Negro Opera Company and served as the director of music for the National Baptist Convention for six years, as well as directing community and church choirs. Whenever he had time, he arranged music, and eventually he became known as an accomplished composer. His best-known arrangements are "O What a Beautiful City," "Trampling," "I Want Jesus to Walk with Me," which was composed for Marian Anderson, and the Gullah spirituals "Let Us Break Bread Together" and "Soon I Will Be Done." He also composed many other works of music, including *Freedom Suite*, for chorus, narrator, and orchestra; *The Man from Nazareth*, a spiritual musical; and *Julius Sees Her*, a musical comedy.

William Levy Dawson (1899–1990), composer, choir director, and teacher, was credited with developing the Tuskegee Institute Choir into an internationally renowned choir, known for their performance of Negro spirituals. Dawson entered Tuskegee Institute at age thirteen, graduating in 1921, and later he received a music degree at the Horner Institute of Fine Arts and a master's degree at the American Conservatory of Music. Dawson's best-known works are his choral arrangements of the Gullah Geechee songs "Soon Ah Will Be Done," "Mary Had A Baby," and "Ev'ry Time I Feel the Spirit," and his *Negro Folk Symphony*, which received international recognition in 1934 under the direction of Leopold Stokowski, director of the Philadelphia Orchestra. The symphony's three movements are "The Bond of Africa," "Hope in the Night," and "O Let Me Shine." Although a reviewer praised his work for its "imagination, warmth, drama, and sumptuous orchestration," Dawson, not completely satisfied with his work, flew to West Africa in 1952, where he revised his symphony, infusing it with the spirit of the native music he listened to intently during his visit.[30]

Sing Hallelujah!

One of the most popular Gullah Geechee performing groups is the Hallelujah Singers, who embody the Gullah culture in every way—song, word, manner, and dress. This ensemble was formed by Dr. Marlena Smalls, herself of Gullah lineage, in 1990, in the historic town of Beaufort, South Carolina, where this African American culture is alive and strong. Speaking about the mission of the Hallelujah Singers, Smalls says, "This Gullah thing is really an African thing, so it gives us a truer picture of who we are, and I [want] to connect with others that we are more alike than we are different."[31]

The group combines singing with storytelling, helping to explain in a uniquely historic and personable manner who the Gullah are, where they originated, and what influence they have on today's culture. "Before we learned about this culture," explains Smalls, "the African was just a former slave. But understanding Gullah is the key to humanizing our race and showing that our ancestors came to this country with their own history, rituals, and customs." The Hallelujah Singers are known for the inventive ways in which they interweave music with narration, present miniature dramatizations of many of the unique personages, rituals, and ceremonies that have played a vital role in shaping their culture, and stimulate their audiences to become participants rather than just listeners. They have three professional recordings: *Gullah: Songs of Hope, Faith, and Freedom* (1997), *Joy: A Gullah Christmas* (1998), and *Gullah: Carry Me Home* (1999).

Dr. Marlena Smalls and the Hallelujah Singers have earned much acclaim, many awards, including the Jean Laney Harris Folk Heritage Award for South Carolina, and have performed around the country and abroad. In addition, they have made appearances on the television shows *Good Morning America*, the *Today* show, the *Crook & Chase* show, and in the award-winning film *Forrest Gump*, with Smalls playing the part of Bubba's mama. As part of its bicentennial celebration, the Library of Congress designated the Hallelujah Singers a "Local Legacy of South Carolina."

The Georgia Sea Island Singers continue to preserve the Gullah culture and traditions after nearly a century of singing and touring the world, including performances at the Olympic Games in Mexico and Lillehammer, Norway.

As previously mentioned, Lydia Parrish and later Bessie Jones were important early influences on the singers' song repertoire and their unique song making that draws upon the rich reservoir of African American culture on St. Simons Island, Georgia. The Georgia Sea Island Singers have performed for college students, civil rights workshops, folk festivals, and museums, as well as on radio and television shows and before world leaders.

Frankie Sullivan Quimby, the leader of the group, was born and raised on the Georgia Sea Islands in a family able to trace its roots squarely back to Africa, to the Foulah tribe, which came from the town of Kianhah in the District of Temourah in the Kingdom of Massina on the Niger River. The oldest of thirteen children, she is descended from enslaved Africans on the Hopeton and Altama Plantations in Glynn County, Georgia. As she likes to say, "We are a strong people who know how to survive, and we want everyone to know where we came from."[32]

Frankie's late husband, Doug, was born in Baconton, Georgia, where his family members were sharecroppers who sometimes earned less than $10 in cash for a year's work, and he had been singing since the age of four. His grandfather spoke only Gullah, and to this day there are isolated pockets on small islands along the coast where Gullah Geechee is used more often than English. He began his professional career in 1963, joining the Sensational Friendly Stars, a well-known gospel group, and six years later he became a member of the Georgia Sea Island Singers. He was best known for his deep bass voice, especially when singing sea chanteys and call-and-response songs with the audience. One of his most powerful songs was "Freedom, Freedom over Me," which recounts the very tragic and moving story of Ebo Landing on St. Simons Island, where eighteen Geechee men chose death over enslavement.

The Sea Island Singers often conveyed the Gullah language to their audiences in several different ways: the rice dance, work songs of the Sea Islands, gospel music, call-and-response, hand clapping, sailors' chanteys, the "shout" (which originated in religious services in the pray's houses on the old plantations), and "body percussion," in which the human body (the "hambone") is used as a percussion instrument. As demonstrated most effectively by Doug, it was a memorable performance in which his hands, lightning quick, used his body as a "drum," producing an astonishing variety of sounds by beating on his thighs, chest, and other parts of his body. Customarily the performer chants, *"Hambone, hambone, where you been?"* Known also as the "Juba dance," this action is often performed by groups jiving together around in circles, clockwise and then counterclockwise, all in rhythm with stomping, patting the body, and slapping, and ending with a step called the "long dog scratch."

> *Hambone, hambone,*
> *Where you been?*
> *Round the corner*
> *An' back agin.*
> *Hambone, hambone,*
> *Where's your wife?*
> *In the kitchen*
> *Cookin rice!*

Ron and Natalie Daise are among the most talented Gullah singers, educators, storytellers, authors, artists, and actors in the world. Along with son Simeon and daughter Sara, they are truly the "First Family of Gullah." Their remarkable show *Gullah Gullah Island* was for many Americans their first time hearing the word "Gullah" and experiencing this unique culture. During an interview with the *Los Angeles Times* in 1996, Natalie explained the central aims of the show: "Daddy can get mad, . . . Mommy can get sick. We like showing the humanity of the parents. Of course, we do burst into song all the time, but we really do that at home, too. We're just sort of good guys on the show. Sometimes, because we're parents, we're firm good guys, but I think good parenting is being a good guy."[33] The popularity and excellence of *Gullah Gullah Island* resulted in the 1995 Parent's Choice Award and nominations for the NAACP Image Award, Daytime Emmy Award, and Writers Guild of America Award. In 1996, *TV Guide* named the show one of the "10 best children's shows" and during its original broadcast, it was Nickelodeon's highest-rated preschool show, averaging more than 750,000 viewers per episode. The show was so influential that visitors to the Sea Islands often ask for directions to Gullah Gullah Island.

Natalie, who was born in Rochester, New York, grew up in a house that was full of music. "My dad sang baritone, my mom contralto, my great-grandmother had a strong lead voice, and my two brothers and I filled in the spaces." She has done more than fill spaces as a singer and has drawn rave reviews for her one-woman show *Becoming Harriet Tubman*. "Through narrative and music, five real-life characters tell the story of how a seemingly insignificant little girl becomes an historical icon."[34] She has presented the show at the Piccolo Spoleto Festival in Charleston, South Carolina, the International Gullah Geechee and African Diaspora Conference in Conway, South Carolina, and the United Solo Theatre Festival in New York City.

Natalie's first love, however, may be painting. "Painting is crucial to my well-being. It is my primary means of expression, and the thing I do most consistently."[35] Her paintings include elements of African iconography, food items, colorful garb, abstract designs, gold and silver or copper leaf, and other elements that mimic a Byzantine style. She has been involved in many art shows, including the Slave Dwelling Conference Exhibit in North Charleston, the Group Show at the Beach Institute in Savannah, Georgia, and Feast Your Eyes: Celebrating the Food of the South at the Franklin G. Burroughs–Simeon B. Chapin Art Museum in Myrtle Beach, South Carolina.

Ron Daise is a fourth-generation Gullah, the youngest of nine children born in the Cedar Grove community of St. Helena Island, South Carolina. When he was growing up, however, he says that he and his family were not proud of their origins. But later that all changed as they learned more and more about their background and its significance. "I'm glad that my wife and I have been helpful in changing this outlook among other people of Gullah heritage," he says. "The songs, the stories, the speech, the crafts, the superstitions, and the dietary practices of the Gullah people have influenced the world culture." After earning a degree in mass media from Hampton University in Virginia, Daise returned to his home and became the first African American news reporter for the *Beaufort Gazette*. In this capacity, he spoke to many of the elders on the island, who provided him with a wealth of material he later incorporated into his book *Reminiscences of Sea Island Heritage*. Several books followed, in addition to new exciting projects like "Gullah Geechee Wisdom Cards Guidebook" a set of spirit cards produced by him and Natalie Daise, who served as illustrator. This product received the 2017 South Carolina African American Heritage Commission's Project Award. Ron's newest endeavor is *We Wear the Mask: Unraveled Truths in a Pre-Gullah Community* and *Turtle Dove Done Drooped His Wings: A Gullah Tale of Fight or Flight*, which are stories for adult and high school readers that celebrate contemporary Gullah Geechee culture.

Ron is currently Vice President for Creative Education at Brookgreen Gardens in Murrells Inlet, South Carolina, where his accomplishments, in part, have garnered him the 2019 South Carolina Governor's Distinctive Achievement Award. In this capacity, he has developed and implemented participatory interpretive tours, presentations, exhibits, and events at Brookgreen Gardens that promote cultural heritage, positioning it as an interpretive center for Gullah Geechee heritage for its three hundred thousand annual guests. Through his curation, the Gullah Geechee Gaardin exhibit at Brookgreen Gardens showcases a unique, multisensory, permanent exhibit highlighting the place of Gullah Geechee people in the history of Americana.

Ron's awards are many and include induction into the 2013 Penn Center 1862 Circle and the 2008 South Carolina African American Heritage Commission's Lifetime Achievement Award. He and Natalie received the 2019 Foundation for Leadership Education Lifetime Achievement Award and the 1996 South Carolina Order of the Palmetto, the state's highest honor. Ron is a past chairman and charter member of the Gullah Geechee Cultural Heritage Corridor Commission, is a charter member of the Sea Island Translation Team and Literacy Project, and presented at the United Nations for the 2016 International Day of Remembrance observance for victims of the transatlantic slave trade.

Reflecting upon their career, Natalie says she's grateful for all they have accomplished and experienced.

For the most part, it has been a lot of fun. It's also been a challenge to live by our talents. We realize that many people never have that opportunity. When I was a little girl dreaming of what I would be when I grew up, it never occurred to me that I could tell stories for a living. Or that the things that made me unique (my imagination, love of music, passion for words) would create and shape the life I would lead as an adult. Now I know that the very best thing that anyone can do, regardless of their age, is to be themselves to the best of their ability. If I can pass that on to my children, along with a deep trust in God, it will be my greatest accomplishment.

"SWING LOW, SWEET CHARIOT"

English Version

Swing low, sweet chariot,
Coming for to carry me home.
Swing low, sweet chariot,
Coming for to carry me home.

I looked over Jordan, and what did I see,
Coming for to carry me home?
A band of angels coming after me,
Coming for to carry me home.

Swing low, sweet chariot,
Coming for to carry me home.
Swing low, sweet chariot,
Coming for to carry me home.

If you get there before I do,
Coming for to carry me home,
Tell all my friends I'm coming too,
Coming for to carry me home.

Swing low, sweet chariot,
Coming for to carry me home.
Swing low, sweet chariot,
Coming for to carry me home.

Gullah Version

When dat ar ole chariot comes,
I'm gwine to lebe you,
I'm boun' for de promised land,
Frien's, I'm gwine to lebe you.

I'm sorry, frien's, to lebe you,
Farewell! oh, farewell!
But I'll meet you in de mornin',
Farewell! oh, farewell!

I'll meet you in de mornin',
When you reach de promised land;
On de oder side of Jordan,
For I'm boun' for de promised land.

Note: This is a typical example of a call-and-response chant as practiced most often in churches, with the preacher singing one line and the congregation, in unison, responding with the next line. The response is often the same from verse to verse, as in the case of the top version: "Coming for to carry me home."

—CHAPTER TWELVE—

ROOTS

When historian Joseph Opala began to investigate Gullah origins in West Africa in the 1970s, very little was known about the subject. Since Lorenzo Turner's groundbreaking work in the 1940s, few scholars seemed interested in investigating a Gullah–Sierra Leone connection, but Opala found Emory Campbell, himself a Gullah and a respected leader, and the two of them brought worldwide attention to the survival of the West and Central African retentions among the enslaved people in the Sea Islands region. As discussed in chapter 1, they organized a visit, in 1988, of the president of Sierra Leone, the late Joseph Saidu Momoh, who was so overwhelmed by the similarities between Gullahs and Sierra Leoneans that he invited a Gullah delegation to his country. The 1989 Gullah Homecoming involving Joe Opala, Emory Campbell, Doug and Frankie Quimby, Cornelia Bailey, and so many other distinguished leaders was a historic moment of reconnection between the descendants of the Africans who were forcibly taken and those who stayed behind powerless to save their loved ones. The Gullahs had, in essence, found a home to call their own, and the Sierra Leoneans had found a family to call their own.

The 1997 Moran Family Homecoming and Priscilla's Homecoming in 2005 inspired even more interest in the Gullah–Sierra Leone connections from government officials, scholars, and the general public, who realized the immense historical importance in understanding the West and Central African influences on Black music, food, art, storytelling, language, and naming practices in America. During these trips, the Gullah visitors encountered Sierra Leoneans with common masculine names they knew from home such as Sorie, Tamba, and Sanie, and feminine names like Kadiatu, Fatimata, Hawa, and Isata. Lorenzo Turner recorded these very names in the Lowcountry sixty years earlier, and they now realized more clearly that they had come home, or at least to one of the principal homes where their ancestors originated. Meeting the Loko, Kono, Soso, and Kisi tribes in Sierra Leone, they understood the origins of other Gullah names that were used during their grandparents' time. The Gullah visitors also saw *shukublay* baskets made with the same coil technique as the sweetgrass baskets so typical of Gullah culture, and "country cloth" blankets made of long strips sewn together just like traditional Gullah strip quilts.

Joe Opala should certainly be recognized for the role he played in organizing the homecomings. The documentary films based on these events—*Family Across the Sea*, *The Language You Cry In*, and *Priscilla's Homecoming* (in preparation)—have been seen by countless people on both sides of the Atlantic and have helped restore family ties severed in the slave trade more than two centuries ago. Opala's subsequent study of the Black Seminoles proved equally important as he and other scholars identified Gullah communities far from the coastal regions of the Corridor.

Black Seminoles

Enslaved Africans escaped, as early as the late 1700s, from rice plantations in South Carolina and Georgia and formed their own freed settlements on

OVERLEAF: A large group of enslaved people standing in front of buildings on Smith's Plantation, Beaufort, South Carolina, circa 1862. *Library of Congress, LC-USZ62-67819.*

the Florida frontier. These Gullahs built thatched-roof houses surrounded by fields of corn and swamp rice, and they maintained friendly relations with the mixed populations of refugee Native American Indians. As a result of increased interaction and intermarriage between the two groups, they came to view themselves as parts of the same loosely organized tribe, in which Black members held important positions. According to Opala, the continued growth of this multiethnic group eventually led to conflicts with the Americans and inevitable war:

> In 1818, General Andrew Jackson led an American army into Florida to claim it for the United States, and war finally erupted. The Blacks and Indians fought side-by-side in a desperate struggle to stop the American advance, but they were defeated and driven south into the more remote wilderness of central and southern Florida. General Jackson (later President) referred to this First Seminole War as an "Indian and Negro War." In 1835, the Second Seminole War broke out, and this full-scale guerrilla war would last for six years and claim the lives of 1,500 American soldiers. The Black Seminoles waged the fiercest resistance because they feared that capture or surrender meant death or return to slavery—and they were more adept at living and fighting in the jungles than their Indian comrades.[1]

A key figure in the Second Seminole War was John Cavallo (also known as Gopher John and John Horse), who was born in 1812 from the union of the Seminole Chief Charles Cavallo and a Black woman near present-day Gainesville and Lake City, Florida. In May 1836, "one of the severest battles fought during the war" occurred close to Lake Thonotossa, says historian Anthony Dixon. "Most likely it is during this period that John Cavallo allied with Chief Alligator and Chief Osceola as they became the principal Seminole war chiefs in the regions surrounding Tampa Bay leading up to Alachua. John probably became the Black Seminole leader most active in efforts to unify the Black Seminoles and plantation slaves of the Florida Territory's western frontier."[2] His effectiveness prompted the American commander General Thomas Jesup to tell the War Department, that this was "a Negro and not an Indian war." When the army finally captured John Cavallo and the rest of the Black Seminoles, officers refused to return them to slavery—fearing that these seasoned warriors, accustomed to their freedom, would wreak havoc on the Southern plantations.[3]

Between 1830 and 1850, the U.S. Army forcibly displaced approximately sixty thousand American Indians of the Five Civilized Tribes from Southeastern United States to areas west of the Mississippi River, mainly in Oklahoma. This shameful event, known as the Trail of Tears, also involved thousands of the Indians' Black slaves and five hundred Black Seminoles who had fought alongside them in the Seminole Wars. Although promised freedom in Oklahoma by the army, Black Seminoles faced re-enslavement, forcing John Cavallo, now known as John Horse, to travel to Washington, D.C., to lobby federal officials for a treaty ensuring separate land for the Black Seminoles. However, Attorney General John Mason ruled that the Black Seminoles were "functionally fair game for slave raiders," and when John returned to Oklahoma, he found his sister's children had been taken and lost forever."[4] Seeing no other choice, John Horse and Chief Wildcat led their people across Texas and the Rio Grande River into Coahuila, Mexico, where they would be free.

Opala and other scholars have identified small pockets of Black Seminole communities still existing in parts of Mexico, Texas, Oklahoma, and even the West Indies.

> The "Black Indians" live on Andros Island in the Bahamas where their ancestors escaped from Florida after the First Seminole War. The "Seminole Freedmen," the largest group, live in rural Seminole County, Oklahoma, where they are still official members of the Seminole Indian Nation. The "Mascogos" dwell in the dusty desert town of Nacimiento in the state of Coahuila in Northern Mexico. And, finally, the "Scouts" live in Brackettville, Texas, outside the walls of the old fort where their grandfathers served in the U.S. Cavalry. These groups have lost almost all contact with one another, but they have all retained the memory of their ancestors' gallant fight for freedom in the Florida wilderness.[5]

In 2012, the U.S. National Park Service sponsored the Sixth Annual National Underground Railroad Conference that brought together many of the Black Seminole groups for the first time. A keynote speaker was actor Louis Gossett Jr., who himself is a Black Seminole. This conference explored how enslaved Africans relentlessly pursued their freedom into Spanish Florida, the Caribbean Islands, Indian Territory (Oklahoma), Texas, and Mexico, creating in the process new cultural identities in these regions. At the historic conference, the University of Florida conducted interviews of Black Seminoles, who could still remember the exploits of their forefathers and the importance of their mixed ancestry. Marie Veronica Warrior speaks about a legacy that was kept from her:

> When I read about John Horse and Colonel Bullis and all those folks back then, it's amazing to hear the facts of my [ancestors] who I had no idea about coming up in school. To hear this now and to be able to learn this and hear all that my dad has to give, to be able to share that with my kids, to carry that legacy on it's not just a blessing but it's an opportunity that could've gotten side tracked if somebody didn't take the time to document what they could for those of us following in their footsteps.... [We] have relatives in Nacimiento, Rositas, Aguas Calientes, just deeper into Mexico from my dad's side.... Even with my mom's side they're down around Rio Grande, Mexico.... When you see a lot of the Hispanics coming from those areas, quote unquote Hispanic, they're as dark as we are, kinky hair but speak no English. It's very likely that they're part of this migration of Seminoles into Mexico marrying the Hispanic women and they're probably an extension.[6]

Another Black Seminole, Matthew Griffin, discusses the importance of the southern version of the Underground Railroad.

> We talk about the Underground Railroad and certainly we draw a lot of attention to Harriet Tubman and other pioneers. Long before Blacks were escaping and going North, they were coming south to Florida. They came south to Florida to seek refuge from the oppression that they were being faced with on the plantations. Being here in Florida, they were able to basically, get a new start. When they joined up with the Seminole Indians here in Florida, the Seminoles took them in, welcomed them, you know, with open arms. Basically, the Seminoles adopted them into their tribe, and the Blacks and the Seminoles were helpful to each other in many different ways. So, basically, with the Underground Railroad, you see a system of people [who] are being oppressed and are trying to escape the situation that they're in at that current time and trying to go and find a better place. That's certainly the connection between the Seminoles and the Black Seminoles here in the state of Florida.[7]

In 2019, writer Wes Ferguson documented two Black Seminole sisters from San Antonio, Texas, who returned to the village of Nacimiento de los Negros in Coahuila, Mexico, for the Juneteenth celebration. The village name means

"Birth of Blacks," and Corina Harrington and Miriam Torralba were born and raised there until moving to Texas as small children. "We never knew Juneteenth," said Harrington. "The June 19 festival and reunion is known as el Día de los Negros, the Day of the Blacks." The journey of the two sisters back to Mexico is, in many ways, reminiscent of the path their ancestors, John Horse and Chief Wildcat, made 179 years earlier as they fled from Oklahoma.

> The morning before Juneteenth, Corina Harrington and her sister Miriam Torralba left San Antonio shortly after sunrise and headed south to Mexico, retracing a portion of the same route their African American ancestors followed in 1850 when they escaped slavery in the United States and fled to freedom south of the border. . . .
>
> Although few Black people remain in northern Mexico, the region was once home to thousands who escaped slavery in the United States. Mexico outlawed slavery in 1829, an underlying factor in Texas's declaration of independence seven years later. In 1836, there were an estimated 5,000 slaves in Texas, a number that ballooned by 1860 to 182,500—more than 30 percent of the state's population.[8]

At the 2019 el Día de los Negros celebration, children recited songs passed down from their Mascogo ancestors, who sang in an English dialect that survives only in the lyrics of slave-era spirituals. Several women wore the long, polka-dotted pioneer dresses they believe to be traditional, and the day ended with a village-wide "Dance of the Blacks." The discoveries of Gullah Geechee descendants in Texas, Oklahoma, Mexico, and the Caribbean islands show the immense reach of the Gullah Geechee culture that survived the transatlantic slave trade, the atrocities of slavery, the Seminole Wars, the Trail of Tears, and the even the lack of acknowledgment in history books.

Sierra Leone Next Step Tour

It has been more than thirty years since the first Gullah Homecoming, but the seeds planted from this historic trip continue to bear fruit on both sides of the Atlantic. This event exemplified the essence of Sankofa, a word from the Akan tribe in Ghana associated with the proverb "Se wo were fi na wosankofa a yenkyi" (It is not wrong to go back for that which you have forgotten). Another interpretation of Sankofa is "go back to the past and bring forward that which is useful." The second and third homecomings continued to build important bonds between Gullah descendants and their new extended Sierra Leone families and prompted increased interest from universities. In 2011, six years after Priscilla's Homecoming, Kenyon College began conducting field interviews on St. Helena Island and established a Gullah Digital Archive. Beginning in 2013, the University of Connecticut collaborated with the Georgia Historical Society and Penn Center on a series of summer workshops for K–12 teachers for their National Endowment of the Arts grant "Gullah Voice: Traditions and Transformations." But it was the 2019 International Gullah Geechee and African Diaspora Conference at Coastal Carolina University that generated interest in a fourth, more intentional journey back to Sierra Leone. One of the participants at the conference was Sierra Leonean Amadu Massally, who envisioned a homecoming unlike any other ever attempted.

Amadu Massally, who lives in Texas, organized a homecoming he titled the Sierra Leone–Gullah Connection Next Step Tour, which was the largest Gullah Geechee homecoming not only to Sierra Leone but Africa to date. Massally, founder and CEO of Fambul Tik, a United States–based Sierra Leonean organization whose name translates into "Family Tree," has guided experiences between the Gullah Geechee people and Sierra Leoneans since 2006. The large scope of the 2019 Next Step Tour is shown in Massally's post-trip report:

> Following a model based on slavery, resistance, and abolition, they started out with a visit to Bunce Island, a slave fortress in Sierra Leone that has some strong links to the United States, as it once existed to send enslaved Africans directly to plantations in South Carolina and decades later, Georgia. The second aspect of the historical tour showed resistance to the Trans-Atlantic Slave Trade and saw the guests visit Old Yagala in the northern and mountainous region of Sierra Leone, where Africans resisted the slave trade. The third aspect saw the participants visit Freetown, which was a depot for formerly enslaved people [who] were either taken to Freetown from the West or "recaptured" at sea and dropped off in Freetown.... The guests visited Senehun Ngola, a small village in Sierra Leone, the origin of a Mende song recorded in Harrisneck, Georgia, by Lorenzo Dow Turner in 1937. And the visit to Rogbonko Mathaka, the shuku blay (sweet grass basket) capital of Sierra Leone, brought a seventh generation Gullah-Geechee woman whose family has been sewing sweetgrass grass baskets for over 200 years. Those villagers who had never seen anyone work their trade from outside their village let alone from outside their country, were simply in awe.[9]

The Sierra Leone Next Step Tour lasted from December 27, 2019, to January 7, 2020, and brought together more than fifty Gullah Geechee scholars and leaders mainly from South Carolina and Georgia. The delegation included Ron, Natalie, Sara, and Simeon Daise, actors and performing artists; Victoria Smalls, executive director of the Gullah Geechee Cultural Heritage Corridor Commission; Veronica Gerald, professor emeritus, Coastal Carolina University; Anita Singleton Prather, storyteller; Nakia Wigfall, a seventh-generation basket maker; Wilson Moran, community leader and son of Mary Moran; Winston Relaford, community historian; and Cynthia Schmidt, the ethnomusicologist who traced the "Mende Song."

"When the plane landed, the tears just kept coming," says Singleton-Prather, "and I just couldn't get them to stop. You know you hear about a place. You dream about a place and have all kinds of imaginations about it, but when you get there you realize that's where your family started."[10] In one of the most poignant moments of the trip, Wigfall recalls, "We all came into the village, and they were playing instruments that they made from materials from their neighborhood like bamboo. They were dancing and of course putting me out front, making me feel like a queen, very special. When I came to Sierra Leone, I had a mission. I wanted to sit and make baskets with a basket maker. Sitting there with those basket makers brought back memories of when my cousins and my sisters would sit around making baskets and talking, telling jokes—having a good time."[11] As Wigfall interacted with the villagers at Rogbonko Mathaka, the artistry of Gullah Geechee basketry had come full circle back to its place of origin.

When the Gullahs visited Old Yagala, they faced a hike up a steep hill to a historic place of safety for the villagers. Massally described it as a "mesa where the Africans moved their village to defend themselves against slave invaders who were also Africans. While up there, they could see for miles away as we went up there and saw for ourselves. Yes, this place is really a special place." After completing the hike, Winston Relaford expressed his emotions: "It was a hard climb up the hill, but I was determined to make it. What gets me more than anything is the tenacity and the ingenuity of the people to come up here to get away from the enemy. And now today it's very surreal. It tells me that they had a desire to be free, There's nothing like freedom."[12]

Following the Next Step Tour, many of the participants spoke of their experiences at the 2020 International Gullah Geechee and African Diaspora Conference at Coastal Carolina University. In a panel discussion, they shared the value in finally understanding the origins of their Gullah Geechee culture and the importance of passing forward this knowledge to others in their communities, especially the younger generation. This fourth homecoming also prompted Anita Singleton Prather to bring four Sierra Leone tourism students—Ibrahim Jabbie, Sheku Fofanah, Mohamed Alpha Jalloh, and Tensie Sia Blessing Momoh, who attend Limkokwing University in Freetown—to Beaufort, South Carolina, in 2022. Three decades after President Joseph Saidu Momoh's momentous trip to Penn Center, these students will be making the same journey of discovery to a place where their ancestors were taken. These young people, nicknamed "Bunce Island Warriors," worked for Amadu Massally's Fambul Tik organization during the Next Step Tour, where they interacted with Singleton Prather and other members of the delegation. Their professionalism was impressive as they often traveled ahead of the delegation to check on the roads, hotel accommodations, and food preparations. When it came to the attention of Singleton Prather that these students had little hope of getting tourism jobs in Sierra Leone, where you typically have to know someone who can help you get a job, she lobbied Congressman James Clyburn and his representatives, who helped secure their approval to travel to the U.S.

In fall 2022, the four Sierra Leoneans were exchange students at the University of South Carolina Beaufort, where they will be able to complete their coursework and internship in the Lowcountry. As mentioned in chapter 10, the University of South Carolina Beaufort's Sea Islands Institute features the Center for Events Management and Hospitality Training, where these students will gain experience at hotels in Hilton Head, South Carolina, one of the country's top tourist destinations. During their time in Beaufort, these students will also have additional work experience at the Original Gullah Festival, Penn Center, and Gullah Geechee Cultural Heritage Corridor Commission. Singleton Prather believes that the presence of these students from Sierra Leone in the Lowcountry will help the younger generation of Gullahs understand the origins and global importance of their culture. Moreover, Singleton Prather hopes that these students will return to Sierra Leone as consultants who can help to modernize the tourist industry in their country. "They will be equipped to organize and even find the necessary resources to improve the experience for visitors to Sierra Leone."[13]

Emmy Award–winning producer Betsy Newman captured the Sierra Leone Next Step Tour in her 2020 documentary titled *Gullah Roots*, which was sponsored in part by South Carolina Educational Television and South Carolina Humanities. This hour-long film follows "leaders of the South Carolina and Georgia Gullah Geechee community as they experience a homecoming in Sierra Leone, and it dives deep into South Carolina's ties with West Africa, educating viewers about Gullah heritage, including spiritual, musical and artistic traditions." The goal of this project is to raise awareness about the Gullah Geechee community and its ties to West Africa, examine the challenges many in that community face today, and show the progress they have made since the first homecoming to Sierra Leone thirty years ago.[14]

Final Thoughts about the Future

Where does the Gullah culture go from here? Few people can predict it more persuasively than Emory Campbell, who has contributed so much to this book and in so many ways to the Lowcountry community in which he lives. He says, "The future of the Gullah culture is bright not only because of its current popularity but also because of the increasing efforts to preserve its vital elements. The publication of the *Special Resource Study* by the National Park Service . . . has provided a very solid access to the public for accurate information about the culture and the boundaries of the Gullah Corridor." Public awareness of this culture will certainly encourage local, state, and federal officials to offer more assistance to Gullah Geechee communities. However, any discussion of the future of the Gullah Geechee must begin and end with their land, for it is the root of their culture and in many ways defines who they are.

Campbell is thoroughly familiar with the Gullah outlook on land, property rights, and related matters. "Although the use of the land is changing," he says of the Lowcountry and Sea Islands, "we still have many who raise part of their own food, who fish the waters, who hunt in the forests, and who do so using the methods of their forebears rather than modern-day equipment and techniques. In some places there is still a nineteenth-century aura, with evenly rowed farms, dusty roads overhung with trees where no tall trucks can pass, trails where only mules and marsh tackies can navigate, and dense forests of palmetto, pine, and live oak—relics of a laid-back era that all of us strive to protect."

Campbell places great emphasis on "the human connection—the value of a child getting to know his or her heritage—of finding self-worth, of putting more value in the family and its members, not only where they live, but where they came from. This connection requires an educational focus both on this side of the sea, here in America, and that side of the sea, in our case, Africa. We must work to ensure that our own children, and the adults understand their culture and heritage."[15] Campbell has echoed this opinion many times, particularly when he was executive director of Penn Center, which has become a rallying place for individuals and groups who want to preserve the Gullah culture and language, and when he was working as a volunteer for more than two decades helping to produce the translation of the New Testament into the Gullah language. When asked to reflect about the first homecoming trip, Campbell said, "The main wound is healed now because I know there is a place that I can call home. I know where home is now. Before then, someone described the Negro in America as a person without roots, but now I know I have roots and have been healed."[16]

ACKNOWLEDGMENTS

Wilbur Cross:

This book could never have been written without going to many key institutions and organizations that have been for many years compiling information about the Gullah culture and peoples. Most pertinent among these because of its specific attention to this subject is the *Low Country Gullah Culture Special Resource Study*. This is far and away the most comprehensive, updated, and accurate resource available. It is the result of research by the National Park Service over a period of more than five years in the Southeast. Within its structure, it also provides multitudes of references to valuable sources.

A close second for my research was the Beaufort County (South Carolina) Library. The main county library in the historic town of Beaufort has one of the South's largest collections of materials on the Gullah language and the Sea Island culture, including many illustrations and documents. The Hilton Head Island branch library was also a source of solid information and personal assistance. Much of my original research, even before I ever embarked on the Gullah story, was conducted at Penn Center on St. Helena Island, the institution that was founded in 1862 as a school to teach freed slaves and that is now a center for the study of the Gullah culture and language. Back in the 1990s, I served on its advisory board for eight years and was inducted into the study of African American affairs. There I "discovered" the absorbing information about the Gullah culture, language, and peoples.

Other institutions that have been invaluable for research have been the South Carolina Historical Society in Charleston, the Avery Research Center, and the South Carolina State Museum, which has a key department devoted to African American culture and research, including major entries on the Gullah language and history in the South. Also invaluable were the Institute for African American Studies at the University of Georgia, the Penn Center collection at the University of North Carolina, and the extensive collections relating to the Gullah/Geechee culture that have been established at many other universities, including Hampton University, Fisk University, the University of South Carolina, James Madison University, South Carolina State University,

Savannah College of Art and Design, Duke University, Yale University, the University of Virginia, and the Technical College of the Low Country (South Carolina).

On a personal level, I am deeply indebted to Dr. Emory Shaw Campbell, who has been my chief mentor on this subject for the past fifteen years, who wrote the foreword for this book, and who is frequently mentioned herein for his continuing devotion to and work on behalf of the Gullah/Geechee people, both today and in the past. Close behind him in my gratitude for assistance is Dr. Joseph Opala, who stands at the top of the list of scholars researching the Gullah culture and its roots in West Africa. He is mentioned and quoted many times in this text, and he is responsible for much vital material that otherwise would never have become part of our story.

Among others who have provided valuable information or assistance have been Grace Morris Cordial, South Carolina Resources Coordinator of the Beaufort County Public Library System; Dr. Julius Scott, who not only helped in providing information but also helped keep up my morale during some trying times; Marquetta Goodwine, commonly known as "Queen of the Gullah/Geechee Nation," an exuberant voice for Gullah, a frequent publisher, and the hostess of many broadcasting programs in this field; Walter Greer, a good friend and noted artist who started his career depicting remote Gullah neighborhoods and structures; Veronica Gerald, a specialist in Gullah history, foods, and cooking; and the Honorable James Clyburn of South Carolina, who wrote the preface for a history of Penn Center that I am coauthoring with Dr. Campbell, and who made possible the vital Gullah/Geechee Heritage Corridor bill to help preserve and protect the Gullah culture in America.

Eric Crawford:

First, I give thanks to my Lord and Savior Jesus Christ for his guidance in the completion of this second edition of *Gullah Culture in America*. To the Cross family, I am deeply honored that you allowed me to follow in Wilbur's large footsteps. His keen observations and exceptional research truly guided my writing and made this project possible. Equally important was the invaluable feedback provided by noted scholars such as Veronica Gerald, Joseph Opala, Anita Singleton Prather, Emory Campbell, Zenobia Harper, Amadu Massally, Ronald Daise, Victoria Smalls, Jessica Berry, and Cyrus MacFoy. I am humbled that they took time to read through portions of this book for me.

Like Wilbur, I recognize the contributions of numerous libraries and mu-seums throughout the Lowcountry and Columbia, South Carolina. In par-ticular, I thank the staffs at the Lineberger Memorial Library and the South Carolina State Library for demonstrating a willingness to go over and beyond in finding missing sources for this book. To the students at Benedict College, I thank you for your feedback and helpful suggestions in making this book of interest to the younger generation.

As always, I recognize my parents, Pastor Timothy and Dr. Bessie Craw-ford, who remain the benchmarks for my life. I am fortunate to call them "dad" and "mommy." To my son, Sean Timothy Crawford, I am a proud father who is grateful to have had a small part in bringing you into this world. Con-tinue to trust in the Lord's plan for your life. I am also thankful for the support of my brother, Dwayne Crawford, and his wife, Kathy; Angie; my nephew, Andre; and nieces, Taylor and Kayla Marie.

Last, I reflect on the past sixteen years since I first traveled to St. Helena Is-land and met the late Deacon James Garfield Smalls, Minnie Gadson, Deacon Joseph Murray, and Rosa Murray. During this time, their willingness to share their culture has shaped my scholarship and, to a large extent, my life. I am eternally grateful for their friendship and trust, and I look forward to the next chapter in our journey in Gullah Geechee song.

NOTES

Chapter 1

1. "A Work in Progress," Infoplease, accessed August 9, 2022, https://www.infoplease
.com/history/black-history/a-work-in-progress.
2. Edward Ball, *Slaves in the Family* (New York: Farrar, Straus, and Giroux, 2017), xi.
3. Edward Ball interviewed by Marsha Barber, "All in the Family," *Mountain Xpress*,
posted January 13, 1999, accessed August 10, 2022, https://mountainx.com/arts
/art-news/0113ball-php.
4. Paul Davis, "Buying and Selling Human Beings: Newport and the Slave Trade,"
Slavery in Rhode Island Series, accessed March 31, 2022, https://stories.usatoday
network.com/slaveryinrhodeisland/buying-and-selling-the-human-species/.
5. Herb Frazier, "Sierra Leone Homecoming," *Charleston Post and Courier*, July 24,
2005, 1F–2F.
6. John H. Tibbetts, "Living Soul of Gullah," *Coastal Heritage* 14, no. 4 (Spring
2000), accessed May 24, 2002, https://www.scseagrant.org/living-soul-of-gullah/.
7. Kip D. Zimmerman et al., "Genetic Landscape of Gullah African Americans," *American Journal of Physical Anthropology* 175 (4) (April 2021): 913. See
Philip Morgan, *African American Life in the Georgia Lowcountry: The Atlantic World and the Gullah Geechee* (Athens: University of Georgia Press, 2011),
81. Morgan discusses the large Black majority existing in the South Carolina
Lowcountry in 1775. The state's population included approximately seventy
thousand whites and one hundred thousand Blacks. Nearly seventy-three
thousand Blacks were in Beaufort, Charleston, and Georgetown.
8. Peter McCandless, *Slavery, Disease, and Suffering in the Southern Lowcountry* (New
York: Cambridge University Press, 2011), 129.
9. Stacey Close, "Elderly Slaves of the Plantation South: Somewhere Between
Heaven and Earth" (PhD diss., Ohio State University, 1992), 83, https://etd
.ohiolink.edu/apexprod/rws_etd/send_file/send?accession=osu1487779
914824944&disposition=inline.
10. Tibbetts, "Living Soul of Gullah."
11. Michelle Paynter, "Missing Boater Rescued From Uninhabited Island," WTOC
News, April 6, 2006, accessed August 10, 2022, https://www.wtoc.com/story
/4737412/missing-boater-rescued-from-uninhabited-island/.
12. Margaret Washington Creel, *A Peculiar People: Slave Religion and Community-
Culture Among the Gullahs* (New York: New York University Press, 1988), 15–17.
13. Tibbetts, "Living Soul of Gullah."

Chapter 2

1. Jonathan Prousky, "Repositioning Individualized Homeopathy as a Psychother-apeutic Technique with Resolvable Ethical Dilemmas," *Journal of Evidence-Based Integrative Medicine* 23 (August 27, 2018): 1.

2. "Laura Towne (1825–1901)," *Only a Teacher: Schoolhouse Pioneers* series, PBS North Carolina, accessed July 12, 2022, https://www.pbs.org/onlyateacher /lauratowne.html.

3. Willie Lee Nichols Rose, *Rehearsal for Reconstruction: The Port Royal Experiment* (Oxford: Oxford University Press, 1964).

4. Laura Matilda Towne and Rupert Sargent Holland, *Letters and Diary of Laura M. Towne Written from the Sea Islands of South Carolina, 1862–1884* (Cambridge, MA: Riverside Press, 1900), 22–23.

5. Towne and Holland, *Letters and Diary of Laura M. Towne*, 22–23.

6. Towne and Holland, *Letters and Diary of Laura M. Towne*, 20, 22.

7. Towne and Holland, *Letters and Diary of Laura M. Towne*.

8. Eric Crawford, *Gullah Spirituals: The Sound of Freedom and Protest in the South Carolina Sea Islands* (Columbia: University of South Carolina Press, 2021), 37.

9. Towne and Holland, *Letters and Diary of Laura M. Towne*, 10–11.

10. Holland, ed., *Letters and Diary of Laura M. Towne*, 93.

11. Towne and Holland, *Letters and Diary of Laura M. Towne*, 87.

12. Towne and Holland, *Letters and Diary of Laura M. Towne*, 78.

13. Towne and Holland,

14. Charlotte Forten Grimké, *The Journals of Charlotte Forten Grimké* (New York: Oxford University Press, 1988), 394.

15. Grimké, *The Journals of Charlotte Forten Grimké*, 396.

16. Grimké, *The Journals of Charlotte Forten Grimké*, 391.

17. See Louise Ware, *George Foster Peabody: Banker, Philanthropist, Publicist* (Athens: University of Georgia Press, 1951), 115.

18. Towne and Holland, *Letters and Diary of Laura M. Towne*, 156.

19. Towne and Holland, *Letters and Diary of Laura M. Towne*, 222.

Chapter 3

1. Interview by Wilbur Cross with Emory Campbell.

2. Erica Chayes Wida, *The Sinking Islands of the Southern US*, BBC Travel, accessed April 18, 2022, https://www.bbc.com/travel/article/20180904-the-sinking -islands-of-the-southern-us.

3. Unpublished papers in the historical archives at Penn Center, St. Helena Island, SC.

4. Unpublished papers in the historical archives at Penn Center, St. Helena Island, SC.

5. Unpublished papers in the historical archives at Penn Center, St. Helena Island, SC.

6. Unpublished papers in the historical archives at Penn Center, St. Helena Island, SC.

7. Unpublished papers in the historical archives at Penn Center, St. Helena Island, SC.

8. Unpublished papers in the historical archives at Penn Center, St. Helena Island, SC.

9. Betty Joyce Nash, "The Sea Island Hurricane of 1893," *Economic History* 10, no. 1 (Winter 2006): 46.

10. Nash, "The Sea Island Hurricane of 1893," 45.

11. Shepherd McKinley, "History: Phosphate in S.C." *Statehouse Report*, April 13, 2022, https://www.statehousereport.com/2015/06/12/history-phosphate-in-s-c.

12. James Giesen, "The South's Greatest Enemy? The Cotton Boll Weevil and Its Lost Revolution, 1892–1930" (PhD diss., University of Georgia, 2004), 312.

13. Joseph McGowan, "History of Extra-Long Staple Cottons" (master's thesis, University of Arizona, 1960), 146–47, https://repository.arizona.edu/bitstream/handle/10150/553949/AZU_TD_BOX256_E9791_1960_82.pdf?sequence=1.

14. "Ballad of the Boll," Track 3 on Pete Seeger, *American Favorite Ballads, Volume 4*, Folkways Records, FW2323, 1961, vinyl record.

15. Jenny Hersh and Sallie Ann Robinson, "The History of Daufuskie Island," Haig Point Foundation, accessed April 15, 2022, https://www.haigpointfoundation.org/news/the-history-of-daufuskie-island.

16. Pat Conroy, *The Water Is Wide: A Memoir* (New York: Dell, 1972), 10.

17. Michael Haines, "Fertility and Mortality in the United States," *EH.Net Encyclopedia*, edited by Robert Whaples, accessed March 19, 2008, https://eh.net/encyclopedia/fertility-and-mortality-in-the-united-states/.

18. Michael Wolfe, *The Abundant Life Prevails: Religious Traditions of Saint Helena Island* (Waco, Texas: Baylor University Press, 2000), 104–5.

19. Wolfe, *Abundant Life Prevails*, vi.

20. Ralph Robert Middleton, interview by Eric Crawford, Saint Helena Island, SC, April 20, 2009.

21. J. Tracy Power, "I Will Not Be Silent and I Will Be Heard: Martin Luther King, Jr., the Southern Christian Leadership Conference and Penn Center," South Carolina Department of Archives and History, Columbia, SC, 5.

22. Hugh Gibson, "Radical Meetings Shrouded in Secrecy," *Charleston News and Courier*, March 13, 1964.

23. David Garrow, "Where Martin Luther, Jr., Was Going," *Georgia Historical Quarterly* (Winter 1991): 722–26.

24. Martin Luther King Jr., "A New Sense of Direction" (speech at St. Helena Island, SC), November 28, 1967, Carnegie Council for Ethics in International Affairs, accessed April 17, 2022, https://www.carnegiecouncil.org/media/article/a-new

-sense-of-direction-1968. This site gives the incorrect year (1968) for the speech.
King's last trip to Frogmore was November 28, 1967. See Orville Burton, *Penn
Center: A History Preserved* (Athens: University of Georgia Press, 2014), 82. King's
SCLC had four retreats at Penn Center in September 1965, November 1966,
May 1967, and November 1967.

25. Martin Luther King Jr., The Trumpet of Conscience: Dr. King's Final Testament
on Racism, Poverty, and War (1968; Boston: Beacon Press, 2010), 14–15.

26. Katherine Charron, *Freedom's Teacher: The Life of Septima Clark* (Chapel Hill:
University of North Carolina Press, 2012), 2.

27. Wolfe, *Abundant Life Prevails*, 112. The Siceloffs were heavily influenced by the
teachings of Quaker theologian John Puschin.

28. Courtney Siceloff and Elizabeth Siceloff, "A New Birth of Freedom on Saint Helena Island," 1950, Penn School Papers, reel 16.

29. Wolfe, *Abundant Life Prevails*, 113.

30. Wolfe, *Abundant Life Prevails,* 116.

31. Wolfe, *Abundant Life Prevails*, vii.

32. Wolfe, *Abundant Life Prevails*, vi.

Chapter 4

1. Paul deVere, "Emory Campbell: Coming Home," *Celebrating Hilton Head*, accessed July 20, 2022, https://www.celebratehiltonhead.com/article/1291/emory
-campbell-coming-home.

2. Don McKinney, "Family Ties: A Visit with the Campbells of Hilton Head Island,"
Sandlapper: The Magazine of South Carolina, Spring 1999, 34.

3. McKinney, "Family Ties," 35.

4. Erin Walsh, "Islander to Receive Education Award," *Island Packet,* April 5, 2005.

5. Emory Campbell and Ayoka Campbell, *Gullah Cultural Legacies: A Synopsis of
Gullah Traditions, Customary Beliefs, Artforms and Speech on Hilton Head Island
and Vicinal Sea Islands in South Carolina and Georgia* (Hilton Head, S.C.: Gullah
Heritage Consulting Services, 2008), 12.

6. Campbell and Campbell, *Gullah Cultural Legacies*, 1, 12–13.

7. Gary Lee, "In the Land of the Gullahs," *Washington Post,* accessed July 19, 2022,
https://www.washingtonpost.com/archive/lifestyle/travel/1998/09/20/in-the
-land-of-the-gullahs/5a42ca20-11f5-4d58-8bf2-143e96e42f1f/.

8. Mayukh Sen, "Vertamae Smart-Grosvenor Is the Unsung Godmother of American
Food Writing," *VICE*, accessed April 21, 2022, https://www.vice.com/en/article
/evmbwj/vwetamae-smart-grosvenor-vibration-cooking-profile.

9. Sen, "Vertamae Smart-Grosvenor."

10. Vertamae Smart Grosvenor, interview by Tracy Dingmann, *New Mexico in Focus*, February 10, 2012, 4:56–5:10, https://www.youtube.com/watch?v=TWNQ3nr1R3M.

11. Tambay Obenson, " 'Daughters of the Dust' Auteur Julie Dash Developing New

Doc 'Travel Notes of a Geechee Girl,'" *IndieWire*, accessed April 20, 2022, https://www.Indiewire.com/2019/05/julie-dash-vertamae-smart-grosvenor-geechee -girl-1202131370/.

12. Cornelia Walker Bailey, "I Am Sapelo," *Golden Isles Navigator*, accessed July 15, 2022, http://www.gacoast.com/navigator/iamsapelo.html.

13. Bailey, "I Am Sapelo."

14. Bailey, "I Am Sapelo."

15. Bailey, "I Am Sapelo."

16. Bailey, "I Am Sapelo."

17. Cornelia Walker Bailey, "I Am Sapelo," *Georgia Isles: Navigator*, accessed July 15, 2022, http://www.gacoast.com/navigator/iamsapelo.html.

18. Cathy Harley, "Making a Name for Herself," *Beaufort* (SC) *Gazette*, December 5, 2006.

19. Anita Singleton Prather, "Gullah Roots: Promo," South Carolina ETV, September 20, 2020, educational video, 0.00–0.16, www.youtube.com/watch?v=f0W3dr Emyto. *Mahei* is the Mende word for chief and *jiagie* means role model.

20. Althea Natalga Sumpter, "Black Cultural Heritage in the Southern Story," accessed April 23, 2022, https://www.altheasumpter.com/gullah-geechee.html.

21. Sumpter, "Black Cultural Heritage."

22. Sumpter, "Black Cultural Heritage."

23. Althea Natalga Sumpter, "Black Cultural Heritage in the Southern Story," accessed July 15, 2022, https://www.altheasumpter.com/scholarship.html.

24. Althea Sumpter, interview by Steve Goss, *Morning Edition*, WABE, February 12, 2014.

25. Harley, "Making a Name for Herself."

26. Undated news release from Gallery Chuma of Charleston, SC, 2006.

27. Undated news release from Gallery Chuma of Charleston, SC, 2006.

28. Undated news release from Gallery Chuma of Charleston, SC, 2006.

29. Undated news release from Gallery Chuma of Charleston, SC, 2006.

30. *The Hub and Arts Daily*, "Off the Wall and Onto the Stage: Dancing the Art of Jonathan Green," SC Arts Commission, accessed April 26, 2022, https://www .scartshub.com/arts_daily//off-the-wall-and-onto-the-stage--dancing-the-art-of -jonathan-green-2/.

31. Undated news release from Gullah Heritage Trail Tours, Charleston, SC, 2007.

32. Philip Simmons, interview by Mary Douglas, April 4–5, 2001, transcript, Smithsonian Archives of American Art, accessed July 16, 2022, https://www.aaa.si.edu /download_pdf_transcript/ajax?record_id=edanmdm-AAADCD_oh_226990.

33. John Michael Vlach, "Keeper of the Gate: Philip Simmons Ironwork in Charleston, South Carolina," Lowcountry Digital History Initiative, accessed April 24, 2022, https://ldhi.library.cofc.edu/exhibits/show/philip_simmons/philip -simmons-keeper-of-the-g.

34. Vlach, "Keeper of the Gate."

35. National Heritage Fellowships, "Philip Simmons: Ornamental Ironworker," National Endowment for the Arts, accessed April 24, 2022, https://www.arts.gov/honors/heritage/philip-simmons.

36. Vlach, "Keeper of the Gate."

37. Theresa Leninger-Miller, "Minnie Evans," in *Notable Black American Women, Book 2*, ed. Jessie Smith (New York: Gale Research, 1996), 206.

38. Katherine Murrell, "More About the Artist Minnie Evans, 1892–1987," *Folkstreams*, accessed April 25, 2022, https://www.folkstreams.net/contexts/more-about-the-artist-minnie-evans-1892-1987.

39. "Minnie Evans," Anthony Petullo Art Collection, accessed April 27, 2022, https://www.petulloartcollection.org/minnie-evans/.

40. Leninger-Miller, "Minnie Evans," 206. According to Miller, Evans memorized the Bible and developed a personal cosmography with biblical imagery from the books of Ezekiel, Samuel, and Revelation.

41. Regenia Perry, "Minnie Evans," Smithsonian American Art Museum, accessed April 25, 2022, https://www.americanart.si.edu/artist/minnie-evans-1466.

42. Murrell, "More About the Artist Minnie Evans."

43. "Minnie Evans," Anthony Petullo Art Collection.

44. Bessie Jones and Bess Lomax Hawes, *Step It Down: Games, Plays, and Stories from the Afro-American Heritage* (Athens: University of Georgia Press), 12.

45. Bessie Jones and John Stewart, *For the Ancestors: Autobiographical Memories* (Athens: University of Georgia Press, 1989), 92–93.

46. Jones and Hawes, *Step It Down*, xii.

47. Jones and Stewart, *For the Ancestors*, 144.

48. Jones and Stewart, *For the Ancestors*, 51.

49. Jones and Hawes, *Step It Down*, 37–38. See Paul Harrison, Victor Leo Walker, and Gus Edwards, *Black Theatre Ritual Performance in the African Diaspora* (Philadelphia: Temple University Press, 2010), 335. The authors give an alternative spelling of juba (giouba) and state that it referred to an African step dance.

50. Josh Dunson, "Slave Songs at the 'Sing for Freedom,'" *Broadside* 46 (May 30, 1964).

51. The Stranger Cemetery is also known as Union Memorial Cemetery.

52. "Bessie Jones," WBSS Media: The Soul Purpose, accessed July 16, 2022, https://wbssmedia.com/artists/detail/3739#:~:text=Alan%20Lomax%2C%20who%20first%20encountered,Courage%20of%20American%20Black%20traditions.

53. See Joel McEachin and Robert Jones, "American Beach Historic District," National Register of Historic Places Nomination Form (Washington, DC: U.S. Department of the Interior, National Park Service, 2001), Section 8, page 2, https://npgallery.nps.gov/NRHP/GetAsset/bd23b68d-080a-464b-bda5-03317296. Abraham Lincoln Lewis worked his way up from a water boy to foreman of a lumber mill. Responding to a need for health and burial insurance, he joined with six others to found the Afro-American Industrial and Benefit Association in 1901.

54. Russ Rymer, "Beach Lady," *Smithsonian Magazine*, June 3, 2003, accessed April 30, 2022, https://www.smithsonianmag.com/history/beach-lady-84237022/.

55. Carol Williams, "A Minority at Its Leisure," Tumucuan Ecological and Historic Preserve Florida, accessed April 30, 2022, https://www.nps.gov/timu/learn/historyculture/ambch_minorityatleisure.htm.

56. Rymer, "Beach Lady."

57. Rymer, "Beach Lady."

58. Carol Alexander, "Humble Beginnings: A Museum Takes Shape," A. L. Lewis Museum at American Beach, Florida, accessed April 30, 2022, https://american beachmuseum.org/about/.

59. Rymer, "Beach Lady." For more information on American Beach refer to Marsha Dean Phelts, *The American Beach Cookbook* (Gainesville: University Press of Florida, 2008); Marsha Dean Phelts, *American Beach for African Americans* (Gainesville: University Pres of Florida, 2010); and McEachin and Jones, "American Beach Historic District," Section 8.

60. Robert Lee, executive director of Seabrook retirement community, interview by Wilbur Cross, Hilton Head Island, SC, May 2006.

61. Robert Lee interview by Wilbur Cross.

Chapter 5

1. National Park Service, *Low Country Gullah Culture Special Resource Study*, F-20.

2. Albert Raboteau, *Slave Religion: The "Invisible Institution" in the Antebellum South* (New York: Oxford University Press, 1980), 8.

3. Margaret Creel, *A Peculiar People: Slave Religion and Community-Culture Among the Gullahs* (New York: New York University Press, 1988), 52.

4. Roger Pinckney, *Blue Roots: African-American Folk Magic of the Gullah People* (St. Paul, MN: Llewellyn Publications, 1998), 73–74.

5. Howard Thurman, *Jesus and the Disinherited* (Boston: Beacon Press, 2022), 30–31.

6. Creel, *A Peculiar People*, 263.

7. Patricia Jones-Jackson, *When Roots Die: Endangered Traditions on the Sea Islands* (Athens: University of Georgia Press, 1987), 79.

8. Jones-Jackson, *When Roots Die*, 77–78.

9. Jones-Jackson, *When Roots Die*, 91, 77–82.

10. Michael Wolfe, *The Abundant Life Prevails: Religious Traditions of Saint Helena Island* (Waco, TX: Baylor University Press, 2000), 40.

11. Henry Mitchell, *Black Preaching: The Recovery of a Powerful Art* (Nashville, TN: Abingdon Press, 1995), 45–46.

12. Ella Anderson Clark, "The Reminiscences of Ella Anderson Clark," MS. pp. 41–42. James Osgood Andrew Clark Papers, Stuart A. Rose Manuscript, Archives, and Rare Book Library, Emory University, Atlanta, GA.

13. National Park Service, *Low Country Gullah Culture Special Resource Study*, 309.

14. Creel, *A Peculiar People*, 277.

15. Elizabeth Jacoway, *Yankee Missionaries in the South* (Baton Rouge: Louisiana State University Press, 1980), 104–5.

16. William Pollitzer, *The Gullah People and Their African Heritage* (Athens: University of Georgia Press, 2005), 137.

17. William Francis Allen, Charles Pickard Ware, and Lucy McKim Garrison, *Slave Songs of the United States* (New York: A. Simpson, 1867), xiii–xiv; Patricia Guthrie, *Catching Sense: African American Communities on a South Carolina Sea Island* (Westport, CN: Bergin & Garvey, 1996), 96. Guthrie observed thirty-forty people attending a pray's house service on St. Helena Island.

18. David Thorpe to John Mooney, January 25, 1863, Dabbs Papers, Thorpe Series, Southern Historical Collection, University of North Carolina at Chapel Hill, Chapel Hill, NC.

19. Guthrie, *Catching Sense*, 100.

20. J. Duncan Hite, "Sandy Islanders Take Another Step—Now They Have Phones," *Florence (SC) Morning News*, May 7, 1972. The residents of the island routinely left their doors and even church unlocked up until the end of the twentieth century.

21. Creel, *A Peculiar People*, 278.

22. Guthrie, *Catching Sense*, 115.

23. See Creel, *A Peculiar People*, 286. Minutes, Beaufort Baptist Church, October 7, 1849, 271–74, Baptist Collection, Furman University, Greenville, SC.

24. C. Eric Lincoln, "In the Presence of the Holy Spirit," interviewed by *Washington Post*, June 7, 1997.

25. See Creel, *A Peculiar People*, 292. Watkins, "Bush School," 673–74; Michael Jackson, *The Kuranko: Dimensions of Social Reality in a West African Society* (New York: St. Martin's, 1977), 214, n. 1; Bureau of Folkways, Liberia, *The Traditional History and Folklore of the Gola Tribe in Liberia, Volume II* (Monrovia, Liberia: Bureau of Folkways, 1961), 15–21.

26. David Thorpe to John Mooney, January 25, 1863.

27. Raboteau, *Slave Religion*, 227.

28. Shelly O'Foran, *Little Zion: A Church Baptized by Fire* (Chapel Hill: University of North Carolina Press, 2006), 185.

29. William Allen, Charles Pickard Ware, and Lucy McKim Garrison, *Slave Songs of the United States* (New York: A. Simpson, 1867), xiii.

30. William Dargan, *Lining Out the Word* (Berkeley: University of California Press, 2006), 91.

31. James Calemine, "The McIntosh County Shouters," *The Bitter Southerner*, accessed May 5, 2022, https://bittersoutherner.com/mcintosh-county-shouters.

32. Art Rosenbaum and Johann S. Buis, *Shout Because You're Free: The African American Ring Shout Tradition in Coastal Georgia* (Athens: University of Georgia Press, 1998), 105–6.

33. Robert F. Thompson, *The Four Moments of the Sun* (Washington, DC: National

Gallery of Art, 1981), 54, 28. Other examples of the use counterclockwise movement in Western Africa are Marion Kilson, "The Ga Naming Rite," *Anthropos* 64/64 (1968/1969): 904–20. Kilson discusses the counterclockwise movement during the libation portion of the Ga naming rite. Arthur Powell and Oshon Temple, "Seeding Ethnomathematics with Oware: Sankofa," *Teaching Children Mathematics* 7, no. 6 (February 2001): 369–75. Powell and Temple reveal the counterclockwise movement of seeds in the Oware game from Ghana.

34. Corey Stayton, "Kongo Cosmogram: A Theory in African American Literature" (master's thesis, Clark Atlanta University, 1997), 4–5.

35. Sterling Stuckey, *Slave Culture: Nationalist Theory and the Foundations of Black America* (New York: Oxford University Press, 1987), 12.

36. Wolfe, *The Abundant Life Prevails*, 26.

37. Nate Anderson, "The Word from Geecheetown," *Christianity Today*, January 1, 2006, accessed July 20, 2022, https://www.christianitytoday.com/ct/2006 /january/9.22.html.

38. Emory Campbell, interviews by Wilbur Cross.

39. Emory Campbell, interviews by Wilbur Cross.

40. "Bahamas Folklore," Bahamas Gullah-Geechee Connection, accessed July 20 and 22, https://gullahgeecheeconnection.wordpress.com/bahamas-folklore -gullahgeechee-coneection/.

Chapter 6

1. Roger Pinckney, *Blue Roots: African-American Folk Magic of the Gullah People* (Orangeburg, SC: Sandlapper Publishing, 2003), 91–92.

2. Albert Raboteau, *Slave Religion: The "Invisible Institution" in the Antebellum South* (New York: Oxford University Press, 2004), 276.

3. Unidentified, collected by Genevieve Wilcox Chandler and Hagar Brown, "Uncle Gabe's Conjuh Ball," *South Carolina Folk Tales: Stories of Animals and Supernatural Beings*, compiled by Workers of the Writers' Program of the Works Program Administration in the State of South Carolina (Columbia, 1941), 103. Scholars question the effectiveness of the enslaved conjurer's medicine on white plantation owners. See Marli Frances Weiner and Mazie Hough, *Sex, Sickness, and Slavery: Illness in the Antebellum South* (Urbana: University of Illinois Press, 2014), 180. The authors quote an unnamed man who said that "a conjurer couldn't make ole master stop whipping him."

4. Mary Granger, ed., *Drums and Shadows: Survival Studies among the Georgia Coastal Negroes* (Athens: University of Georgia Press, 1940), 41.

5. Granger, *Drums and Shadows*, 89.

6. Andrew Jacobs, "In a Historic Black Hamlet, Wal-Mart Finds Resistance," *New York Times*, March 6, 2006, accessed May 18, 2022, https://www.nytimes.com /2004/03/06/us/in-a-historic-black-hamlet-wal-mart-finds-resistance.html.

7. Granger, *Drums and Shadows*, 90.

8. Granger, *Drums and Shadows*, 91.

9. V. E. Kelly, *A Short History of Skidway* (Athens: University of Georgia Press, 2003), 209.

10. Vennie Deas-Moore, "Home Remedies, Herb Doctors, and Granny Midwives," *The World & I Journal*, January 1987, 480.

11. Cornelia Walker Bailey, *God, Dr. Buzzard, and the Bolito Man: A Saltwater Geechee Talks about Life on Sapelo Island, Georgia* (New York: Anchor Books, 2000), 202.

12. National Park Service, *Low Country Gullah Culture Special Resource Study*, 191.

13. Pinckney, *Blue Roots*, 91–92, 94.

14. National Park Service, *Low Country Gullah Culture Special Resource Study*, 191.

15. National Park Service, *Low Country Gullah Culture Special Resource Study*, 191.

16. Jack Montgomery, "Chapter One: Beneath the Spanish Moss: The World of the Root Doctor," *Western Kentucky University TopSCHOLAR*, accessed May 18, 2022, https://digitalcommons.wku.edu/cgi/viewcontent.cgi?article=1002 &context=dlts_fac_pub.

17. National Park Service, *Low Country Gullah Culture Special Resource Study*, 303.

18. Pinckney, *Blue Roots*, 6.

19. Jack Montgomery, "Chapter One: Beneath the Spanish Moss: The World of the Root Doctor," *Western Kentucky University TopSCHOLAR*, accessed May 18, 2022, https://digitalcommons.wku.edu/cgi/viewcontent.cgi?article=1002 &context=dlts_fac_pub.

20. Montgomery, "Chapter One: Beneath the Spanish Moss."

21. Jeffrey Anderson, *Conjure in African American Society* (Baton Rouge: Louisiana State University, 2005), 130.

22. Anderson, *Conjure in African American Society* (Baton Rouge: Louisiana State University, 2005), 131.

23. Bailey, *God, Dr. Buzzard, and the Bolito Man*, 187–88.

24. "Hant House" and "Bring Back Us Teef," collected by Genevieve Wilcox Chandler, in *South Carolina Folk Tales*, compiled by Workers of the Writers Program of the Works Progress Administration in the State of South Carolina (Columbia, 1941), 78, 75–76; Zackie Knox, interviewed by Genevieve Chandler, August 25, 1936, WPA Mss.

25. "Hant House" and "Bring Back Us Teef."

26. Alicia O'Brien, "The Development of the Gullah Church"(master's thesis, University of Miami, 2006), 30.

27. Charles Joyner, *Down by the Riverside: A South Carolina Slave Community* (Urbana: University of Illinois Press, 1984), 150.

28. Bob Yellin Carawan and Ethel Raim, *Ain't You Got a Right to the Tree of Life?: The People of Johns Island, South Carolina, Their Faces, Their Words, and Their Songs* (New York: Simon and Schuster, 1967), 108.

29. "Hag," collected by Genevieve Wilcox Chandler, in *South Carolina Folk Tales*, 90.

30. "Trus' Gawd," collected by Genevieve Wilcox Chandler, in *South Carolina Folk Tales*, 86–89.

31. Carawan and Raim, *Ain't You Got a Right to the Tree of Life?* 106.

32. O'Brien, "The Development of the Gullah Church," 32.

33. Thomas Jackson Woofter, *Black Yeomanry: Life on St. Helena Island* (New York: H. Holt, 1930), 78. See Rossa Cooley, *Homes of the Freed* (New York: Negro University Press, 1970), 59–64. Cooley discusses her "Community Class" of nurses who were motivated to learn as much as they could from the nurse instructor.

34. Federal Writers' Project and Library of Congress, *Georgia Slave Narratives: A Folk History of Slavery in Georgia from Interviews with Former Slaves* (Bedford, MA: Applewood Book, 2006), 245.

Chapter 7

1. John Bennett, "Gullah: A *Negro Patois*," *South Atlantic Quarterly* 7, 4 (October 1908): 332. See also William Allen, Charles Ware, and Lucy Garrison, *Slave Songs of the United States* (New York: A. Simpson and Company, 1867), xxiv. In Allen's view, "A stranger, upon first hearing these people talk, especially if there is a group of them in animated conversation, can hardly understand them better than if they spoke a foreign language, and might, indeed, easily, suppose this to be the case."

2. Patricia Jones-Jackson, *When Roots Die: Endangered Traditions on the Sea Islands* (Athens: University of Georgia Press, 1997), 133.

3. "Gullah Culture," *NOW*, pbs.org, January 24, 2003.

4. Lorenzo Dow Turner, *Africanisms in the Gullah Dialect, by Lorenzo Dow Turner* (Chicago: University of Chicago Press, 1949), 254.

5. Turner, *Africanisms*, 12.

6. Turner, *Africanisms*, v.

7. Turner, *Africanisms*, 257.

8. Lorenzo Dow Turner Collection, Indiana University, Archives of Traditional Music, Accession: 86/107/F.

9. Joseph E. Holloway, *Africanisms in American Culture* (Bloomington: Indiana University Press, 2005), 56.

10. William Pollitzer, *The Gullah People and Their African Heritage* (Athens: University of Georgia Press, 2005), 113.

11. Turner, *Africanisms*, 218.

12. Charles Joyner, *Down by the Riverside: A South Carolina Slave Community* (Chicago: University of Illinois Press, 1984), 198.

13. Joyner, *Down by the Riverside*, 199.

14. Joyner, *Down by the Riverside*, 210.

15. Joyner, *Down by the Riverside*, 197, 223.

16. Jones-Jackson, *When Roots Die*, 132.

17. Jones-Jackson, *When Roots Die*, 133.

18. Jones-Jackson, *When Roots Die*, 136.

19. Jones-Jackson, *When Roots Die*, 139–40.

20. Jessica Berry, "Use of Copula and Auxiliary BE by African American Children with Gullah Geechee Heritage" (PhD diss., Louisiana State University, 2015), 2, https://digitalcommons.lsu.edu/gradschool_dissertations/3513.

21. Berry, "Use of Copula and Auxiliary BE," 9.

22. Berry, "Use of Copula and Auxiliary BE," 9–10.

23. Berry, "Use of Copula and Auxiliary BE," 5.

Chapter 8

1. Jeffrey Young, "Slavery in Antebellum Georgia," *New Georgia Encyclopedia*, accessed on June 2, 2022, https://www.georgiaencyclopedia.org/articles/history-archaeology/slavery-in-antebellum-georgia/.

2. Office of the Comptroller of the Currency, "The Freedman's Saving Bank: Good Intentions Were Not Enough; A Noble Experiment Goes Awry," accessed on June 2, 2022, https://www.occ.treas.gov/about/who-we-are/history/1863-1865/1863-1865-freedmans-savings-bank.html#:~:text=1863%2D1865-,The%20Freedman's%20Savings%20Bank%3A%20Good%20Intentions%20Were%20Not%20Enough,A%20Noble%20Experiment%20Goes%20Awry&text=Like%20much%20else%20that%20came,sense%20of%20high%20moral%20purpose.

3. Matthew Cressler, "Five Years after Shooting, Mother Emanuel Uneasily Adapts as Pilgrimage Site," *Religion News Service*, accessed June 2, 2022, https://religionnews.com/2020/06/17/five-years-after-shooting-mother-emanuel-uneasily-adapts-as-pilgrimage-site/.

4. Debbie Elliott, "5 Years After Charleston Church Massacre, What Have We Learned?" *South Carolina Public Radio,* accessed June 2, 2022, https://www.npr.org/2020/06/17/878828088/5-years-after-charleston-church-massacre-what-have-we-learned.

5. Dartinia Hull, "'Not Everything Is Pretty Here': Charleston Tourism Reckons with Slavery and Racism," *CNN Travel*, accessed June 2, 2022, https://www.cnn.com/travel/article/charleston-south-carolina-tourism-racism/index.html.

6. Herb Frazier, "Swamp Used by Freedom-Seekers Recognized on Underground Railroad List," *Charleston City Paper*, accessed June 2, 2022, https://charlestoncitypaper.com/swamp-used-by-freedom-seekers-recognized-on-underground-railroad-list/. See also Tim Lockley, "Runaway Slave Communities in South Carolina," *History in Focus*, accessed June 5, 2022, https://archives.history.ac.uk/history-in-focus/Slavery/articles/lockley.html. Lockley discusses other maroon communities in South Carolina located in swamps in Colleton County and the Savannah and Santee Rivers.

7. Douglas Martin, "Charles E. Fraser, 73, Dies; Developer of Hilton Head," *New*

York Times, accessed June 2, 2022, https://www.nytimes.com/2002/12/19
/business/charles-e-fraser-73-dies-developer-of-hilton-head.html.

8. National Park Service, *Low Country Gullah Culture: Special Resource Study and
Final Environmental Impact Statement* (Atlanta: National Park Service, Southeast
Regional Office, 2005), 83.

9. National Park Service, *Low Country Gullah Culture: Special Resource Study and
Final Environmental Impact Statement* (Atlanta: National Park Service, Southeast
Regional Office, 2005), 84.

10. Andrew W. Kahrl, "From Commons to Capital: The Creative Destruction of
Coastal Real Estate, Environments, and Communities in the US South," *Transat-
lantica American Studies Journal* Issue 2, 2020, accessed June 3, 2022, https://
journals.openedition.org/transatlantica/16278.

11. Henrietta Canty, "The Real Daufuskie Island," 1989, Southern Justice Institute
Records, Box 31, Folder "Daufuskie: History and General Articles," Southern Historical Collection, University of North Carolina at Chapel Hill.

12. Kahrl, "From Commons to Capital."

13. Roger Pinckney, "Blue Root Real Estate," *Orion*, accessed July 29, 2022, https://
orionmagazine.org/article/blue-root-real-estate/.

14. Rev. George Weathers, interview with Coastal Carolina University, June 3, 2016.

15. David Farren, interview, May 26, 2015, as cited in Virginia Beach and Dana Beach,
*A Wholly Admirable Thing: Defending Nature and Community on the South Caro-
lina Coast* (Charleston, SC: Evening Post Books, 2019).

16. Rev. George Weathers, interview with Coastal Carolina University, June 3, 2016.

17. Betsy Newman, Beryl Dakers, and Anita Singleton-Prather, *Carolina Stories: Saving Sandy Island* (Columbia: SCETV, 2006).

18. National Park Service, *Low Country Gullah Culture*, 95.

19. Eulis Willis, *Navassa: The Town and Its People, 1735–1991* (Navassa, NC: Eulis
Willis, 1993), 83.

20. Eulis Willis, *Navassa*, 33. Willis argues that the overhead expenses required many
white planters to have secondary occupations as doctors, lawyers, slave traders, and
financiers to supplement their rice profits.

21. Chris Pleasance, "North Carolina's Contaminated Town: Former Rice Farmers
Struggle to Survive on Poisoned Land after Decades of Abuse by Irresponsible
Companies," *Daily-Com*, accessed June 3, 2022, https://www.dailymail.co.uk
/news/article-3267787/North-Carolina's-contaminated-town-Former-rice-farm
ers-struggle-to-survive-on-poisoned-land-after-decades-of-abuse-by-irresponsible
-companies.

22. Martha Waggoner, "Residents of Contaminated Town Wary of Government
Efforts," *Associated Press*, accessed June 3, 2022, https://www.ksl.com/article
/36890245/residents-of-contaminated-town-wary-of-government-efforts.

23. Waggoner, "Residents of Contaminated Town." Mayor Willis is a descendant of a

freedman named Charles Waddell, who founded Navassa when he purchased five acres of land for $100 on December 18, 1875.

24. Amy Roberts and Patrick Holladay, *Gullah Geechee Heritage in the Golden Isles* (Charleston, SC: The History Press, 2019), 33.

25. Sidney Lanier, *Hymns of the Marshes* (New Haven, CT: Yale University Press, 1912), 45–52.

26. David van Nyendael, quoted in P. Amaury Talbot, "The Peoples of Southern Nigeria: A Sketch of Their History, Ethnology, and Languages, with an Abstract of the 1921 Census," *Nature* 121 (1928): 975–77; Basil Davidson, *West Africa Before the Colonial Era: A History to 1850* (London: Longman, 1998), 121.

27. Amy Roberts and Patrick Holladay, *Gullah Geechee Heritage in the Golden Isles* (Charleston, SC: The History Press, 2019), 46.

28. Roberts and Holladay, *Gullah Geechee Heritage in the Golden Isles*, 48.

29. Robert A. Ciucevich, "Glynn County Historic Resources Survey Report Prepared for: The Glynn County Board of Commissioners" (Savannah: M.H.P. Quatrefoil Historic Preservation Consulting, 2009), 151–52.

30. Timothy Powell, "Ebos Landing," *New Georgia Encyclopedia*, accessed June 4, 2022, https://www.georgiaencyclopedia.org/articles/history-archaeology /ebos-landing/.

Chapter 9

1. Jesse Edward Gantt Jr. and Veronica Davis Gerald, *The Ultimate Gullah Cookbook: A Taste of Food, History and Culture from the Gullah People* (Atlanta: Sands Publishing, 2002), 19.

2. Ganntt and Gerald, *The Ultimate Gullah Cookbook*, 16.

3. William S. Pollitzer, *The Gullah People and Their African Heritage* (Athens: University of Georgia Press, 1999), 175.

4. Benjamin Dennis, "South Carolina Hoppin' John with Chef BJ Dennis," South Carolina Department of Parks, Recreation, and Tourism's *Discover South Carolina*, December 3, 2018, https://www.youtube.com/watch?v=s6VqToKrTRk, 6:19.

5. Dennis, "South Carolina Hoppin' John."

6. Joseph Opala, *The Gullah: Rice, Slavery, and the Sierra Leone-American Connection* (Freetown, Sierra Leone: USIS, 2000), 14.

7. Emily Meggett, *Gullah Geechee Home Cooking* (New York: Abrams, 2022), 213.

8. Josephine A. Beoku-Betts, "We Got Our Way of Cooking Things," *Gender & Society* 9, no. 5 (October 1995), 543.

9. Gantt and Gerald, *The Ultimate Gullah Cookbook,* 20.

10. See William Crump, *Encyclopedia of New Year's Holidays Worldwide* (Jefferson, NC: McFarland and Company, 2014), 18–19. Crump offers other possible derivations of this classic Gullah dish. *Hoppin'* may be a corruption of the French Creole term for black-eyed peas, "pois a pigeon." It is known that the term *Hoppin John*

was a name associated with Black enslaved persons during the American colonial era.

11. Gantt and Gerald, *The Ultimate Gullah Cookbook*, 56.

12. William Pollitzer, *The Gullah People and Their African Heritage* (Athens: University of Georgia Press, 2005), 95–97.

13. Beoku-Betts, "We Got Our Way of Cooking Things," 540–41.

14. Priya Krishna, "Kardea Brown Honors Gullah Cuisine and Family Traditions," *Southern Living*, accessed June 10, 2022, https://www.southernliving.com/food /kardea-brown-gullah-cuisine.

15. Latria Graham, "Meet Kardea Brown, the Next Food Network Star," *Garden and Gun*, accessed June 10, 2022, https://gardenandgun.com/articles/meet-next-food -network-star-kardea-brown.

16. Lauren Johnson, "Fifteen Minutes with Kardea Brown," *Charleston*, accessed June 10, 2022, https://charlestonmag.com/features/15_minutes_with_kardea _brown.

17. Krishna, "Kardea Brown Honors Gullah Cuisine."

18. Gantt and Gerald, *The Ultimate Gullah Cookbook*, 36.

19. Emily Meggett, *Gullah Geechee Home Cooking* (New York: Abrams, 2022), 45.

Chapter 10

1. Emory Campbell, "A Sense of Self and Place: Unmasking My Gullah Cultural Heritage," in *African American Life in the Georgia Lowcountry: The Atlantic World and the Gullah Geechee*, ed. Philip Morgan (Athens: University of Georgia Press, 2010), 281. Campbell credits the emergence of his sense of self to scholars (outsiders) and "we" (Gullahs) who were committed to the study of Gullah Geechee culture.

2. Campbell, "A Sense of Self and Place," 289.

3. Emory Campbell and Ayoka Campbell, *Gullah Cultural Legacies: A Synopsis of Gullah Traditions, Customary Beliefs, Artforms and Speech on Hilton Head Island and Vicinal Sea Islands in South Carolina and Georgia* (Hilton Head, SC: Gullah Heritage Consulting Services, 2008), 111, 118–19.

4. Margaret Evans, "Emory Campbell Receives Honorary Doctorate from Sewanee," *Lowcountry Weekly*, accessed June 10, 2022, https://lcweekly.com/culture/emory -campbell-receives-honorary-doctorate-from-sewanee/#:~:text=Emory%20 Campbell%2C%20retired%20Executive%20Director,Saints%20Chapel%20in %20Sewanee%2C%20Tennessee.

5. Bruce Baker, *What Reconstruction Meant: Historical Memory in the American South* (Charlottesville: University of Virginia Press, 2010), 77–78. See Robert Cook, *Troubled Commemoration: The American Civil War Centennial 1961–1965* (Baton Rouge: Louisiana State University Press, 2007), 156. Black veterans took part in the Grand Army of the Republic (GAR), the Union equivalent of the

United Confederate Veterans. As many as eight thousand of them commemorated Decoration Day in Beaufort, South Carolina, in its heyday at the turn of the century. The passing of the veterans dwindled the celebration.

6. Dawna Pazant and Bradford Pazant, "How It All Began," *The Original Gullah Festival*, accessed June 13, 2022, https://www.originalgullahfestival.org/the originalgullahfestival.

7. "Decoration Day," The Gullah Kinfolk Traveling Theatre, accessed August 1, 2022, https://www.gullahkinfolktravelingtheater.org.

8. See Bessie Jones and Bess Lomax Hawes, *Step It Down: Games, Plays, and Stories from the Afro-American Heritage* (New York: Harper & Row, 1972). Jones and Hillery's impressive repertoire of children's games and songs drew the attention of folklorist Alan Lomax and his sister Bess Lomax Hawes, who capture these songs in this popular book.

9. Amy Lotson and Patrick Holladay, *Gullah Geechee Heritage in the Golden Isles* (Charleston, SC: History Press, 2019), 36.

10. Ennis Davis, "Gullah Fest Headed to Springfield This Weekend," *The Jaxson*, accessed June 10, 2022, https://www.thejaxsonmag.com/article/gullah-fest-headed -to-springfield-this-weekend/#:~:text=Gullah%20Fest%20is%20an%20 annual,of%20Jacksonville%27s%20African%20American%20influences.

11. Sapelo Island Cultural and Revitalization Society, "About Us," accessed June 13, 2022, http:/sicars.org/about/.

12. WTOC staff, "Hundreds Enjoy Taste of Gullah Festival," WTOC Channel 11, accessed June 13, 2022, https://www.wtoc.com/story/28051848/hundreds -enjoy-taste-of-gullah-festival/.

13. "Eric Turpin: New NIBCAA Executive Director Helping to Make the Island a Special Place for All," *Hilton Head: Monthly Voice of the Lowcountry*, https://www .hiltonheadmonthly.com/people/intriguing-people/4007-eric-turpin-new -nibcaa-executive-director-helping-to-make-the-island-a-special-place-for-all.

14. The North Carolina Rice Festival, "Education Through Celebration," accessed June 12, 2022. https://www.northcarolinaricefestival.org.

15. National Park Service, *Low Country Gullah Culture: Special Resource Study and Final Environmental Impact Statement* (Atlanta: National Park Service, Southeast Regional Office, 2005), 69.

16. Mount Pleasant Town Council, "Thomasena Stokes-Brown Celebrated for Dedication to Her Community," accessed June 12, 2022, https://www.24 -7pressrelease.com/press-release/478656/thomasena-stokes-marshall-celebrated -for-dedication-to-her-community/.

17. Dale Rosengarten, *Row Upon Row: Sea Grass Baskets of the South Carolina Lowcountry* (Columbia: McKissick Museum, University of South Carolina, 1994), 3.

18. Charles Joyner, *Down by the Riverside: A South Carolina Slave Community* (Urbana: University of Illinois Press, 1984), 122.

19. Michele Roldán-Shaw, "Let the Circle Be Unbroken: An Account of Growing up

Gullah," *Welcome to Bluffton, South Carolina*, accessed June 15, 2022, https://www
.bluffton.com/let-circle-unbroken-account-growing-gullah/.

20. William Brooks, "Thomas Doyle," in *Encyclopedia of American Folk Art*, ed. Ge-
rard C. Wertkin (New York: Routledge, 2004), 65.

21. News release from Gallery Chuma of Charleston, SC, February 17, 2007.

22. Michiel Perry, "Faces of Art: Sonja Griffin Evans Captures the Spirit of Gullah
Culture," *Design Aspire Home*, https://aspiremetro.com/faces-of-art-sonja
-griffin-evans/.

23. University of South Carolina Beaufort, "Sea Islands Institute," accessed June 15,
2022, https://www.uscb.edu/academics/research/sea_islands_institute/index.html.

24. "The Charles W. Joyner Institute for Gullah and African Diaspora Studies,"
Coastal Carolina University, accessed August 1, 2022, https://www.coastal.edu
/joynerinstitute/.

25. The Athenaeum Press at Coastal Carolina University, "At Low Tide: The Voices
of Sandy Island," accessed June 15, 2022, http://theathenaeumpress.com/projects
/at-low-tide/#:~:text=The%20Sandy%20Island%20Cultural%20Initiative%20
is%20working%20on%20documenting%20and,for%20Cultural%20Equity%20
to%20digitize.

26. Georgia Southern University, "Georgia Southern's Gullah Geechee Cultural Heritage Center Opens, Bridges Connections Between Past and Present," https://
news.georgiasouthern.edu/2021/09/29/georgia-southerns-gullah-geechee
-cultural-heritage-center-opens-bridges-connections-between-past-and-present/.

Chapter 11

1. Dena Epstein, *Sinful Tunes and Spirituals: Black Folk Music to the Civil War* (Urbana: University of Illinois Press, 1977), 16.

2. Willis Laurence James and Jon Michael Spencer, *Stars in de Elements: A Study
of Negro Folk Music* (Durham, NC: Duke University Press, 1995), 148. See Eric
Crawford, *Gullah Spirituals: The Sound of Freedom and Protest in the South Carolina Sea Islands* (Columbia: University of South Carolina Press, 2021), 99–100.
The author discusses James's influence on the adoption of the spirituals by civil
rights organizations during the 1960s.

3. Thomas Wentworth Higginson, "Negro. Spirituals," *The Atlantic Online*, accessed
July 26, 2022, https://www.theatlantic.com/past/docs/issues/1867jun/spirit.htm.

4. Bartholomew Rivers Carroll, "An Editorial Trip to Edisto Island," *Chicora* I
(1842): 42, 63.

5. Author consulted *Gullah Bible Online* for accurate spellings of Gullah texts: Wy-
cliff Gullah Translators, *De Gullah Nyew Testament*, accessed July 26, 2022, www
.gullahbible.com.

6. Lydia Parrish, *Slave Songs of the Georgia Sea Islands* (Athens: University of Georgia Press, 1942), 48.

7. Guy Carawan, "That's All Right," *Sing Out! The Folk Song Magazine* 14, no. 2 (April–May 1964): 29.

8. Guy Carawan, Candie Carawan, Julian Bond, and Florence Reece, *Sing for Freedom: The Story of the Civil Rights Movement Through Its Songs* (Montgomery, AL: NewSouth Books, 2007), 99–100.

9. John Howison, *European Colonies in Various Parts of the World, Viewed in Their Social, Moral, and Physical Condition, Vol. 1* (London: Richard Bentley, New Burlington Street, Publisher in Ordinary to His Majesty, 1834), 94. Cited in Epstein, *Sinful Tunes and Spirituals*, 7.

10. Cecilia Conway, "Banjo," in *African American Folklore: An Encyclopedia for Students*, ed. Anand Prahlad (Santa Barbara, CA: Greenwood, 2016), 13.

11. Nic Butler, "A 'Banjer' on the Bay of Charleston 1766," Charleston County Public Library, accessed July 26, 2022, https://www.ccpl.org/charleston-time-machine/banjer-bay-charleston-1766.

12. B. A. Boykin, *Lay My Burden Down: A Folk History of Slavery* (Chicago: University of Chicago Press, 1945), 11. Cited in Eileen Southern, *The Music of Black Americans: A History* (New York: W. W. Norton, 1997), 175.

13. Whitman Meade, *Travels in North America* (New York: C. S. Van Winkle, 1820), 29.

14. Solomon Northup, *Twelve Years a Slave; The Thrilling Story of a Free Colored Man, Kidnapped in Washington in 1841; Sold into Slavery, and After Twelve Years' Bondage Reclaimed by State Authority from a Cotton Plantation in Louisiana* (New York: International Book Co, 1900), 196.

15. Mark Smith, *Stono: Documenting and Interpreting a Southern Slave Revolt* (Columbia, SC: University of South Carolina Press, 2005), 75.

16. Epstein, *Sinful Tunes and Spirituals*, 84.

17. Federal Writers' Project, *Drums and Shadows: Survival Studies Among the Georgia Coastal Negroes: Savannah Unit*. Georgia Writer's Project: Work Projects Administration (Athens: University of Georgia Press, 1940), 62.

18. Theodore F. Seward, *Jubilee Songs: As Sung by the Jubilee Singers, of Fisk University (Nashville, Tenn.) Under the Auspices of the American Missionary Association* (New York: Biglow & Main, 1872), 32.

19. M. F. Armstrong, Helen Wilhelmina Ludlow, and Thomas P. Fenner, *Hampton and Its Students. By Two of Its Teachers, Mrs. M.F. Armstrong and Helen W. Ludlow. With Fifty Cabin and Plantation Songs* (New York: G. P. Putnam's Sons, 1875), 172.

20. Armstrong, Ludlow, and Fenner, *Hampton and Its Students*, 181.

21. Eileen Southern, *The Music of Black Americans: A History* (New York: W. W. Norton, 1997), 231.

22. Nicholas George Ballanta Taylor, *Saint Helena Island Spirituals* (New York: G. Schirmer, 1925), 92. Ballanta-Taylor's "Jedus" spelling replicates the islanders' pronunciation of Jesus.

23. Alfred Emanuel Smith, *New Outlook, Vol. 121* (New York: Outlook Publishing Co., 1919), 343. See also "A Wartime Spiritual," *New York Times*, December 7, 1919.

24. Southern, *The Music of Black Americans*, 280.

25. "Real Value of Negro Melodies," *New York Herald*, May 21, 1893, 28.

26. Harry Burleigh, *The Spirituals of Harry T. Burleigh* (Miami: Belwin-Mills, 1984), 4.

27. James Weldon Johnson, J. Rosamond Johnson, and Lawrence Brown, *The Books of American Negro Spirituals: Including the Book of American Negro Spiritual and the Second Book of Negro Spirituals* (Cambridge, MA: Da Capo Press, 2003), 42–43.

28. James Weldon Johnson, J. Rosamond Johnson, and Lawrence Brown, *The Books of American Negro Spirituals: Including the Book of American Negro Spiritual and the Second Book of Negro Spirituals* (Cambridge, MA: Da Capo Press, 2003), 45.

29. "Hall Johnson," Afrocentric Voices, www.afrovoices.com/hjohnson.html.

30. "William L. Dawson Tribute," Tuskegee University, https://www.tuskegee.edu /student-life/student-organizations/choir/william-l-dawson-tribute.

31. Cele Seldon and Lynn Seldon, "Dr. Marlena Smalls and the Hallelujah Singers," *South Carolina Living: The Best of the Palmetto State*, accessed August 3, 2022, https://scliving.coop/sc-life/sc-life-features/dr-marlena-smalls-and-the-hallelujah -singers/.

32. Sandy Jones, "The Georgia Sea Island Singers," accessed August 3, 2022, http:// www.gacoast.com/navigator/quimbys.html.

33. Lynne Heffley, "Hey, This Huge Yellow Creature Isn't Big Bird: The West African– Flavored 'Gullah Gullah Island' Is a Surprise Hit with Preschoolers on Nickel-odeon," *Los Angeles Time*s, accessed August 3, 2022, https://www.latimes.com /archives/la-xpm-1996-06-01-ca-10603-story.html.

34. EatStayPlay Beaufort, "Natalie Daise Brings Harriet Tubman to Stage in Beau-fort," accessed July 27, 2022, https://www.eatstayplaybeaufort.com /natalie-daise-brings-harriet-tubman-to-stage-in-beaufort/.

35. Adam Parker, "Ron and Natalie Daise, Famous for 'Gullah Gullah Island,' Keep Up the Storytelling," accessed June 27, 2022, https://www.postandcourier.com /features/ron-and-natalie-daise-famous-for-gullah-island-keep-up-the-storytelling /article_bfb42ed6-8a08-11e8-83e6-afb02f47add5.html.

Chapter 12

1. Joseph Opala, "Black Seminoles-Gullahs Who Escaped From Slavery," *The Gul-lah: Rice, Slavery, and the Sierra Leone-American Connection*, accessed July 8, 2022, https://glc.yale.edu/sites/default/files/files/Black%20Seminoles%20.pdf.

2. Anthony Dixon, "Black Seminole Involvement and Leadership During the Sec-ond Seminole War 1835–1842" (PhD diss., Indiana University, 2007), 154. Dixon further qualifies Cavallo's status as a Black Seminole chief by mentioning General Jesup's description of meeting with Chief Abraham, who was "accompanied by a

nephew of the Indian Chief Cloud, and a Negro chief." This Negro chief is believed to be John Cavallo.

3. Opala, "Black Seminoles-Gullahs."

4. Juliette Porter-Mitchell, "Story of John Horse, a Black Seminole Warrior," *Catholic Review*, accessed July 8, 2022, https://www.archbalt.org/story-of-john -horse-a-black-seminole-warrior/.

5. Opala, "Black Seminoles-Gullahs."

6. Marie Veronica Warrior, interview by Marna Weston, July 20, 2012, Samuel Proctor Oral History Program College of Liberal Arts and Sciences Program, accessed July 6, 2022, https://ufdcimages.uflib.ufl.edu/AA/00/06/65/67/00001/URR %20001%20Veronica%20Warrior%206-20-2012ufdc.pdf.

7. Johnnie and Matthew Griffin, interview by Marna Weston, July 20, 2012, Samuel Proctor Oral History Program, College of Liberal Arts and Sciences, University of Florida, accessed July 6, 2022, https://ufdcimages.uflib.ufl.edu/AA/00/06 /63/89/00001/URR%20012%20Johnnie%20and%20Matthew%20Griffin%206 -22-2012ufdc.pdf.

8. Wes Ferguson, "Why This Mexican Village Celebrates Juneteenth: Descendants of Slaves Who Escaped Across the Southern Border Observe Texas's Emancipation Holiday with Their Own Unique Tradition." *Texas Monthly*, July 19, 2019, https:// www.texasmonthly.com/being-texan/mexican-village-juneteenth-celebration/.

9. Fambul Tik, "First Anniversary of the Sierra Leone Next Step Tour," accessed July 9, 2022, https://fambultik.com/blog/first-anniversary-sierra-leone-next -step-tour.

10. "Gullah Roots," *Carolina Stories*, directed and produced by Betsy Newman (2021, South Carolina Educational Television), https://www.pbs.org/video/gullah-roots -tpxcfm/.

11. "Gullah Roots." Wigfall comments that she brought starter baskets over to Sierra Leone to make the sewing process less time consuming.

12. "Gullah Roots."

13. Anita Singleton Prather, interviewed by author, July 8, 2022.

14. South Carolina Humanities, "Gullah Roots Documentary," accessed July 8, 2022, https://schumanities.org/news/gullah-roots-documentary/.

15. Maureen Simpson, editorial, *Island Packet* (Hilton Head Island, SC), December 24, 2006.

16. *Family Across the Sea*, produced by Tim Carrier (1990, South Carolina Educational Television), accessed July 8, 2022, https://www.folkstreams.net/films /family-across-the-sea.

BIBLIOGRAPHY

Bailey, Cornelia Walker. *God, Dr. Buzzard, and the Bolito Man*. New York: Anchor Books, 2000.

Ball, Edward. *Slaves in the Family*. New York: Farrar, Straus, and Giroux, 1998.

Bebey, Francis. *African Music: A People's Art*. New York: Lawrence Hill & Co., 1975.

Bennett, John. *Doctor to the Dead: Grotesque Legends and Folk Tales of Old Charleston*. New York: Rinehart, 1946.

Black, James Gary. *My Friend the Gullah*. Beaufort, SC: Beaufort Book Company, 1974.

Botkin, A. *Lay My Burden Down*. Chicago: University of Chicago Press, 1945.

Bottume, Elizabeth Hyde. *First Days Among the Contrabands*. Boston: Lee and Shephard, 1893.

Branch, Muriel Miller. *The Water Brought Us*. New York: Dutton, 1995.

Brockington, Lee G. *Plantation Between the Waters*. Charleston, SC: History Press, 2006.

Burchard, Peter. *Charlotte Forten: A Black Teacher in the Civil War*. New York: Crown, 1995.

Burlin, Natalie Curtis. *Negro Folk Songs*. New York: G. Schirmer, 1918–19.

Burn, Billie. *An Island Named Daufuskie*. Spartanburg, SC: Reprint Company, 1991.

Campbell, Emory S. *Gullah Cultural Legacies*. Hilton Head Island, SC: Gullah Heritage Consulting Services, 2002.

Christensen, Abigail. *Afro-American Folk Lore Told Round Cabin Fires on the Sea Islands of South Carolina*. New York: Negro University Press, 1969.

Conroy. Pat. *The Water Is Wide*. Boston: Houghton Mifflin, 1972.

Cooley, Rossa B. *Homes of the Freed*. New York: New Republic, 1926.

Creel, Margaret W. *A Peculiar People*. New York: New York University Press, 1988.

———. *School Acres: An Adventure in Rural Education*. New Haven, CT: Yale University Press, 1930.

Dabbs, Edith M. *Face of an Island: Leigh Richmond Miner's Photographs of Saint Helena Island*. New York: Grossman Publishers, 1970.

Dabbs, James McBride. *Haunted by God*. Richmond, VA: John Knox Press, 1972.

Daise, Ronald. *Reminiscences of Sea Island Heritage*. Orangeburg, SC: Sandlapper Publishing, 1986.

Dash, Julie. *Daughters of the Dust*. New York: Dutton, 1997.

Dillard, J. L. *Black English: Its History and Usage in the United States*. New York: Random House, 1972.

Du Bois, William Edward Burghardt. *Souls of Black Folk*. Chicago: McClurg, 1904.

Forten, Charlotte. *The Journal of Charlotte L. Forten*. New York: Dryden Press, 1953.

Franklin, John Hope. *From Slavery to Freedom*. New York: Knopf, 1988.

Fulop, Timothy E., and Albert J. Raboteau. *African-American Religion: Interpretive Essays in History and Culture*. London: Routledge, 1996.

Gantt, Jesse Edward Jr., with Veronica Davis Gerald. *The Ultimate Gullah Cookbook*. Beaufort, SC: Sands Publishing, 2003.

Gates, Henry Louis Jr., et al. *Unchained Memories*. New York: Bullfinch Press, 2002.

Georgia Writers' Project. *Drums and Shadows: Survival Studies Among the Georgia Coastal Negroes*. Works Project Administration (WPA), 1940.

Geraty, Virginia Mixon. *Gullah fuh Oonuh: A Guide to the Gullah Language*. Orangeburg, SC: Sandlapper Publishing, 1997.

Gonzales, Ambrose E. *Black Border* series. Columbia, SC: State Company, 1922.

———. *With Aesop Along the Black Border*. New York: Negro University Press, 1969.

Goodwine, Marquetta L., ed. *The Legacy of Ibo Landing: Gullah Roots of African American Culture*. Atlanta: Clarity Press, 1998.

Green, Jonathan. *Gullah Images: The Art of Jonathan Green*. Columbia: University of South Carolina Press, 1996.

Grosvenor, Vertamae. *Vertamae Cooks in the Americas' Family Kitchen*. San Francisco: KQED Books, 1996.

———. *Vibration Cooking, or the Travel Notes of a Geechee Girl*. New York: Doubleday, 1970.

Guthrie, Patricia. *Catching Sense*. Westport, CT: Bergin & Garvey, 1996.

Harper, Michael S., and Anthony Walton. *The Vintage Book of African American Poetry*. New York: Random House, 2000.

Holland, Rupert Sargent, ed. *Letters and Diary of Laura M. Towne Written from the Sea Islands of South Carolina, 1862–1884*. New York: Negro University Press, 1912, 1969.

Holloway, Joseph E., and Winifred K. Vass. *The African Heritage of American English*. Bloomington: Indiana University Press, 1993.

———. *Africanisms in American Culture*. Bloomington: Indiana University Press, 1990.

Jacoway, Elizabeth. *Yankee Missionaries in the South*. Baton Rouge: Louisiana State University Press, 1980.

Johnson, Guion Griffis. *A Social History of the Sea Islands, with Special Reference to St. Helena Island, South Carolina*. Chapel Hill: University of North Carolina Press, 1930.

Johnson, Guy B. *Folk Culture on St. Helena Island, South Carolina*. Chapel Hill: University of North Carolina Press, 1930.

Jones, Bessie. *For the Ancestors: Autobiographical Memories Collected and Edited by John Stewart*. Urbana: University of Illinois Press, 1983.

Jones, Charles Colcock. *Gullah Folk Tales from the Georgia Coast*. Athens: University of Georgia Press, 2000.

Jones-Jackson, Patricia. *When Roots Die: Endangered Traditions on the Sea Islands.* Athens: University of Georgia Press, 1987.

Joyner, Charles. *Down by the Riverside.* Chicago: University of Illinois Press, 1984.

———. *Folk Song in South Carolina.* Columbia: University of South Carolina Press, 1971.

———. *Shared Traditions: Southern History and Folk Culture.* Urbana: University of Illinois Press, 1999.

Kiser, Clyde Vernon. *Sea Island to City.* New York: Columbia University Press, 1932.

Kuyk, Betty M. *African Voices in the African American Heritage.* Indianapolis: Indiana University Press, 2003.

Longsworth, Polly I. *Charlotte Forten, Black and Free.* New York: Thomas Y. Crowell, 1920.

McTeer, J. E. *Adventures in the Woods and Waters of the Low Country.* Beaufort, SC: Beaufort Book Company, 1972.

———. *Fifty Years as a Lowcountry Witch Doctor.* Beaufort, SC: Beaufort Book Company, 1976.

Mitchell, Faith. *Hoodoo Medicine: Gullah Herbal Remedies.* Columbia, SC: Summerhouse Press, 1999.

Montgomery, Michael. *The Crucible of Carolina.* Athens: University of Georgia Press, 1994.

Moutoussamy-Ashe, Jeanne. *Daufuskie Island: A Photographic Essay.* Columbia: University of South Carolina Press, 1982.

Opala, Joseph. *The Gullah: Rice, Slavery, and the Sierra Leone–American Connection.* Freetown, Sierra Leone: USIS, 1987.

Parrish, Lydia. *Slave Songs of the Georgia Sea Islands.* New York: Farrar, Straus and Giroux, 1942.

Pinckney, Roger. *Blue Roots: African-American Folk Magic of the Gullah People.* St. Paul, MN: Llewellyn Publishers, 1998.

Pollitzer, William S. *The Gullah People and Their African Heritage.* Athens: University of Georgia Press, 1999.

Rawley, James. *The Transatlantic Slave Trade.* New York: Norton, 1981.

Robinson, Randall. *The Debt: What America Owes to Blacks.* New York: Dutton, 2000.

Robinson, Sallie Ann. *Gullah Home Cooking the Daufuskie Way.* Chapel Hill: University of North Carolina Press, 2003.

Rose, Willie Lee Nichols. *Rehearsal for Reconstruction: The Port Royal Experiment.* New York: Vintage Books, 1964.

Sea Island Translation Team. *De Good Nyews Bout Jedus Christ Wa Luke Write: The Gospel According to Luke.* New York: American Bible Society, 1994.

———. *De Nyew Testament.* New York: American Bible Society, 2005.

Stoddard, Albert Henry. *Gullah Animal Tales from Daufuskie Island, South Carolina.* Hilton Head Island, SC: Push Button Publishing Company, 1995.

Turner, Lorenzo Dow. *Africanisms in the Gullah Dialect.* Chicago: University of Chicago Press, 1949.

Twining, Mary Arnold, and Keith E. Baird. *Sea Island Roots: African Presence in the Carolinas and Georgia.* Trenton, NJ: Africa World Press, 1991.

Weir, Robert M. *Colonial South Carolina.* Columbia: University of South Carolina Press, 1997.

Whaley, Marcellus S. *The Old Types Pass: Gullah Sketches of the Carolina Sea Islands.* Boston: Christopher Publishing House, 1925.

Wolfe, Michael C. *The Abundant Life Prevails.* Waco, TX: Baylor University Press, 2000.

Wood, Peter. *Black Majority.* New York: Knopf, 1974.

Woofter, Thomas Jackson. *Black Yeomanry: Life on St. Helena Island.* New York: Henry Holt and Company, 1930.

Yetman, Norman, ed. *Voices from Slavery.* Mineola, NY: Dover Publications, 1972.

Films and Video Recordings

Amistad. The story of the slave ship and the slaves who revolted and took over the vessel, eventually finding freedom in the New World. A reproduction of the *Amistad,* based at Mystic Seaport in Connecticut, makes regular voyages to many ports where visitors can observe what slaves had to endure while being transported from Africa to American ports in both the North and the South.

Conrack. The engaging story of a young white teacher assigned to an isolated Sea Island populated largely by poor Black families. Working with young children who are illiterate, he finds a way to spark their lagging interest in being educated, guiding them to knowledge about reading, writing, and arithmetic that will help them in later life. This film is the story of noted author Pat Conroy and his personal experience on remote Daufuskie Island, South Carolina.

Daughters of the Dust. A hauntingly lovely story set in the Sea Islands off the Georgia coast a century ago, the film portrays the unique culture of the Gullah people by focusing on a typical local family as its members struggle with the option of leaving their island and heading north. The climax comes when on the eve of their intended departure memories of their ancient history and roots appear in highly dramatic visions. The film was created by Julie Dash, a noted director, as a tribute to her Gullah ancestors.

Fah de Chillun: Gullah Traditions. A music video that teaches children about the Gullah culture in a lively manner that they can understand and appreciate. The Hallelujah Singers, wearing traditional costumes and with colorful set designs as backdrops, perform Gullah songs and skits, interacting with each other and the young audience.

Family across the Sea. A vivid story of the ways in which the Gullah people have retained their ties to their homeland in West Africa despite centuries of oppression and hardship. This film chronicles the journey of a small band of Gullah people from South Carolina, Georgia, Florida, and Oklahoma to Sierra Leone, West Africa, in 1989, with the goal of tracing their roots.

Free at Last. The detailed stories of civil rights heroes and events that are of historical importance.

Garden of Gold. This film is a brief presentation about the "Rice Kingdom" in the days of the large plantations in the Sea Islands, where rice was one of the major crops. It explores the agricultural methods used to grow rice and examines how many slaves were imported from West Africa because of their proficiency in the planting, growing, and processing of rice. The film was produced in conjunction with the establishment of the Georgetown County, South Carolina, Rice Museum and includes a short history of that institution as well.

God's Gonna Trouble the Water. Who are the Gullah? What binds these peoples together? This story is told through spirituals and remembrances featuring the renowned Hallelujah Singers, the Gullah Praise House Shouters, and local sea islanders. The film features rare vintage footage, old audio recordings, and vivid commentary.

Gullah Tales. The story opens with Maum Nancy, an elderly slave woman, telling stories to children, both Black and white, on a Georgia plantation in the 1830s. Then it shifts to a dramatization of two typical Gullah animal and human "trickster" tales, in which the actors try to outsmart each other. In all, the sequences also provide an authentic depiction of Gullah culture and language.

The Language You Cry In. This award-winning "Story of a Mende Song" is a remarkable detective tale based on African and African-inspired music and reaching across hundreds of years and thousands of miles from eighteenth-century Sierra Leone in West Africa to the Gullah people of the present-day Sea Islands of the Carolinas and Georgia. The film also recounts the remarkable story of how the Gullahs of today have retained strong links with their African past.

My Name Ain't Eve. This film explores the way that African Americans name their children traditionally or through more contemporary methods.

Palmetto Places: St. Helena Island. This film celebrates the Gullah culture as it exists today on one of the largest Sea Islands in the Carolinas. Viewers are taken on a trip around the island, visiting key places, such as the ruins of an old chapel, a Gullah museum, a Gullah restaurant, and Penn Center, once Penn School, founded in 1862.

Penn Center. A history of Penn School, founded in 1862 and still in existence as Penn Center, situated on St. Helena Island, South Carolina, and dedicated to the history and preservation of the Gullah language, culture, and heritage.

Remnants of Mitchellville. A documentary film focusing on the history of Mitchellville, a village established on Hilton Head Island, South Carolina, in 1862 by the Union commander to provide homes for some 1,500 freed slaves, with the idea that they could live there and earn a living largely as wage-earning laborers for the occupying Union forces on the island. Today, this is a historic site visited on Gullah tours.

Robert Smalls: A Patriot's Journey from Slavery to Capitol Hill. The story of a little-known hero who commandeered a Confederate ship during the Civil War and de-

livered it to the Union fleet. Smalls eventually became the first African American to
serve in Congress.

Saving Sandy Island. How the Gullah residents of a small island in South Carolina
took very positive and successful steps to preserve the isolation and natural wonders
of their environment and protect it from the encroachments of developers, even to
the extent of blocking the efforts of mainland citizens to plan a bridge to the island.

The Story of English: Part V, Black on White. An examination of Black English, or Gullah, and its influence on American speech in the South. The film traces the origins
of this language from West Africa to modern times and characterizes the people
who spoke it along an old slave-trade route. It also uses traditional music and song
to explain the powerful influence of the Gullah culture on the people of the Sea
Islands.

The Strength of These Arms: White Rice, Black Labor. The life of Gullah slaves as seen
from an archaeological perspective, starting with the excavation of slave quarters
at Middleburg Plantation in South Carolina. The film shows how enslaved people
from West Africa brought their skills to the southern plantations and includes some
rare footage of Gullah descendants of enslaved people working in rice fields in the
1940s.

Tales of the Land of Gullah for Kids. An educational presentation that focuses on both
the plight and accomplishments of the first African slaves who landed on the shores
of the Carolinas. The film is enlivened by fables, songs, and stories.

Tales of the Unknown South. This title is actually a reference to three separate films
about the Carolinas: (1) *The Half-Pint Flask*, the impressive and startling story of a
man who disturbs a Gullah grave in order to acquire a souvenir for a collection but
fails to reckon with something horrible in the grave; (2) the tale of a woman from
the deep backwoods whose home is threatened when a developer starts purchasing
the Gullah lands in her neighborhood; and (3) an incident in which a Black girl en-
rolls in a previously all-white school and faces unknown personal danger.

Unchained Memories. Readings from the narratives of formerly enslave people, based
on the Federal Writers' Project of the Works Progress Association (WPA) in the
1930s, which was commissioned during the Great Depression to interview members
of the last living generation of African Americans born into slavery and compile
their memories of bygone years. An HBO documentary film described as "in their
words, our shared history."

Voices of Color film series. An ongoing initiative designed to highlight the range and
depth of the African American experience, giving voice to this subject area. It was
launched on the twentieth anniversary of the noted award-winning film *The Color
Purple.*

When Rice Was King. How rice cultivation made the southern colonies among the
richest in America in the eighteenth and nineteenth centuries and made possible
the lavish homes and lifestyles of the planters in these regions. Although the Gullah
connections are minimal, the film includes many examples of Gullah language and

work songs and succeeds in explaining the nature and extent of rice cultivation and the making of the "Rice Kingdom."

Will to Survive: The Story of the Gullah/Geechee Nation. An hour-long TV documentary in celebration of Black History Month, this film documents the ways in which the Gullah peoples have established homes and communities in America and have continued the traditions of their African ancestors. The setting is Sapelo Island, Georgia, one of the last remaining Gullah communities that is still intact.

Yonder Come Day. This film documents the efforts of Bessie Jones, the last active member of the Georgia Sea Island Singers, to pass on the songs, games, and traditions of the Gullah past to new generations. Born in 1902, Jones learned many of the songs from her grandfather, who had been brought to America from Africa and died at age 105.

Sound Recordings

Avery Research Center. *Spiritual Society Concerts.* Fifty-six spirituals performed by three generations of the amateur Spiritual Society between 1936 and 1995.

———. *Spiritual Society Field Recordings.* Nineteen spirituals performed by African American congregations in the Carolina Lowcountry between 1936 and 1939. Six of these also include performances by the champion "street criers" at the 1936 Azalea Festival.

———. *Spirituals of the Carolina Low Country.* The music and Gullah lyrics of forty-nine spirituals that were recorded by the Society for the Preservation of Spirituals between 1922 and 1931. Also available is a guide to all of the spirituals collected by the Society, describing where to find them and the form in which they are available.

Daise, Ron. *De Gullah Storybook.* Narrated by Ron Daise and Natalie Daise. A counting book with English and Gullah poems. GOG Enterprises.

———. *Little Muddy Waters.* Compact disk narrated by Ron Daise and Natalie Daise. A story based on Gullah folk tales, which also includes a Gullah song, "*Respec Yo Eldas.*" GOG Enterprises.

———. *Sleep Tight: Night Songs and Stories.* From the *Gullah, Gullah Island* series. GOG Enterprises.

———. *We'll Stand the Storm and Other Spirituals.* Beaufort, SC, collection. Folkway Records.

———. *Johns Island, South Carolina: Its People and Songs.* A collection of field recordings that includes secular and religious songs of the Gullah culture.

Goodwine, Marquetta ("Queen Quet"). *Hunnah Chillun.* A collection of recordings of traditional Gullah Geechee spirituals, stories, history, and dance music.

———. *Hunnah Hafa Shout Sumtines.* Gullah Roots Productions.

Hallelujah Singers. *Songs of Hope, Faith, and Freedom.* The first of many recordings by this noted group, including "Carry Me Home," featuring Gullah melodies that span the period of history between the 1860s and the birth of the blues in the 1920s.

Jones, Bessie. *Put Your Hand on Your Hip, and Let Your Backbone Slip*. Songs and games from the Georgia Sea Islands. A compact disk with thirty-one songs sung by Jones, accompanied by tambourine and various adult and children singers.
———. *So Glad I'm Here*. An album intended to preserve the rich Gullah heritage. Rounder Records.
———. *Step It Down. A recording of children's games*. Rounder Records.
Jones, Bessie, with John Davie and Bobby Leecan. *Georgia Sea Island Songs*. Local performers sing a variety of chants resembling African counterparts, as well as more modern selections. Compact disk. New World Records.
Klein, Thomas, in conjunction with Georgia Southern University. *Lorenzo Dow Turner: Man and Mission*. A recording that covers Turner's work as a key pioneer in studying the Gullah language in the 1920s and 1930s. This project comprises some eighteen hours of oral history recordings of Gullah and Geechee residents of the Sea Islands during 1932 and 1933. The subjects cover just about every phase of living, working, and the arts, and although the tapes are primitive, sometimes with high levels of interference, they have been described as "unique, invaluable, and irreplaceable documents of American and world history."
Lomax, Alan. A selection of the most important works arranged by this noted and exceptional collector is now housed in the American Folklife Center in the Library of Congress. The numerous works related to African American and Gullah music include *Southern Journey*, a thirteen-volume series of original recordings of blues, ballads, hymns, spirituals, reels, shouts, chanteys, and work songs. These selections, recorded by Lomax in extensive travels throughout the southern states, evoke the musical world of the rural South in an era before radio, movies, and television. Notable volumes include *Georgia Sea Islands—Biblical Songs and Spirituals*; *Earliest Times—Georgia Sea Island Songs for Everybody*; *Velvet Voices: African-American Music of the Eastern Shores*; and *Brethren, We Meet Again*.
Magee, Richard, and Mary Magee. *Ride With Me, South Carolina*. A specified objective is "to hear the ancient language of the Sea Islands." RMW Associates.
McIntosh County Shouters. *Slave Songs from the Coast of Georgia*. One of a number of recordings made by this popular group using all of the techniques and accompaniment of the southeastern ring shout, which has been described as "the oldest surviving African American performance tradition on the North American continent," and is pretty much localized to McIntosh County on the Georgia coast.
Moving Star Hall Singers. "Been in the Storm So Long," "Remember Me," "Reborn Again," "See God's Ark A-Moving," and other numbers that have been popular on Johns Island, South Carolina, one of the oldest American communities.
Plantation Singers. "Feelin' Good," "This Little Light of Mine," and other songs particularly oriented to the preservation of the spiritual and sacred music of the Lowcountry.
Smalls, Marlene. *Heritage, Not Hate: Discovering Gullah and Finding Myself*. A combination of narrated personal history and songs from Smalls and the Hallelujah Singers.

Gullah Websites

Providing websites in a book or any other publication with a shelf life of more than two months can be an exercise in frustration because sites change periodically or go off the internet without notice. For a reader of this book who may be seeking such sources, the most practical route is to go to your favorite search engine and simply type in the search bar "Gullah websites." In all likelihood, you will get some references that you do not want and others that are only partly on the mark, but at least you will be in the right field.

Having given this caution, here is a list of Gullah sites that provide excellent information and are more or less permanent.

Abridged Gullah Dictionary. https://gullahtours.com/gullah/gullah-words/.

Avery Research Center. https://avery.cofc.edu/.

Beaufort County, SC, Library. https://www.beaufortcountylibrary.org/.

Low Country Gullah Culture Special Resource Study. https://www.nps.gov/ethnography /research/docs/ggsrs_book.pdf.

Marquetta Goodwine and the Gullah/Geechee Nation. https://gullahgeecheenation .com/gullahgeechee-sea-island-coalition/.

Oxford African American Studies Center. https://oxfordaasc.com/.

The Penn Center: A Link to the Past and a Bridge to the Future. http://www.penncenter .com/.

South Carolina State Museum. https://www.scmuseum.org/.

INDEX